HOCKEY
IN
PORTLAND

FRONT COVER: Art Jones played for the Portland Buckaroos. (Courtesy Scott Petterson.)
COVER BACKGROUND: The 1934–1935 Portland Buckaroos team is pictured here. (Courtesy Scott Petterson.)
BACK COVER: The Portland Buckaroos 1960–1961 Western Hockey League (WHL) playoff championship winning team is pictured with the Lester Patrick Cup. (Courtesy Scott Petterson.)

HOCKEY IN PORTLAND

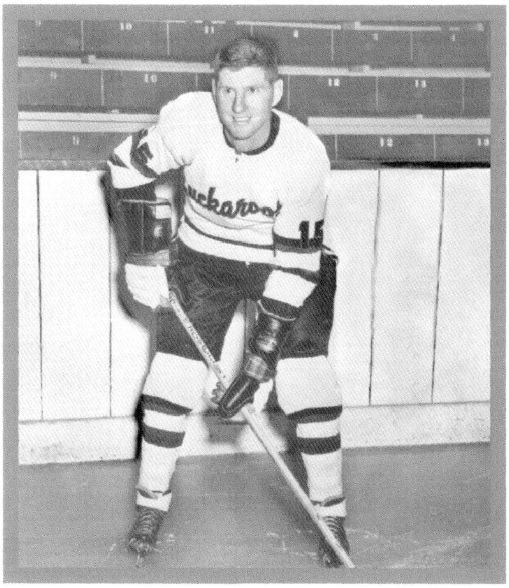

Jim Mancuso and
Scott Petterson

ARCADIA PUBLISHING

ISBN 978-0-7385-4804-3

Published by Arcadia Publishing
Charleston SC, Chicago IL, Portsmouth NH, San Francisco CA

Printed in the United States of America

Library of Congress Catalog Card Number: 2007924201

For all general information contact Arcadia Publishing at:
Telephone 843-853-2070
Fax 843-853-0044
E-mail sales@arcadiapublishing.com
For customer service and orders:
Toll-Free 1-888-313-2665

Visit us on the Internet at www.arcadiapublishing.com

This book is dedicated to Hal Laycoe, "the Professor"—one of the greatest coaches in minor league hockey history.

CONTENTS

ACKNOWLEDGMENTS

Some images in this book are courtesy of Art Brewster (caricature drawings that appeared on the Buckaroos program covers during the 1965–1966 season, in chapter nine), Ernie Fitzsimmons, Gordon Fashoway, Art Jones, Norm Johnson, Dave Kelly, Ed Long, and Arnie Schmautz. We would like to thank Ernie Fitzsimmons and Prof. Edwin Duane Isenberg for their imaging work on the illustrations in this book.

The statistics in this book were obtained from Western Hockey League media guides (various years), Ralph Slate's Hockey Database (www.hockeydb.com), the Society for International Hockey Research (www.sihrhockey.org), and *Total Hockey: The Official Encyclopedia of the National Hockey League* (NHL, second edition).

Other resources used to complete this work include Ray Clow, Ernie Fitzsimmons, Kirk Findlay, *The Hockey News* (various years), Scott Petterson's www.portlandbuckaroos.com, Jim Small, "Icemen: A History of the Western Hockey League" (a commemorative program published for the WHL's 25th anniversary in 1972–1973), the *Oregonian* newspaper, the Oregon Historical Society, and the *Western Hockey World* newspaper (various years in the 1960s).

Please note that the Western Hockey League's (WHL) official all-time statistics, as presented in this book, are counted from the 1948–1949 season of the Pacific Coast Hockey League (PCHL) to the WHL's final season in 1973–1974. The WHL was originally called the PCHL, and the league name change was made prior to the 1952–1953 season to better reflect the geography of the circuit. During its first four seasons, from 1944–1945 to 1947–1948, the PCHL was under the auspices of the Amateur Hockey Association of the United States (AHAUS) and operated as an amateur league. In an historic meeting on January 14, 1948, at the St. Francis Hotel in San Francisco, the directors of the PCHL voted that the league become a professional league for the 1948–1949 season. The PCHL officially kept new all-time statistics and records starting with its first professional season in 1948–1949 and did not include the statistics and records from the league's first four seasons under the AHAUS. Evidence of this record keeping is reflected in WHL media guides, official league publications, and when the WHL officially celebrated its 25th anniversary season in 1972–1973.

A special thanks to my mother, Joan Mancuso, ticket sales representative at the Utica Memorial Auditorium, who got me in free to hockey games in the 1970s and early 1980s.

A special thanks to my wife, Terry Petterson, for all of the love and patience over the last 20-plus years since I started collecting memorabilia.

INTRODUCTION

Professional hockey in Portland began in the 1914–1915 season with the Portland Rosebuds of the Pacific Coast Hockey Association (PCHA). The PCHA was a major league that operated from 1911–1912 to 1923–1924. PCHA champions competed against National Hockey Association (NHA) champions in a playoff for the Stanley Cup from the 1913–1914 season to the 1920–1921 season. The NHA was the forerunner league of the National Hockey League (NHL). In 1915–1916, the Rosebuds captured the PCHA crown and became the first American hockey team to compete for the Stanley Cup title that season. The Rosebuds stayed in Portland until the 1917–1918 campaign and compiled a 38-40 (.487) record over four seasons. Hockey Hall of Famers Tommy Dunderdale, Dick Irvin, and Thomas "Moose" Johnson skated for the PCHA Rosebuds.

Major league hockey returned to Portland in 1925–1926 with a new Portland Rosebuds team, which was a member of the Western Hockey League (WHL). The WHL was previously called the Western Canada Hockey League (WCHL) from 1921–1922 to 1924–1925, but dropped "Canada" from its name when Portland became the only American franchise in league history in 1925–1926. The WCHL champion faced off against the PCHA champion in a playoff in 1921–1922 and 1923–1924 to decide who would play the NHL champions for the Stanley Cup (in 1922–1923, the winners of the PCHL and the NHL met in a semifinal to play the WCHL). The WCHL and the PCHA played an interlocking regular-season schedule in 1922–1923 and 1923–1924. In 1924–1925, the WCHL absorbed the two remaining PCHA teams after Seattle (PCHA) folded and the PCHA terminated operations. The new Rosebuds would only last for one season, as the WHL folded after the 1925–1926 campaign. George Hay and Dick Irvin are hockey Hall of Famers who played for the WHL Rosebuds. The WHL could not compete with the NHL's expansion into the United States and the NHL's player salaries, which led to the sale of WHL players or, in the case of the Rosebuds, the team itself. A NHL expansion team was awarded to Chicago for the 1926–1927 season, and owners of the new franchise bought the entire Rosebuds team, moved the club to the windy city, and renamed the team the Chicago Black Hawks.

After an absence of two seasons, professional hockey returned to Portland with the original Portland Buckaroos of the Pacific Coast Hockey League (PCHL) in 1928–1929. The PCHL was a minor professional league that existed from the 1928–1929 season to the 1930–1931 season. The Buckaroos were members of the PCHL during all three years of the league, and former PCHA star Bobby Rowe was the club's general manager/coach.

Rowe organized a second Portland Buckaroos team in 1933–1934, which brought Portland its first two minor professional hockey championships in 1936–1937 and 1938–1939. The new Buckaroos, who took the ice for eight seasons from 1933–1934 to 1940–1941, were members of a new minor league on the West Coast that operated from the 1932–1933 season to the 1940–1941 season. This league, originally known as the Western Canada Hockey League (WCHL) in its inaugural season in 1932–1933, underwent two name changes to reflect the geographical composition of its teams. The WCHL changed its name to the North West Hockey League (NWHL) for the 1933–1934 season with the addition of United States–based teams. After three seasons as the NWHL, the league changed its label once again to the Pacific Coast Hockey League (PCHL) prior to the 1936–1937 campaign because all of its teams were now located on the coast. The PCHL ceased operations after the 1940–1941 season due to a lack of players brought on by the arrival of World War II.

A new Pacific Coast Hockey League (PCHL) formed as an amateur league in 1944–1945. The PCHL was actually two amateur leagues that banded together to form one circuit—the Southern California Hockey League (SCHL) and the Northwest International Hockey League (NIHL). The Portland Eagles were inaugural members of the PCHL in 1944–1945. The PCHL reorganized into a minor professional league for the 1948–1949 season. The Portland club changed its name to the Portland Penguins in 1949–1950 and had a live penguin as a mascot; it made an appearance before the start of each game. The penguin mascot traveled with the team for away games and rode in Portland coach Jimmy Ward's car. In 1950–1951, the team reverted back to the nickname "Eagles." The Portland Eagles folded after the 1950–1951 campaign because of financial difficulties and a dilapidated arena—the Hippodrome. The Hippodrome had been home to all five Portland professional hockey franchises up to this point (the PCHA and WHL Rosebuds, the original and WCHL/NWHL/PCHL Buckaroos, and the Eagles/Penguins).

With the geography of the league gradually shifting off the coast in the early 1950s, the PCHL became more appropriately named the Western Hockey League (WHL) for the 1952–1953 season. The WHL would develop into one of the greatest minor professional leagues in hockey history.

Minor professional hockey returned to Portland in 1960–1961, and the name Portland Buckaroos was brought back. The Buckaroos spent 14 seasons in the WHL (from 1960–1961 to 1973–1974) and are one of the most successful teams in WHL history. The club is tied for the second most Patrick Cup titles of all time with three (1960–1961, 1964–1965, and 1970–1971). Portland has the greatest all-time regular-season winning percentage in WHL history with an outstanding .597 mark (550-355-101) and has captured the most regular-season titles in WHL history with eight (including a WHL record five in a row). The Buckaroos also hold all-time WHL records for most appearances in the Patrick Cup finals (nine) and most consecutive appearances in the Patrick Cup finals (five). The Buckaroos iced some of the greatest players in WHL history, as well as in minor professional hockey history, including Don Head, Andy Hebenton, Gordon Fashoway, Guyle Fielder, Art Jones, Norm Johnson, Connie Madigan, and Bill Saunders.

The Portland Buckaroos provided area fans with a high caliber of hockey and established themselves as one of the top minor league hockey teams of all time. Portland truly has one of the richest traditions in hockey history.

1

America's First Stanley Cup Challengers

Professional hockey was born in Portland when the Portland Rosebuds became members of the Pacific Coast Hockey Association (PCHA). The New Westminster Royals, a member of the PCHA from 1911–1912 to 1913–1914, transferred to Portland and were renamed the Portland Rosebuds for the 1914–1915 season. The Rosebuds home ice was the Hippodrome in Portland. In their inaugural season in 1914–1915, the Rosebuds, coached by Pete Muldoon, finished second out of three teams in the PCHA with a 9-9 record. The PCHA did not have intra-league playoffs until the 1917–1918 season.

In 1915–1916, the Rosebuds became the first America team to compete for the Stanley Cup, as they finished first in the PCHA with a 13-5 record under new coach Edward Savage (he piloted the team through the 1917–1918 campaign). At that time, the Stanley Cup finals were alternately hosted by the PCHA or National Hockey Association (NHA) winners. Unfortunately for Portland, the finals series was scheduled to be hosted by the NHA champion, the Montreal Canadiens. In a best-of-five series, Montreal edged Portland three games to two to capture its first of 24 Stanley Cup championships.

The Rosebuds were not as successful during the next two seasons, posting losing records. Portland had a 9-15 record in 1916–1917 (finishing third out of four teams) and posted a 7-11 record in 1917–1918 (finishing last out of three teams). The Rosebuds franchise moved to Victoria, British Colombia, for the 1918–1919 campaign and were renamed the Victoria Aristocrats. Charles Tobin is the Rosebuds' all-time leader in points (79), goals (59), and games played (78), while Eddie Oatman holds the club's all-time record for assists (28). Tommy Dunderdale accumulated the most penalties in minutes (PIM) in team history (243).

A new Portland Rosebuds franchise would emerge in the Western Hockey League (WHL) during the 1925–1926 season when the Regina Capitals, a team that existed in that league from 1921–1922 to 1924–1925, transferred to Portland. The Rosebuds, coached by Pete Muldoon, finished fourth out of six WHL teams with a 12-16-2 record and missed the playoffs. The 1925–1926 campaign was the last for the WHL and the Portland Rosebuds.

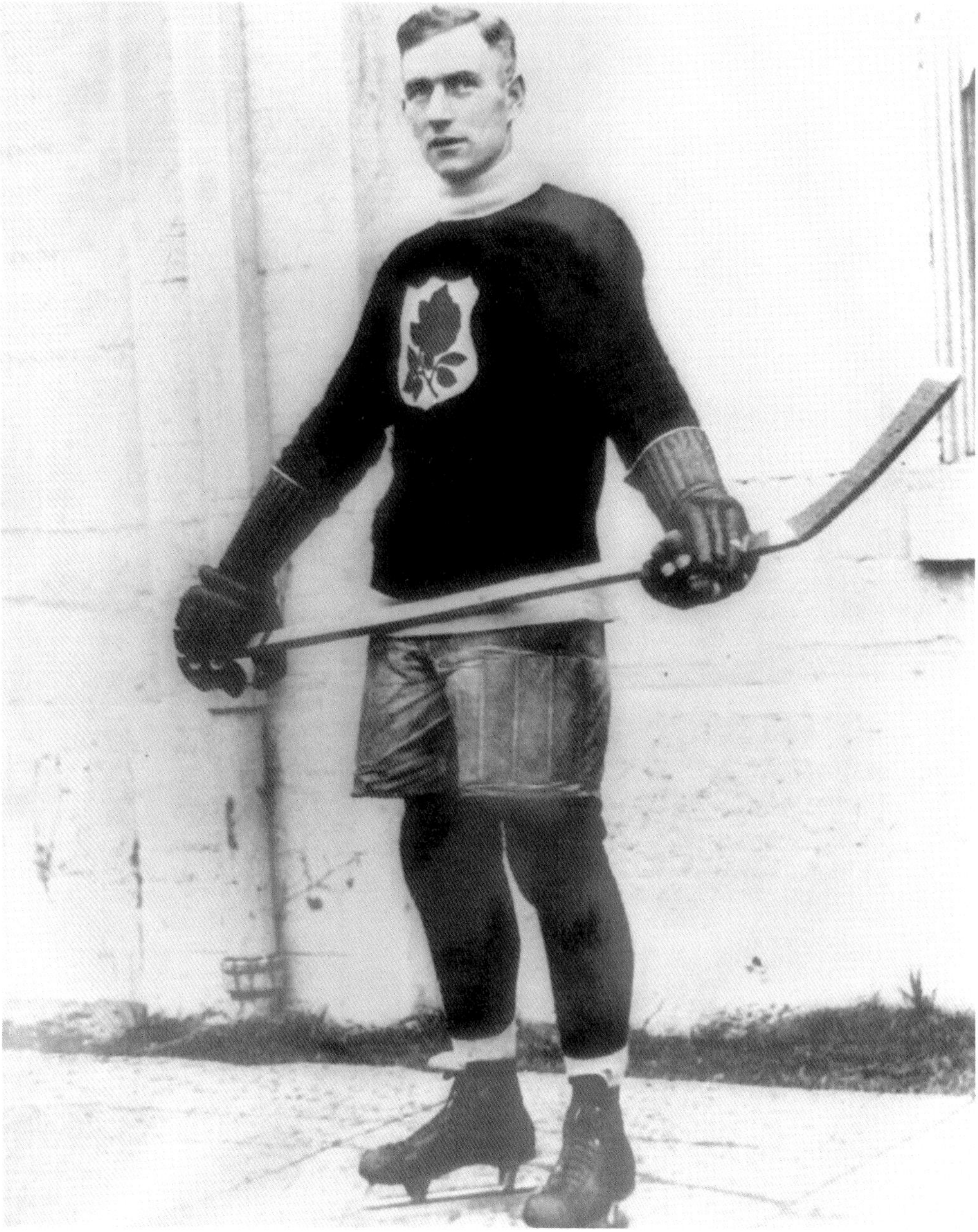

DICK IRVIN (CENTER). Irvin was inducted into the Hockey Hall of Fame in 1958. He played for both Portland Rosebuds franchises. In 1916–1917 with the original Rosebuds, the center garnered 45 points, 35 goals, and 24 PIM in 24 games. In 1925–1926 with the WHL Rosebuds, he led the league in goals with 31, registered 36 points, and had 29 PIM in 30 games. Irvin spent four other seasons in the WCHL/WHL with Regina from 1921 to 1925. He was selected to the WCHL All-Star Team twice (one first-team and one second-team selection) and the PCHA All-Star second team once. The Hall of Famer skated in the NHL from 1926 to 1929 and collected 52 points, 29 goals, and 78 PIM in 94 games.

CHARLES MCVEIGH (CENTER). A veteran of nine NHL seasons, from 1926 to 1935, McVeigh tallied 172 points, 84 goals, and 138 PIM in 397 games. The center skated with Portland in 1925–1926, garnering 11 points, 8 goals, and 14 PIM in 28 games. He also spent time in the WCHL/WHL with Regina from 1921 to 1925. McVeigh played minor pro hockey with London of the International Hockey League (IHL) in 1935–1936.

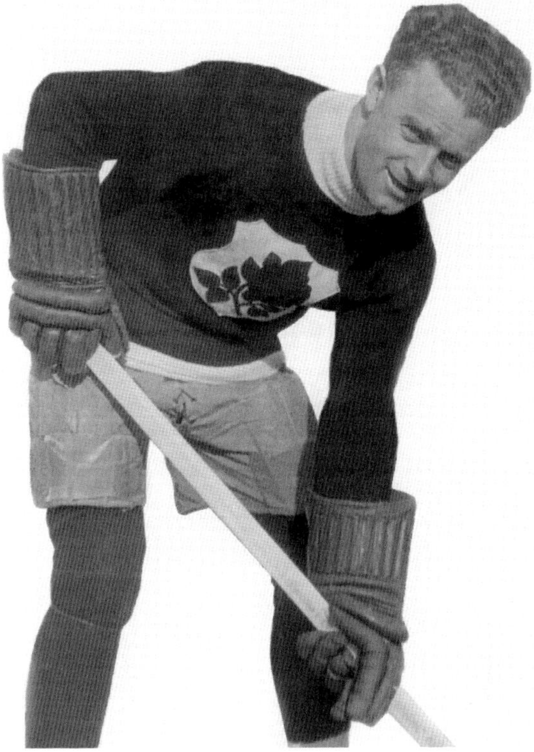

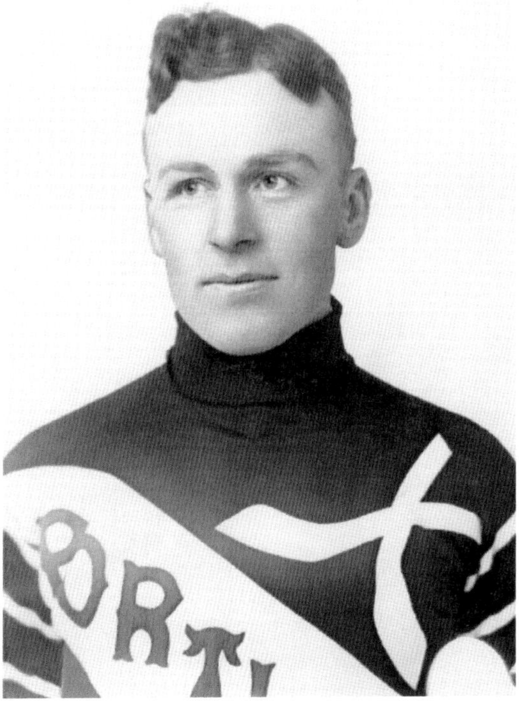

ART THROOP (LEFT WING). Throop skated with the Rosebuds in the team's inaugural season in 1914–1915 and garnered 24 points, 16 goals, and 43 PIM in 18 games. The left-winger also skated in the PCHA with New Westminster in 1913–1914 and spent time in the NHA with Haileybury in 1909–1910 and Toronto in 1912–1913.

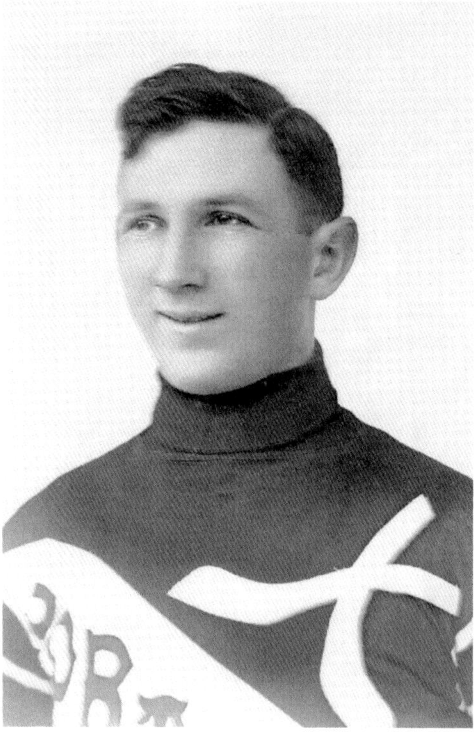

PETE MULDOON (COACH). Muldoon coached the PCHA Rosebuds to a 9-9 (.500) record during their inaugural season in 1914–1915. He returned to Portland in 1925–1926 with the WHL Rosebuds and led the team to a 12-16-8 (.444) record. Muldoon was behind the bench in the NHL with Chicago in 1926–1927 and compiled a 19-22-3 (.466) record. He also piloted Seattle (PCHA) from 1920–1921 to 1923–1924.

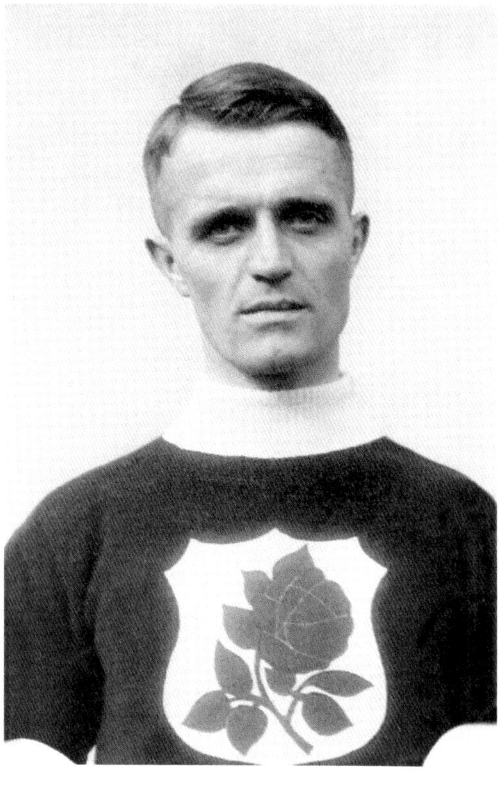

PERCY "PUSS" TRAUB (DEFENSE). A veteran of three NHL seasons, from 1926 to 1929, Traub garnered 6 points, 3 goals, and 217 PIM in 130 games. In 1925–1926 with the WHL Rosebuds, he tallied 4 points, 3 assists, and 66 PIM in 28 games. The defenseman also played in the WCHL/WHL with Regina from 1921 to 1925.

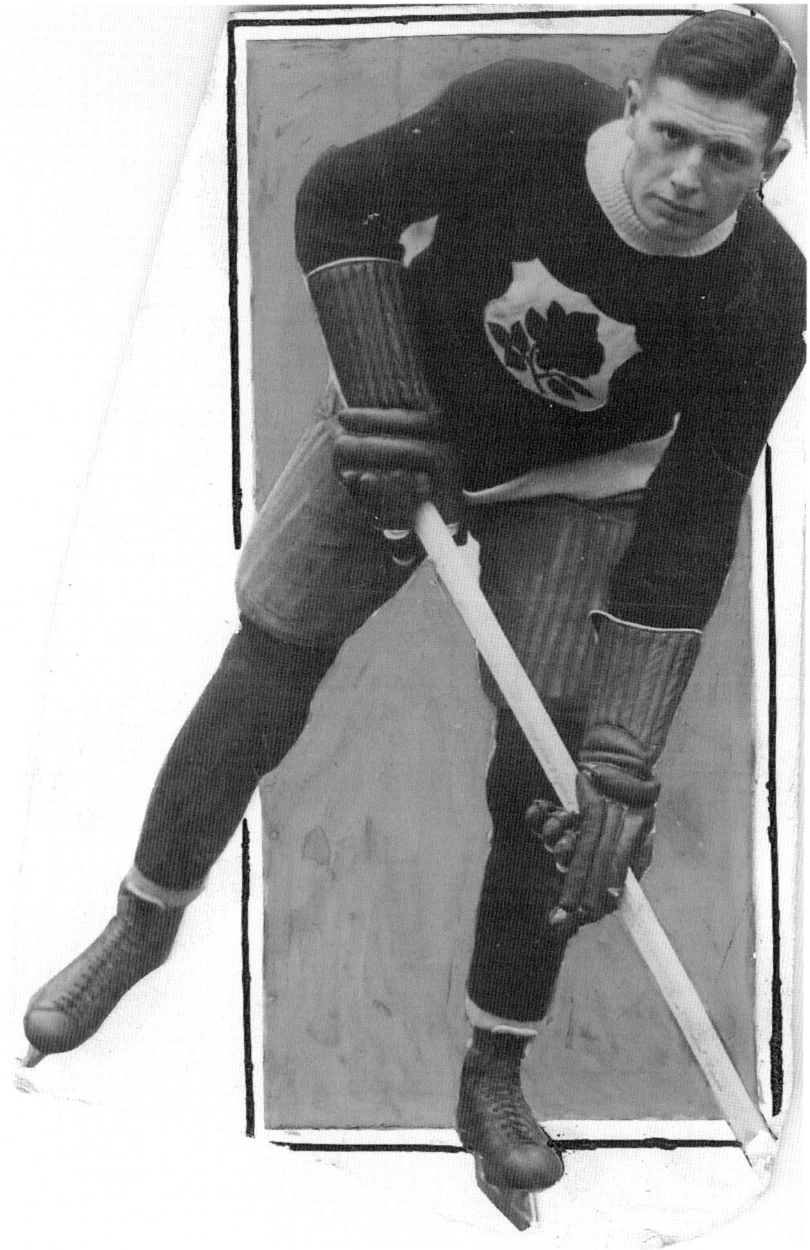

George "The Western Wizard" Hay (Left Wing). In 1925–1926, with the WHL Rosebuds, Hay was named a first team WHL All-Star, tallying 31 points, 19 goals, and 4 PIM in 30 games. The left-winger played seven seasons in the NHL, from 1926 to 1931 and from 1932 to 1934, garnering 134 points, 74 goals, and 84 PIM in 239 games. He was a NHL All-Star in 1927–1928. "The Western Wizard" spent five campaigns in the WCHL/WHL from 1921 to 1926 and was a first-team All-Star four times. Hay was an original Chicago Black Hawk in 1926–1927 and has the distinction of scoring the first NHL goal at the old Chicago Coliseum on November 17, 1926. He was inducted into the Hockey Hall of Fame in 1958.

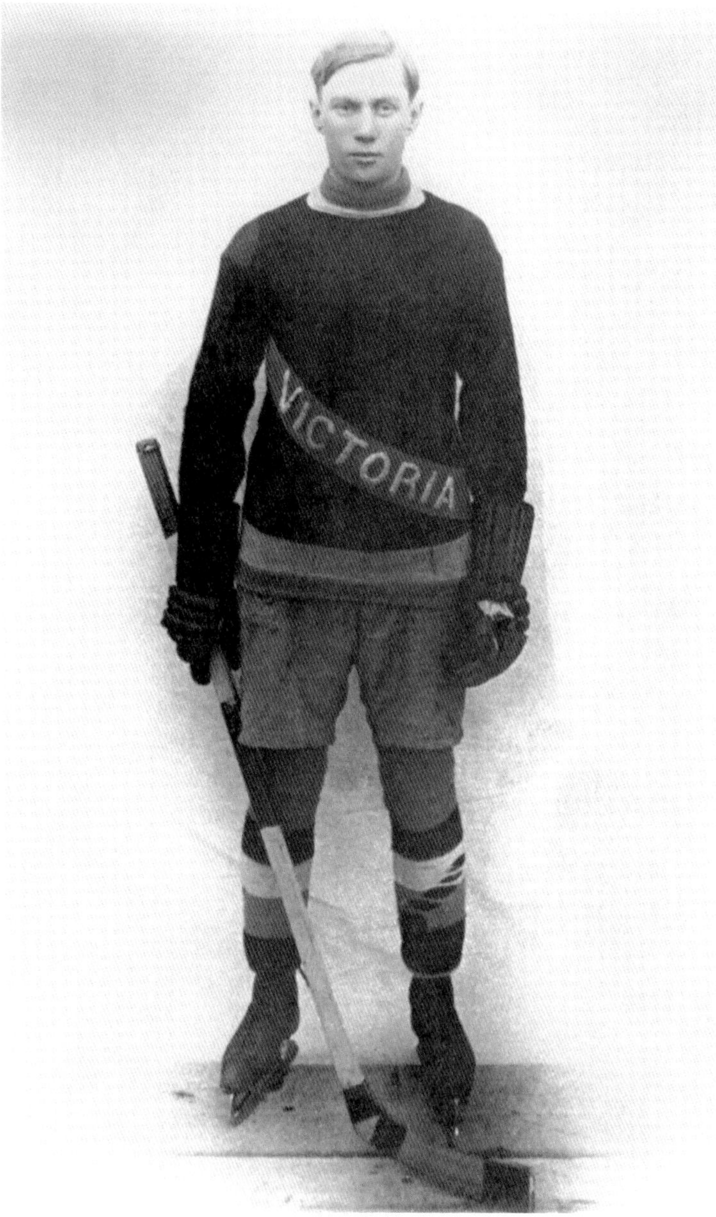

TOMMY DUNDERDALE (CENTER). He was inducted into the Hockey Hall of Fame in 1974. The Australian-born player spent three seasons with Portland, from 1915 to 1918, tallying an all-time team record 243 PIM and the second most goals in team history (50), and registering 63 points in 60 games. The center played 12 campaigns in the PCHA, from 1911 to 1923, and tallied the most goals in league history (194). He was named a PCHA first-team All-Star six times, led the league in goals in three seasons and points in two seasons, and skated for three PCHA championship teams with Victoria (1912–1913 and 1913–1914) and Portland (1915–1916). Dunderdale holds the all-time PCHA single-season PIM record with 141 in 1916–1917. The hockey legend also played major league hockey in the NHA from 1909 to 1911 and in the WCHL/WHL in 1923–1924.

Laudas "Duke" Dukowski (Defense). Dukowski garnered 13 points, 6 goals, and 46 PIM in 29 games with the Rosebuds in 1925–1926. The defenseman spent five seasons in the NHL (the 1926–1927 season, from 1929 to 1931, and from 1932 to 1934), and produced 46 points, 16 goals, and 172 PIM in 200 games. He skated for Stanley Cup–winning Chicago in 1933–1934.

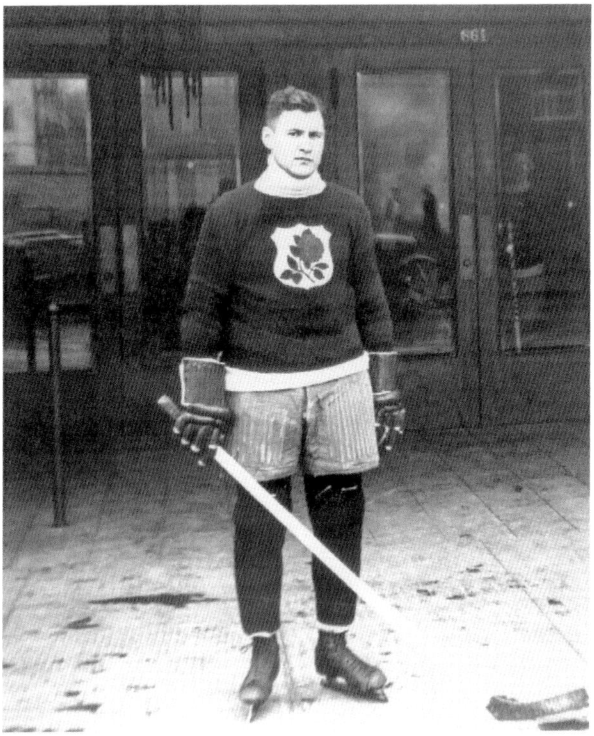

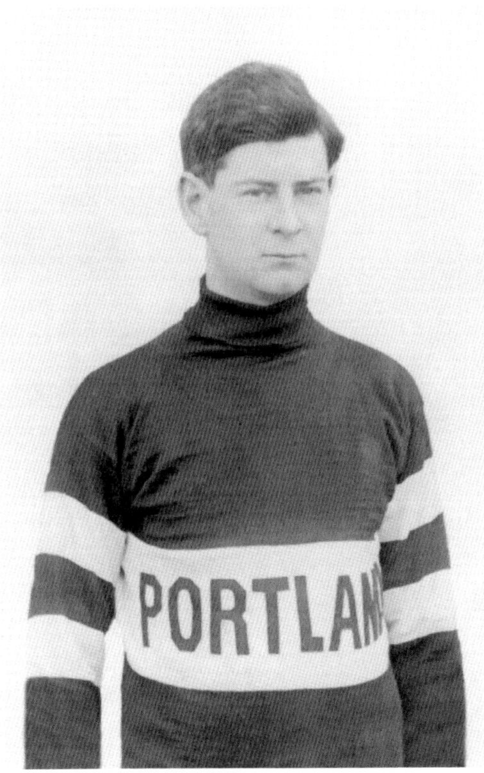

Del Irvine (Defense). In 1915–1916 with Portland, Irvine garnered 7 points, 5 assists, and 21 PIM in 18 games. Before turning pro, the defenseman skated in the Winnipeg Senior Hockey League (WSrHL) with Winnipeg from 1912 to 1915.

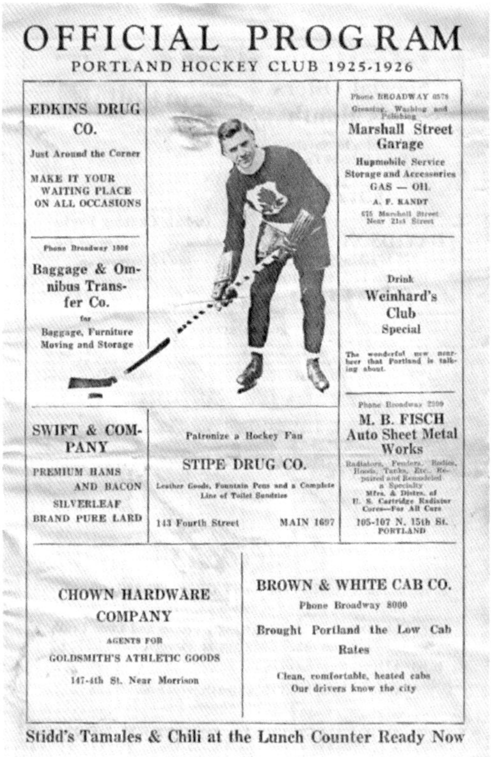

OFFICIAL PROGRAM

PORTLAND HOCKEY CLUB 1925-1926

EDKINS DRUG CO.
Just Around the Corner
MAKE IT YOUR WAITING PLACE ON ALL OCCASIONS

Phone Broadway 1896
Baggage & Omnibus Transfer Co.
for
Baggage, Furniture Moving and Storage

Phone BROADWAY 6578
Greasing, Washing and Polishing
Marshall Street Garage
Hupmobile Service
Storage and Accessories
GAS — OIL
A. F. RANDT
675 Marshall Street Near 21st Street

Drink
Weinhard's Club Special
The wonderful new near-beer that Portland is talking about.

SWIFT & COMPANY
PREMIUM HAMS AND BACON
SILVERLEAF BRAND PURE LARD

Patronize a Hockey Fan
STIPE DRUG CO.
Leather Goods, Fountain Pens and a Complete Line of Toilet Sundries
143 Fourth Street MAIN 1697

Phone Broadway 2209
M. B. FISCH
Auto Sheet Metal Works
Radiators, Fenders, Bodies, Hoods, Tanks, Etc. Repaired and Remodeled a Specialty
Mfrs. & Distrs. of U. S. Cartridge Radiator Cores—For All Cars
105-107 N. 15th St. PORTLAND

CHOWN HARDWARE COMPANY
AGENTS FOR
GOLDSMITH'S ATHLETIC GOODS
147-4th St. Near Morrison

BROWN & WHITE CAB CO.
Phone Broadway 8000
Brought Portland the Low Cab Rates
Clean, comfortable, heated cabs
Our drivers know the city

Stidd's Tamales & Chili at the Lunch Counter Ready Now

ROSEBUDS PROGRAM, 1925–1926. Dick Irvin, Tommy Dunderdale, George Hay, and Thomas "Moose" Johnson are the only players in Portland hockey history to be inducted into the Hockey Hall of Fame.

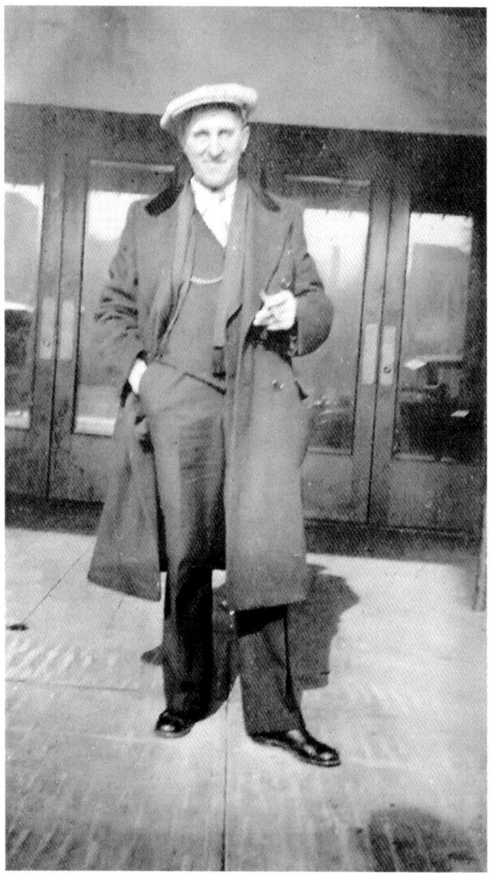

THOMAS "MOOSE" JOHNSON (DEFENSE). Johnson was inducted into the Hockey Hall of Fame in 1952. He skated with the PCHA Rosebuds from 1914 to 1918, producing 45 points, 27 goals, and 140 PIM, while playing in the second-most games in team history (75). Johnson also played in the PCHA with New Westminster from 1911 to 1914 and with Victoria from 1918 to 1922. He was named a PCHA first-team All-Star eight times.

2

The Original Buckaroos

Professional hockey returned to Portland in 1928–1929 with the arrival of the new minor professional Pacific Coast Hockey League (PCHL). Bobby Rowe, manager of Portland's home ice—the Hippodrome—was the general manager and coach of the Portland entry. Rowe nicknamed his team "the Buckaroos" because he felt that name suggested a fighting quality; he chose not to use the traditional Rosebuds name because he believed that label was somewhat effeminate. In 1928–1929, the Buckaroos finished in third place with a 14-17-5 record and made the playoffs. The locals lost in a semifinal round, two-game, total-goals series against the Seattle Eskimos, three goals to one (2-1 and 1-0).

Rowe's club improved to a 20-10-6 record in 1929–1930 and finished in second place. Portland squared off with the first-place Vancouver Lions for the postseason championship (there was no semifinal round). The Lions won their second straight PCHL playoff championship by defeating the Buckaroos three games to one.

In 1930–1931, Portland compiled a 12-15-8 record, finished in third place, and did not qualify for the playoffs. Buckaroo Dave Downie led the PCHL in regular-season points that year with 17. Vancouver won the PCHL playoff championship in 1930–1931 for the third consecutive season to become only one of two teams in minor professional hockey history to accomplish that feat at that time (the Oakland Sheiks of the California Hockey League [CalHL] also won three straight postseason crowns from 1928–1929 to 1930–1931). The Lions would not have a chance to extend their championship reign, as the PCHL folded after only three campaigns because of the financial strains brought on by the Great Depression.

The original Buckaroos compiled a 46-42-19 (.519) record during three PCHL seasons. Red Conn is the franchise's all-time leader in points (44), goals (31), and games played (105), while Earl Armstrong holds the club's all-time record for assists (17). Jack Pratt is the team's all-time PIM king (260). Andy Aitkenhead set all-time team records for career goals against average (GAA) with a 1.34 mark, wins (32), shutouts (22), and games in goal (71).

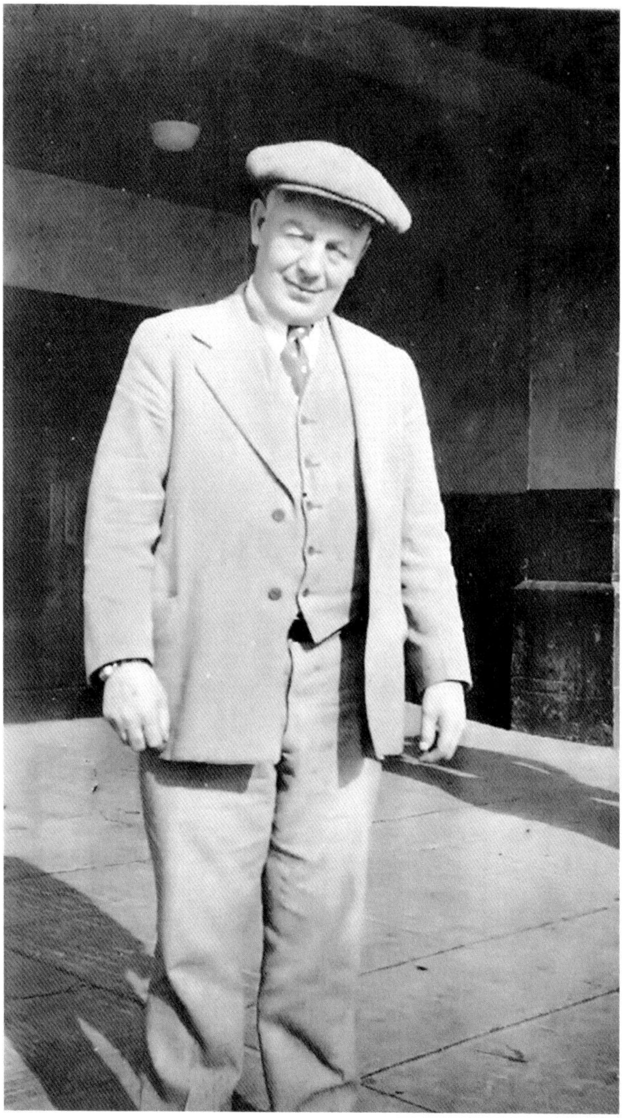

BOBBY ROWE (GENERAL MANAGER/COACH). Rowe coached Portland teams for 11 seasons—the PCHL from 1928–1929 to 1930–1931 and the WCHL/NWHL/PCHL from 1933–1934 to 1940–1941—and compiled a record of 194-172-64 (.526). He delivered two regular-season and playoff championships to the City of Roses in 1936–1937 and 1938–1939. The right wing/defenseman spent 13 seasons in the PCHA and was a member of the first American Stanley Cup winning team in 1916–1917—the Seattle Metropolitans (PCHA). He was a five-time PCHA All-Star and a member of four PCHA championship teams with Victoria (1912–1913 and 1913–1914) and Seattle (1916–1917 and 1918–1919). Rowe played one season in the NHL with the Boston Bruins in the team's inaugural season in 1924–1925 and skated in two seasons in the NHL's forerunner league—the NHA—from 1909 to 1911, with Renfrew. The Portland mentor finished his professional playing career with the Portland Rosebuds (WHL) in 1925–1926, as he skated in two games with the club.

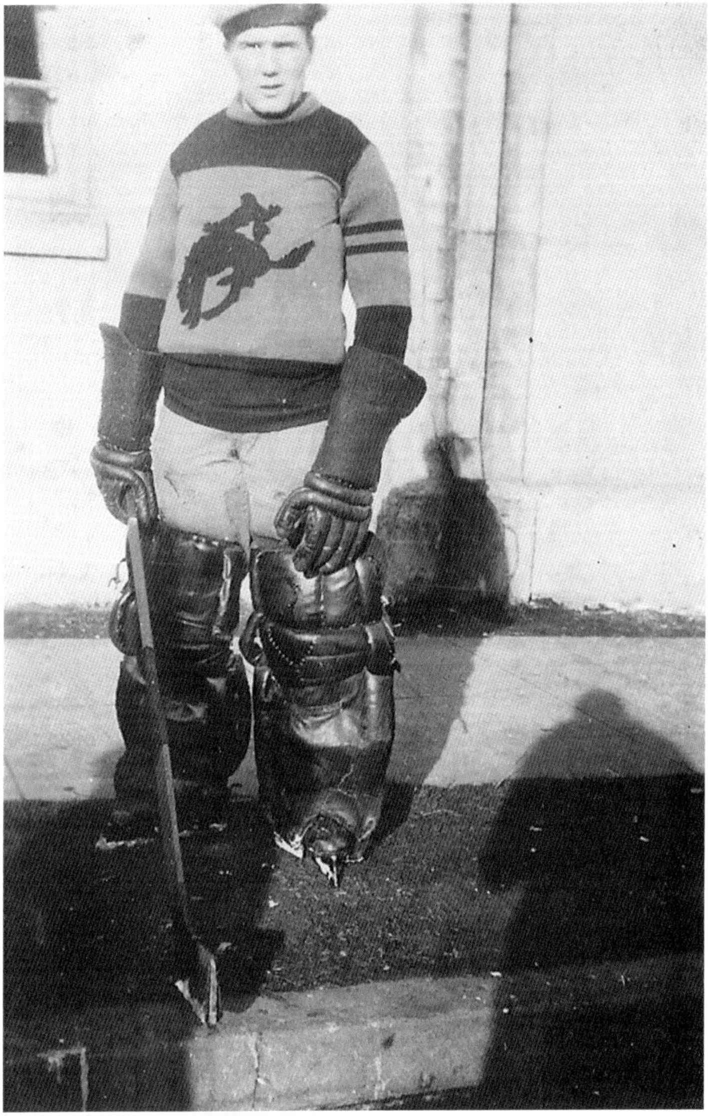

ANDY "THE GLASGOW GOBBLER" AITKENHEAD (GOALIE). He played two seasons with the original Buckaroos from 1929 to 1931, earning a 1.34 GAA, a 32-25-14 record, and 22 shutouts in 71 games. In 1929–1930, he established all-time single-season original Buckaroo records while leading the PCHL that season in GAA (0.94), wins (20), and shutouts (16). Aitkenhead played three seasons in the NHL, from 1932 to 1935, compiling a 2.35 GAA, a 47-43-16 record, and 11 shutouts in 106 games. He won a Stanley Cup with the Rangers in 1932–1933. The Glasgow Gobbler also played with the WCHL/NWHL/PCHL Buckaroos from 1934 to 1941 and had a 2.03 GAA, a 116-76-40 record, and 35 shutouts in 232 games. He led Portland to two PCHL playoff championships in 1936–1937 and 1938–1939. With the WCHL/NWHL/PCHL Buckaroos, Aitkenhead led the league in GAA five times (1934–1935, 1935–1936, 1936–1937, 1938–1939, and 1939–1940) and shutouts twice (1936–1937 and 1938–1939). The netminder also led Saskatoon to a Prairie Hockey League (PrHL) championship in 1927–1928.

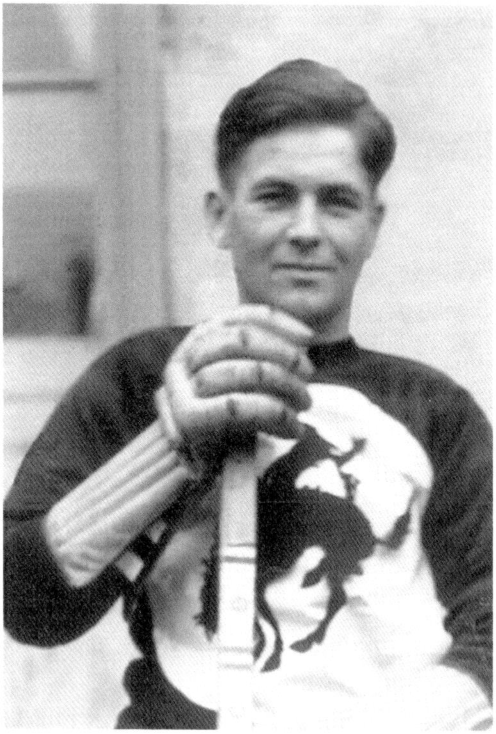

IKE MORRISON (FORWARD). Morrison played five games with the Buckaroos in 1928–1929. He skated in both seasons of the PrHL, from 1926 to 1928; played in the IHL in 1929–1930; and played in the Ontario Professional Hockey League (OPHL) in 1930–1931. The forward participated in the Memorial Cup tournament with Regina of the Regina Junior Hockey League (RJHL) in 1924–1925.

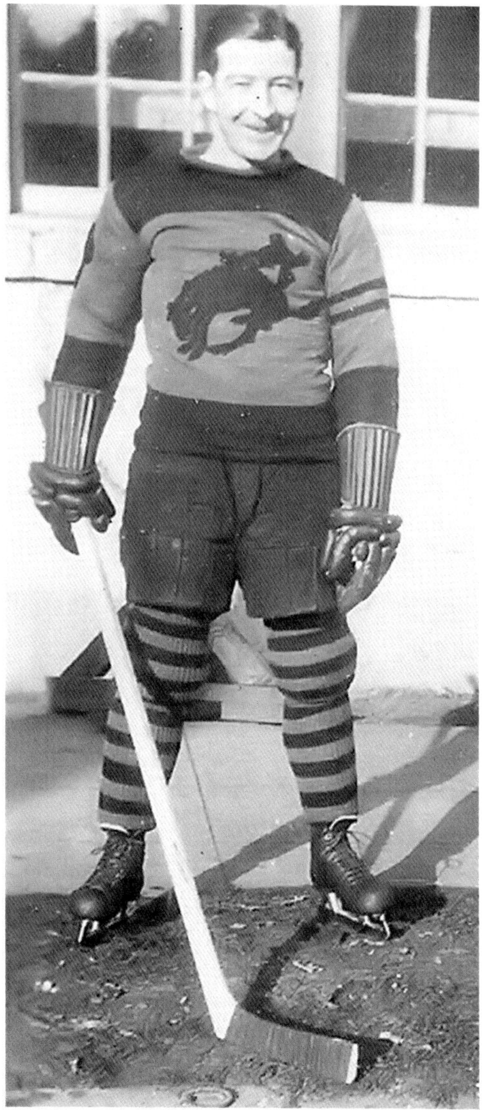

BUSTER HUFFMAN (LEFT WING). Huffman had 6 points, 5 goals, and 6 PIM in 32 games with Portland during the 1929–1930 season. The left-winger played most of his career in the California Professional Hockey League (CalPHL)/California Hockey League (CalHL) between 1925 and 1932. He was a member of three playoff championship teams—with Palais-De-Glace (CalPHL) in 1925–1926, Oakland (CalHL) in 1930–1931, and Prairie Hockey League (PrHL) champion Calgary in 1926–1927.

GORDON TEEL (CENTER). Teel played three seasons with the Buckaroos, from 1928 to 1931, splitting the 1928–1929 campaign between Portland and Vancouver. In his two full seasons with the Buckaroos, from 1929 to 1931, the center produced 17 points, 11 goals, and 113 PIM in 66 games. He won back-to-back Sinclair Trophies with St. Louis, members of the American Hockey Association (AHA), in 1934–1935 and 1935–1936.

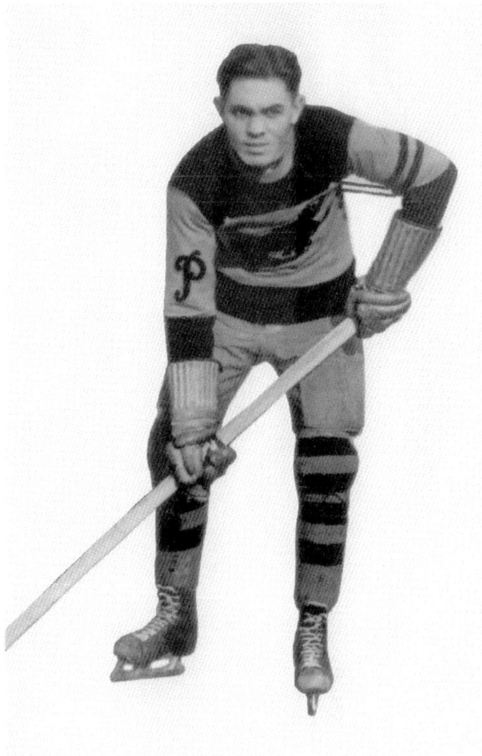

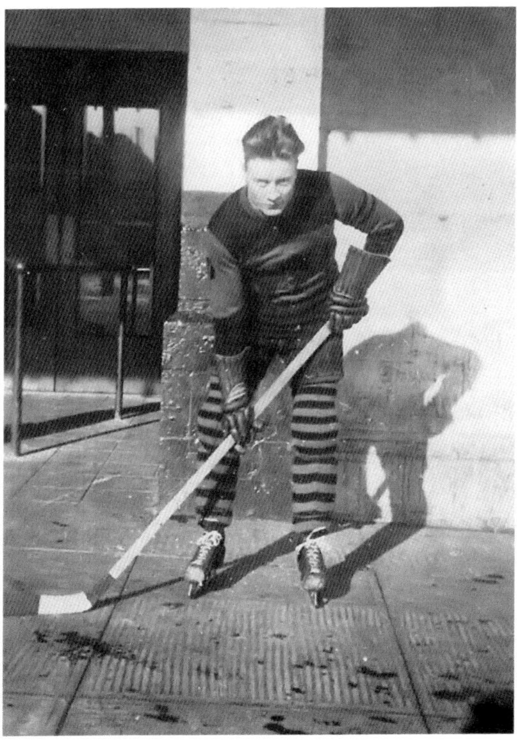

JACK PRATT (CENTER). Pratt is the Buckaroos' all-time penalty minutes leader with 260 PIM. He played with Portland from 1928 to 1930 and collected 16 points and 10 goals in 70 games. The center also skated with the WCHL/NWHL/PCHL Buckaroos in 1935–1936, garnering 34 points, 19 goals, and 43 PIM in 27 games. Pratt skated with Boston (NHL) from 1930 to 1932, registering 2 points and 42 PIM in 37 games.

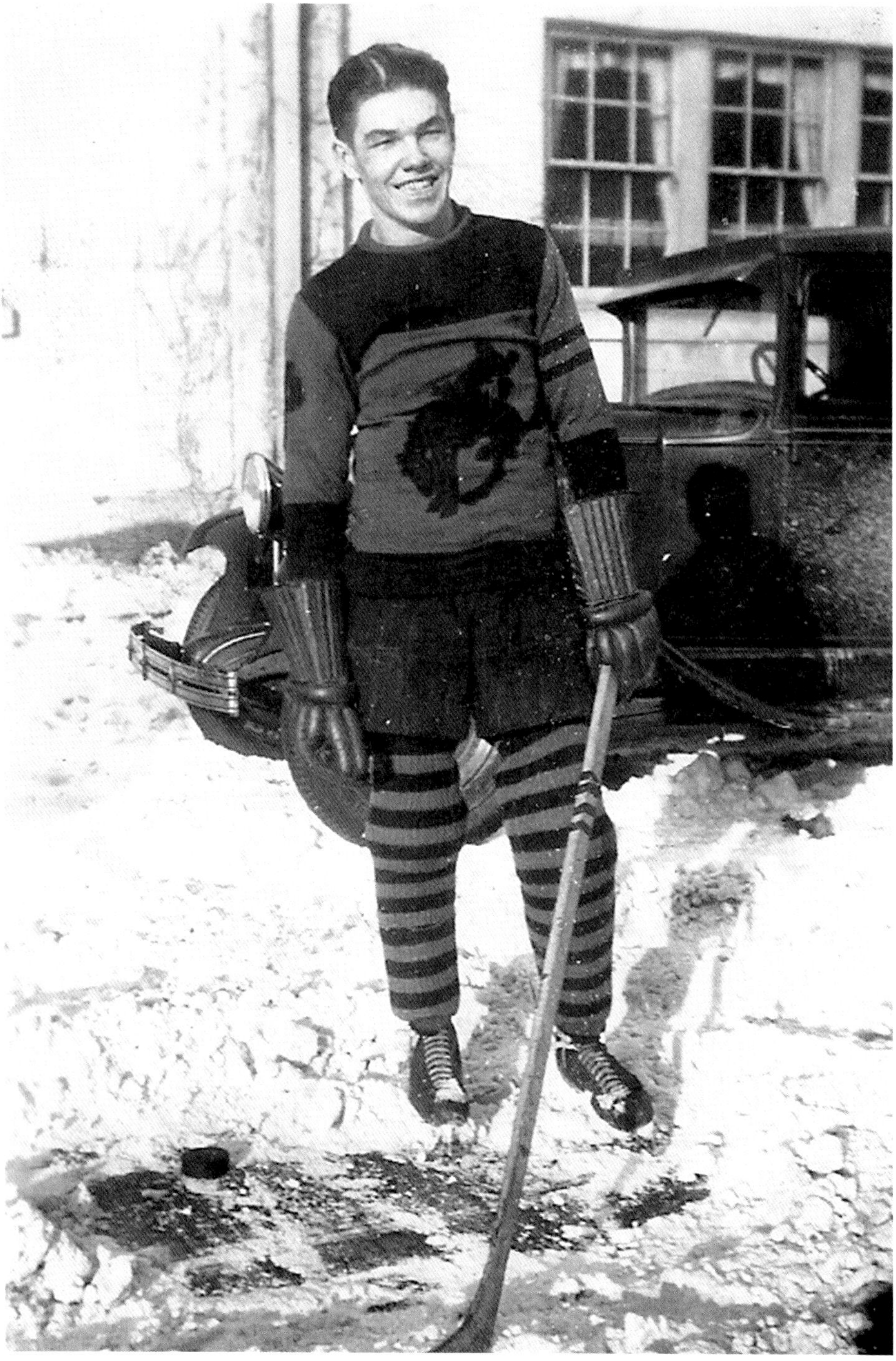

Dave Downie (Center). During three seasons with Portland, from 1928 to 1931, Downie garnered 38 points, 23 goals, and 174 PIM in 87 games. He skated in the NHL with Toronto in 1932–1933 and had one point and two PIM in 11 games. The center also spent time in several other minor professional leagues during his career.

EARL ARMSTRONG (DEFENSE). Armstrong is the Buckaroos' all-time leader in assists (17). He also had 30 points, 13 goals, and 231 PIM in 104 games during three seasons with Portland from 1928 to 1931. The defenseman participated in the Memorial Cup tournament with the Ottawa Gunners of the Ottawa City Junior Hockey League (OCJHL) during the 1927–1928 campaign.

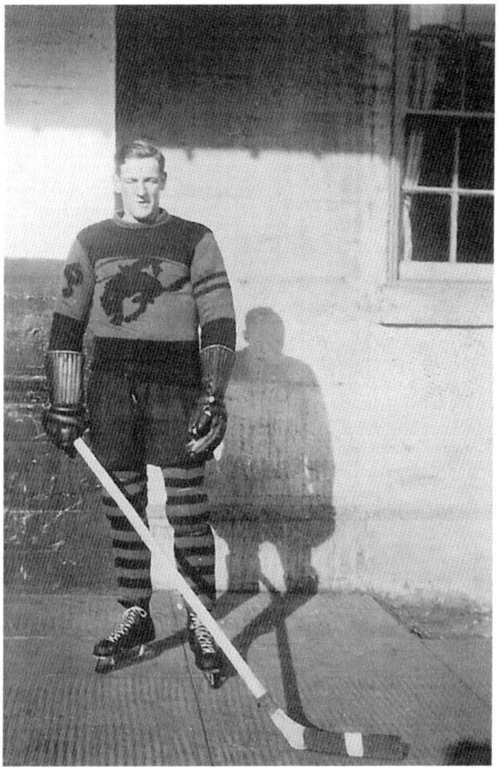

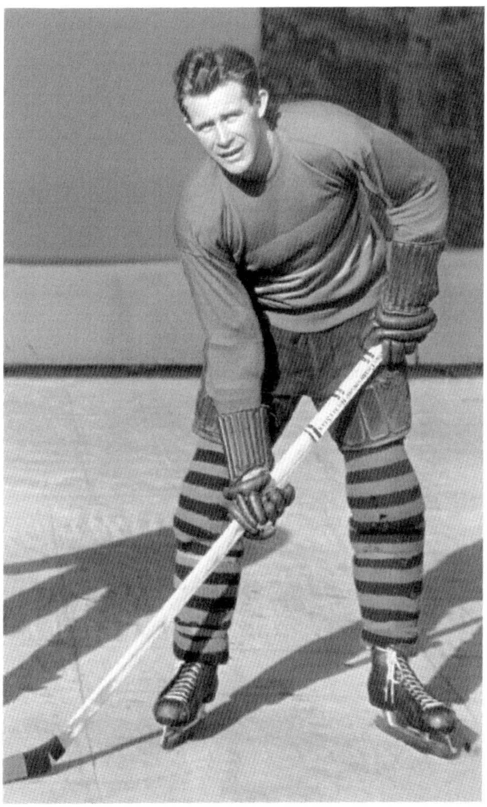

FRANK SINGER (DEFENSE). The defenseman had 1 point and 12 PIM in 10 games with Portland in 1928–1929. Singer also played in the CalHL in 1929–1930 and in the AHA from 1930 to 1932.

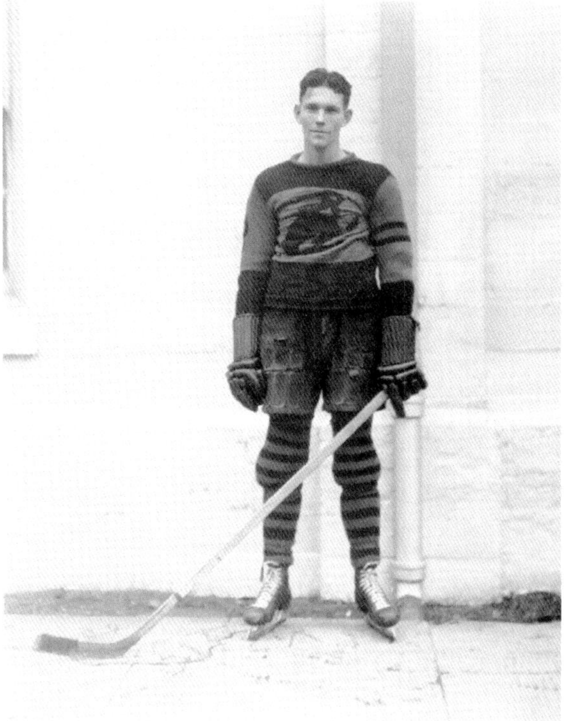

ROLLY ROULSTON (LEFT WING). In 1930–1931, with Portland, the left-winger tallied three points on three goals and accumulated 68 PIM in 34 games. In three NHL campaigns with Detroit from 1935 to 1938, Roulston produced 6 points and 10 PIM in 24 games. He was a member of the Detroit Olympics (IHL), back-to-back Teddy Oke Trophy winning teams in 1934–1935 and 1935–1936.

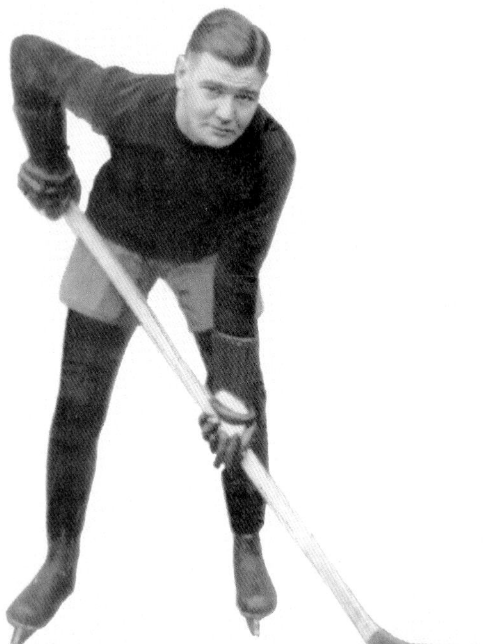

JOHN MCCULLY (DEFENSE). McCully skated in five games with Portland during the 1928–1929 campaign. He also spent time in the Canadian Professional Hockey League (CPHL) from 1928 to 1930 (the CPHL was later known as the IHL), played in the OPHL in 1930–1931, and skated in the Canadian American Hockey League (CAHL) in 1933–1934.

3

Bobby Rowe Brings the Buckaroos Back

Bobby Rowe helped form a new Portland Buckaroos team in the minor professional North West Hockey League (NWHL) in 1933–1934 and was again the team's general manager and coach. The NWHL was known as the Western Canada Hockey League (WCHL) during its first season in 1932–1933. Portland finished in last place in 1933–1934 with a 10-21-3 record and missed the playoffs. Rowe's team had productive seasons in 1934–1935 (15-10-7) and 1935–1936 (18-14-8) but were eliminated in the playoff semifinals against the Vancouver Lions in both seasons by two-games-to-one counts.

The NWHL changed its name to the Pacific Coast Hockey League (PCHL) for the 1936–1937 season because the teams in the league were now all located on the coast. The Buckaroos won the PCHL regular-season and playoff championships in 1936–1937 (21-13-5) and in 1938–1939 (31-9-8). Portland was given a direct bye into the PCHL playoff finals during both seasons for capturing the regular-season crown. In 1936–1937, the Buckaroos swept the Spokane Clippers in the playoff finals three games to none, and they defeated the Seattle Seahawks in the playoff finals four games to one in 1938–1939.

In between the two championship years, the Buckaroos experienced one of the most controversial season endings in minor league hockey history. In 1937–1938, Rowe's club placed third with a 16-18-8 mark and faced Vancouver in the semifinals. Vancouver protested Portland using emergency replacement Lou Holmes (loaned from Spokane) in the second game of the series, which was won by the Buckaroos to even the best-of-three series at one game apiece. The PCHL later ruled that Holmes was an ineligible player and ordered that game two be replayed. Bobby Rowe refused to have the Buckaroos replay the game, and the PCHL ruled game two a Portland forfeit and awarded the semifinal series to Vancouver.

In 1939–1940, the Buckaroos made it to the PCHL playoff finals for the third time in four years, finishing with a 17-18-5 record (second place). In the only playoff series that year, Vancouver beat Portland four games to one in the finals. The locals finished in last place out of four teams in 1940–1941 with a 20-27-1 mark and failed to qualify for the postseason.

The PCHL did not operate in 1941–1942 because of a lack of players brought on by the arrival of World War II. The Buckaroos earned a 148-130-45 (.528) record in their eight seasons in the league.

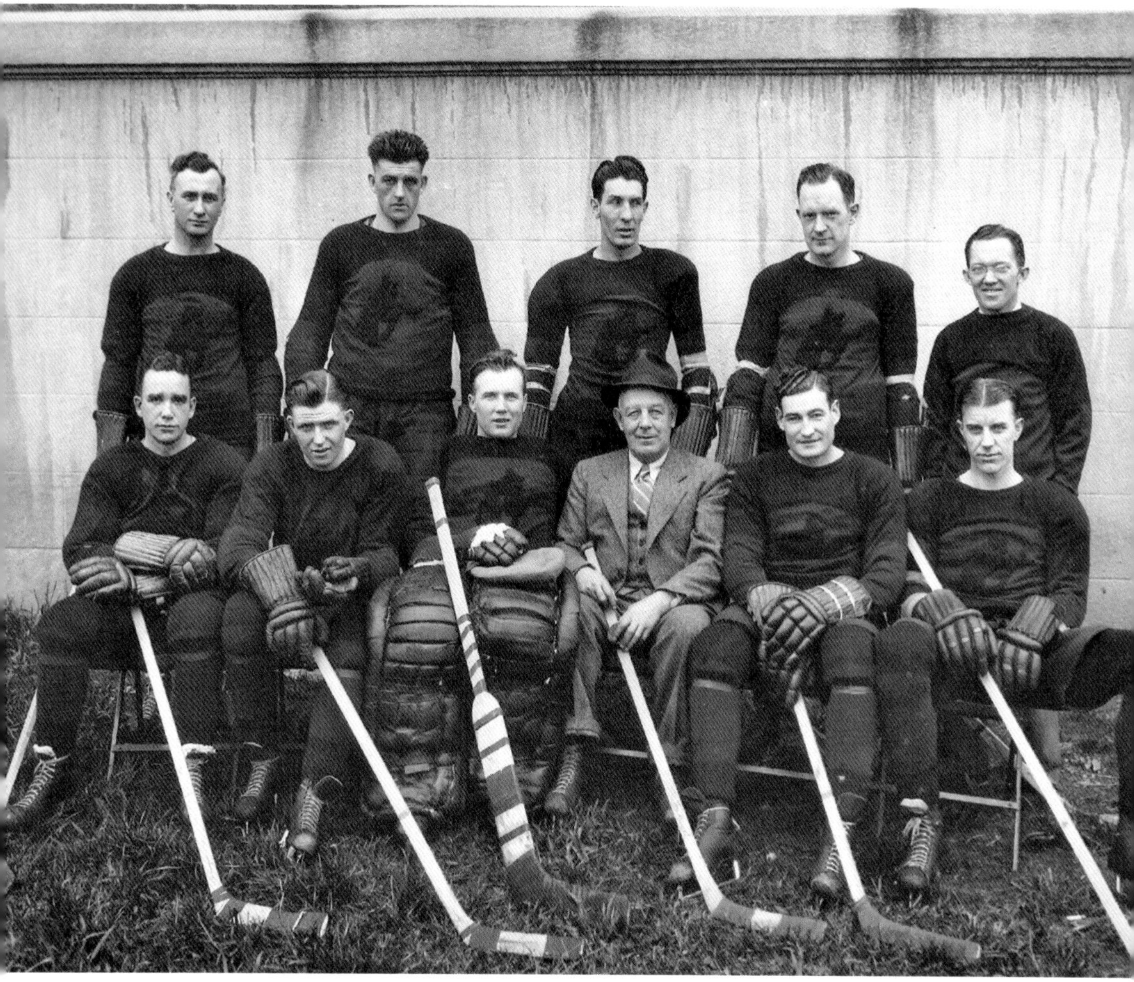

PORTLAND BUCKAROOS, 1934–1935. Pictured here from left to right are the following: (first row) Jim Evans, Jimmy Jempson, Andy Aitkenhead, Bobby Rowe (general manager/coach), Ron "Peaches" Lyons, and John Hemmerling; (second row) Jack Arbour, Moose Munson, Ralph Blyth, Gord Fraser, and unidentified.

Jack Arbour (Defense). In two seasons with Portland, from 1934 to 1936, Arbour compiled 30 points, 17 goals, and 57 PIM in 71 games. The defenseman skated in two NHL campaigns between 1926 and 1929, garnering 6 points, 5 goals, and 56 PIM in 47 games. He was a member of two Teddy Oke Trophy championship teams with Windsor (CPHL/IHL) in 1928–1929 and 1930–1931.

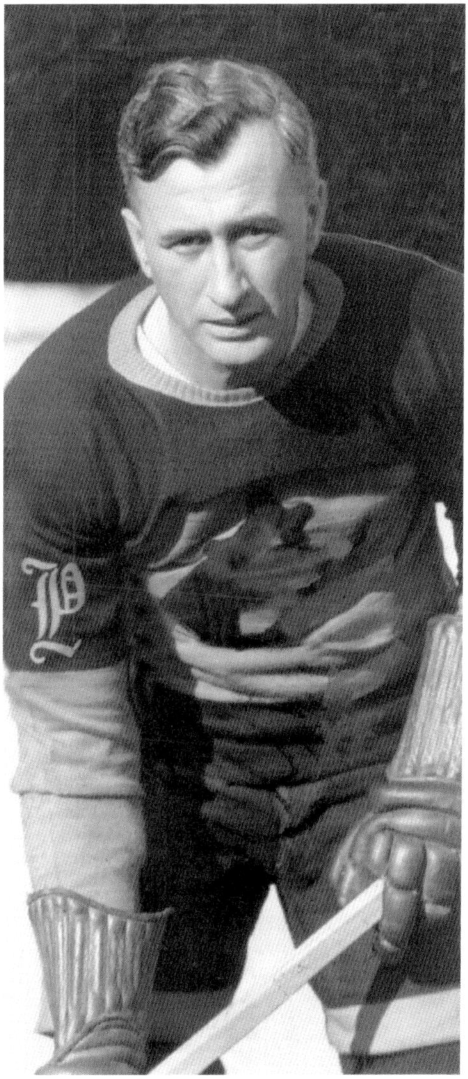

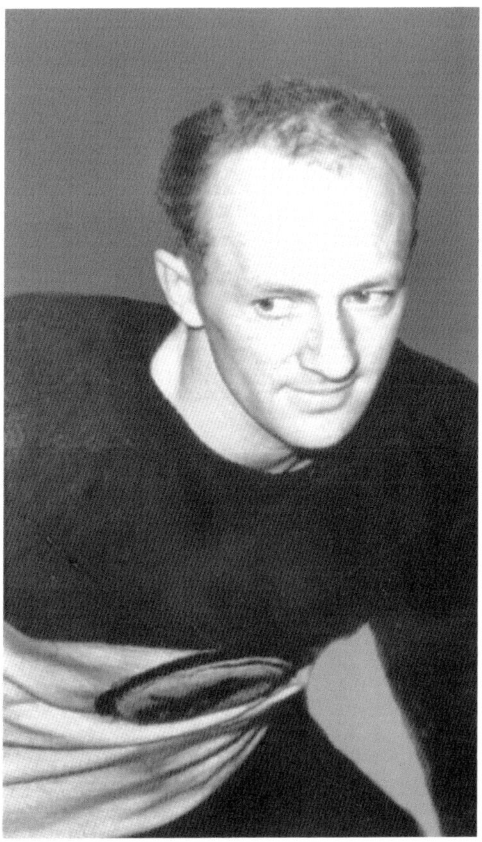

Lou Holmes (Center). Holmes ranks second in points (150), goals (71), and assists (79) in WCHL/NWHL/PCHL Buckaroos' history. The center skated in 133 regular-season games with Portland from 1938 to 1941 and had a stint in the 1937–1938 postseason with the Buckaroos. Holmes also set WCHL/NWHL/PCHL Buckaroos' single-season records for points (74), goals (34), and assists (40) during the team's 1938–1939 PCHL championship year.

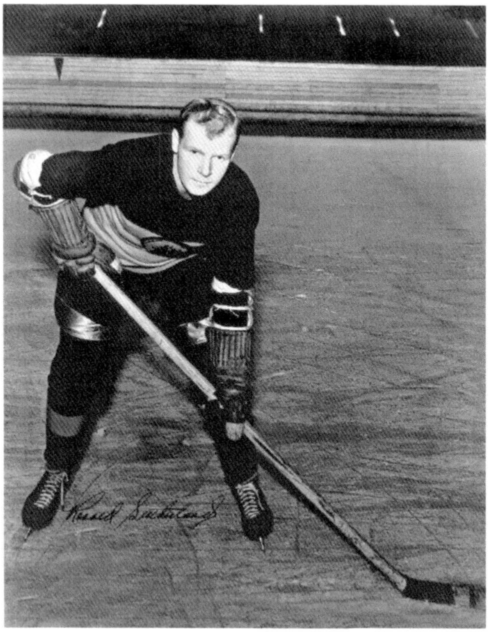

RON SUTHERLAND (DEFENSE). Sutherland is the WCHL/NWHL/PCHL Buckaroos' all-time leader in games played (258) and penalty minutes (481). From 1935 to 1941, the defenseman also garnered 94 points and 44 goals during six seasons with Portland. He was a member of the Buckaroos' 1936–1937 and 1938–1939 championship teams.

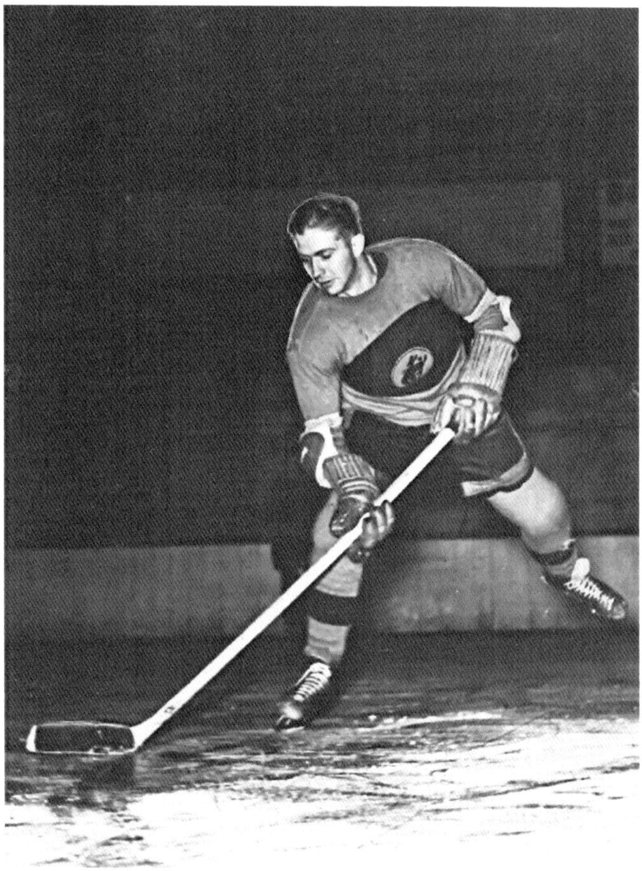

BOB "BUD" GILMOUR (DEFENSE). He was a member of two Portland championship teams in 1936–1937 and 1938–1939. In four seasons with the Buckaroos (in 1933–1934 and from 1936 to 1939), the defenseman tallied 31 points, 13 goals, and 207 PIM in 139 games. He holds the WCHL/NWHL/PCHL Buckaroos' record for most PIM in a single season—109 in 1938–1939. Gilmour won a Central Hockey League (CHL) championship with St. Paul in 1934–1935.

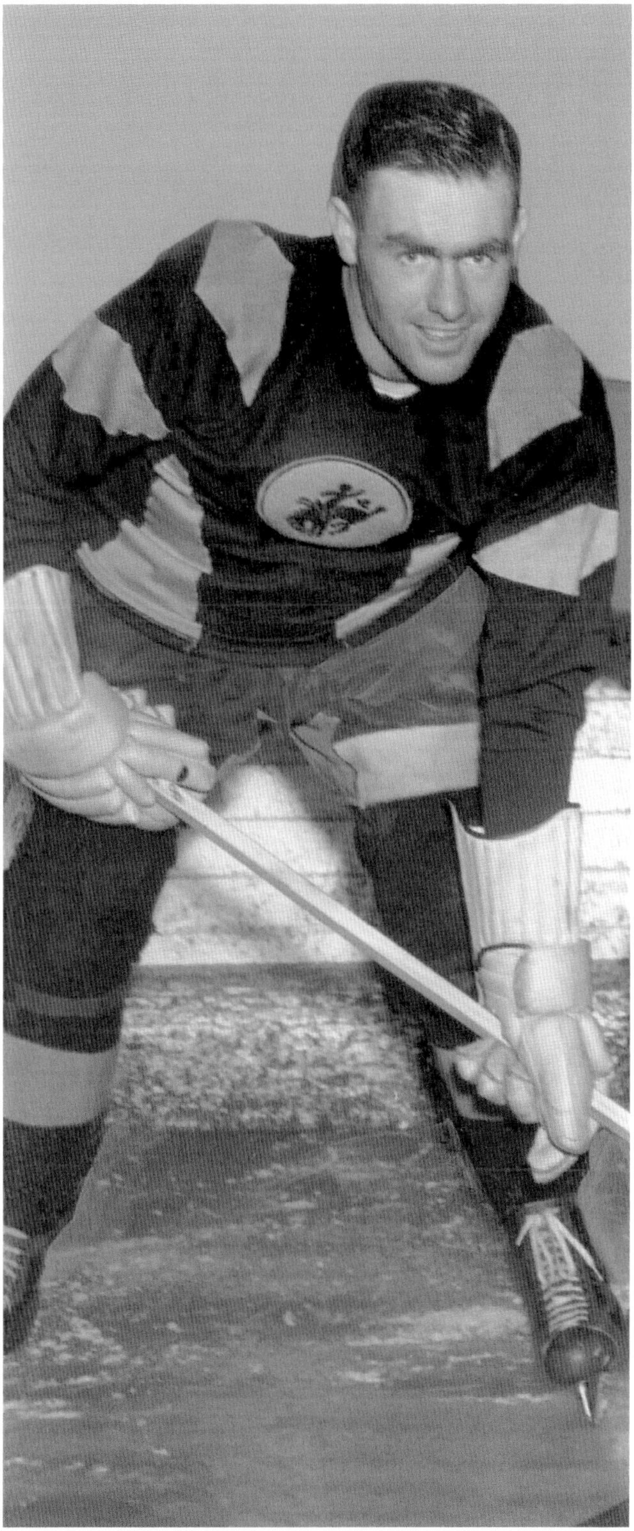

JIM MCFADDEN (CENTER). A veteran of eight NHL seasons, from 1946 to 1954, McFadden accumulated 226 points, 100 goals, and 89 PIM in 412 games. He won a Stanley Cup with Detroit in 1949–1950. The center skated with Portland from 1939 to 1941 and collected 37 points, 22 goals, and 43 PIM in 53 games. McFadden was a member of President's Cup–winning Calgary (WHL) in 1953–1954.

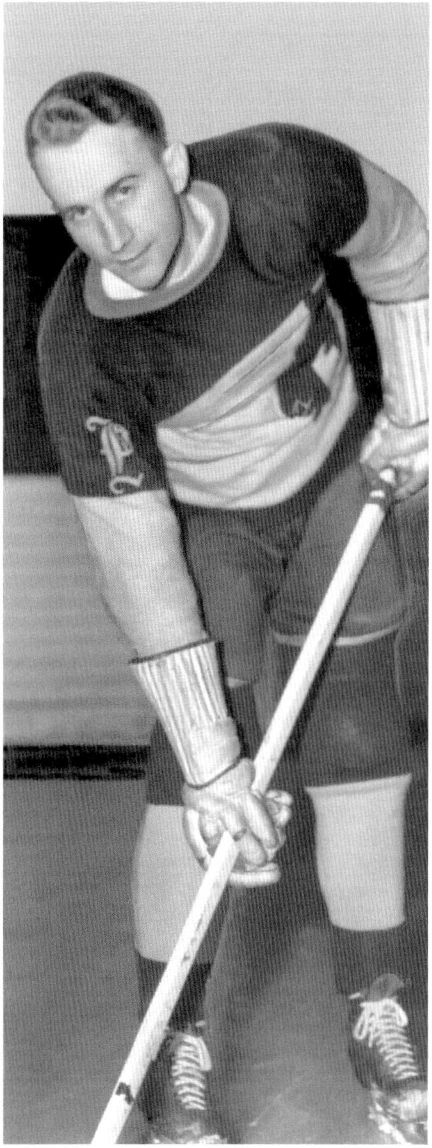

Burt Scharfe (Center). Scharfe was a member of Portland's 1938–1939 championship team. In two seasons with the Buckaroos, from 1938 to 1940, the center produced 73 points, 30 goals, and 38 PIM in 82 games. He also played in the WCHL/NWHL/PCHL with Spokane in 1940–1941 and led the league in points that season. Scharfe spent time in the AHA in 1941–1942.

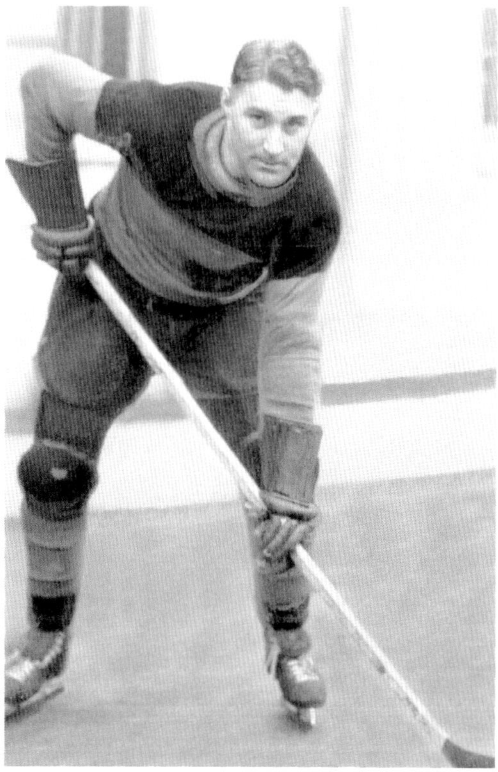

Norm Pridham (Defense). Pridham skated with Portland for two seasons, from 1936 to 1938, and was a member of the 1936–1937 Buckaroos' championship team. In his only full season with Portland, in 1936–1937, the defenseman garnered 4 points, 2 goals, and 29 PIM in 12 games. Pridham played for Tropical Hockey League (TrHL) champion Coral Gables in the league's only season in 1938–1939.

NORMAN "CHUBBY" SCOTT (CENTER). Scott spent six seasons with Portland, from 1934 to 1940, and garnered 9 points, 6 goals, and 43 PIM in 108 games. He was a member of the Buckaroos' 1936–1937 and 1938–1939 championship teams. The center also skated with three other championship teams—Duluth (AHA) in 1926–1927, Edmonton (WCHL) in 1932–1933, and Teddy Oke Trophy–winning Buffalo (IHL) in 1932–1933.

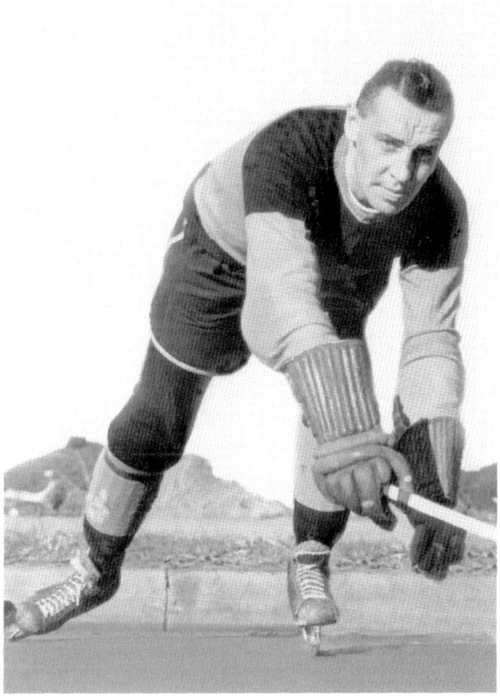

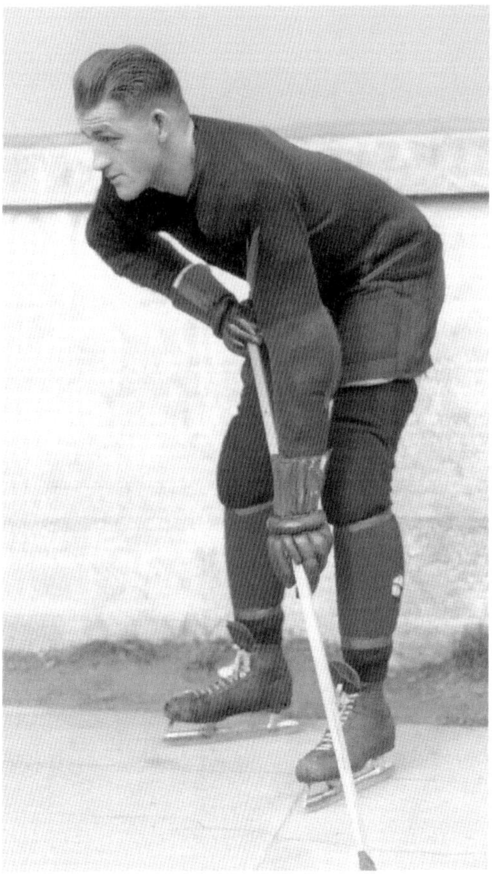

MILFORD "MOOSE" MUNSON (DEFENSE). In two seasons with the Buckaroos (1934–1935 and 1937–1938), Munson garnered 3 points, 2 goals, and 14 PIM in 20 games. The defenseman also played in the CHL from 1932 to 1935 and in the AHA from 1935 to 1938. Munson was a member of St. Paul's (CHL) championship team in 1934–1935.

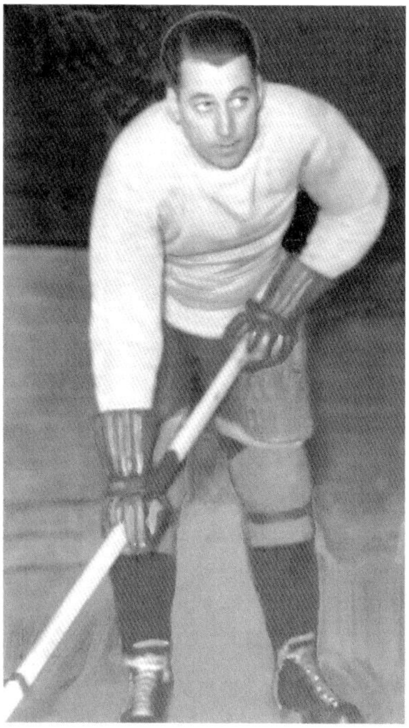

MIKE NEVILLE (CENTER). The center skated with Portland in 1934–1935, garnering six points, three goals, and four PIM in 11 games. Neville spent nine seasons in the CPHL/IHL, from 1926 to 1934 and in 1935–1936, and was a member of three Teddy Oke Trophy–winning teams with Stratford in 1927–1928, Windsor in 1928–1929, and London in 1933–1934. In three NHL campaigns between 1924 and 1931, he tallied 10 points in 65 games.

HERB RHEAUME (GOALIE). In 1933–1934, with Portland, Rheaume had a 3.47 GAA and one shutout in 34 games. He also played in the WCHL/NWHL/PCHL with Regina/Vancouver in 1932–1933, Edmonton in 1934–1935, and Vancouver in 1935–1936. The goaltender spent one season in the NHL with the Canadiens in 1925–1926 and had a 2.92 GAA and a 10-20-1 record in 31 games. Rheaume won a Fontaine Cup championship with Boston (CAHL) in 1928–1929.

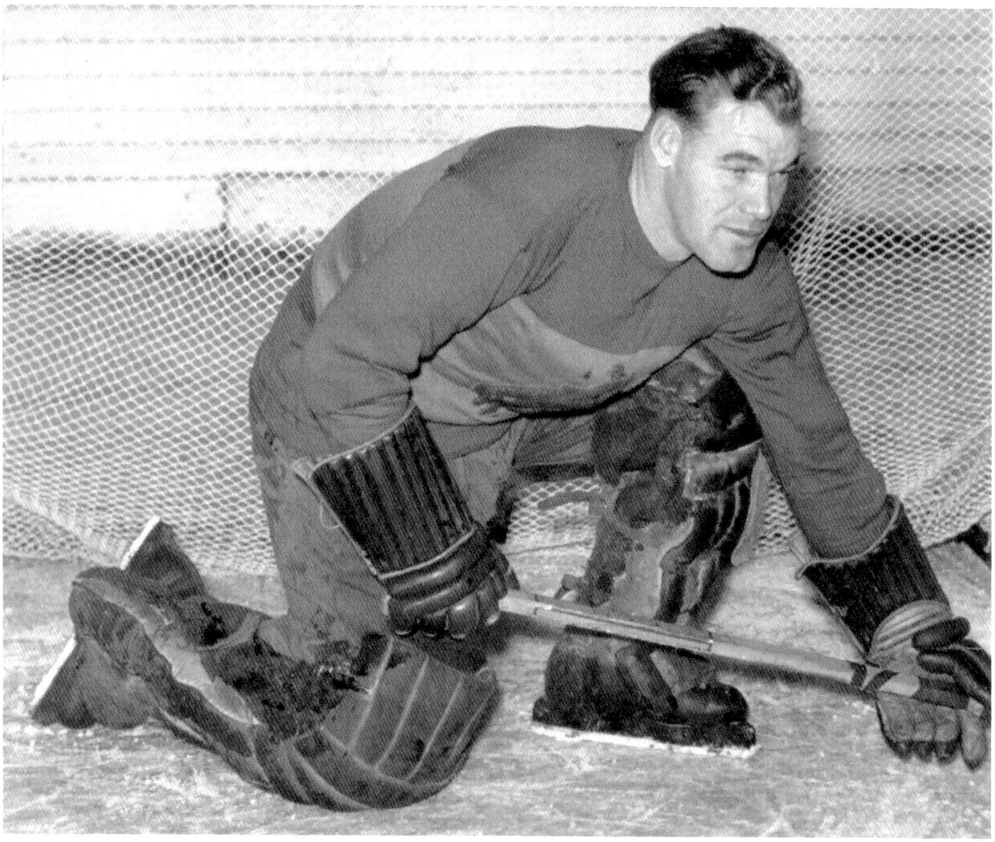

DON OLSON (DEFENSE). In 1939–1940, with Portland, Olson tallied 10 points, 6 goals, and 4 PIM in 18 games. The defenseman skated in the AHA from 1933 to 1941 and won a Sinclair Trophy championship with St. Louis (AHA) in 1937–1938.

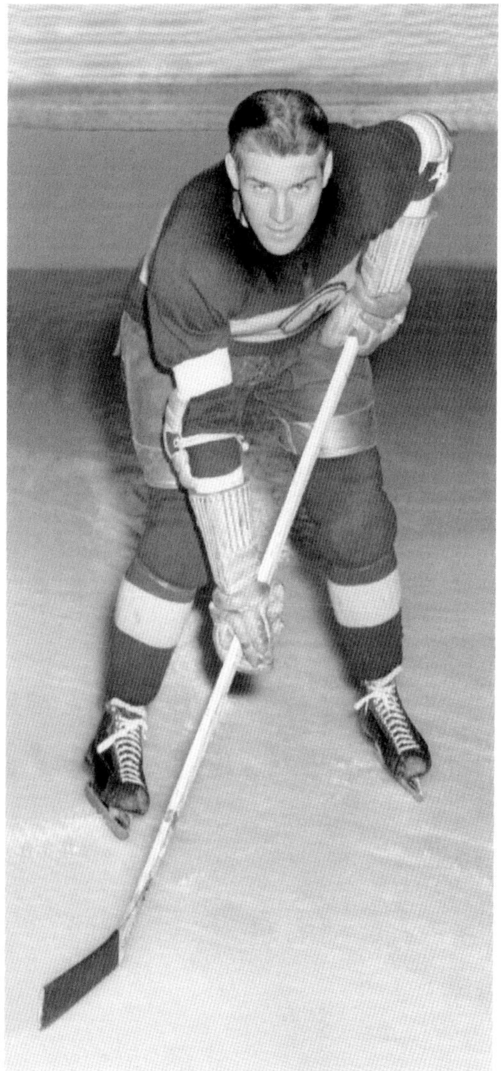

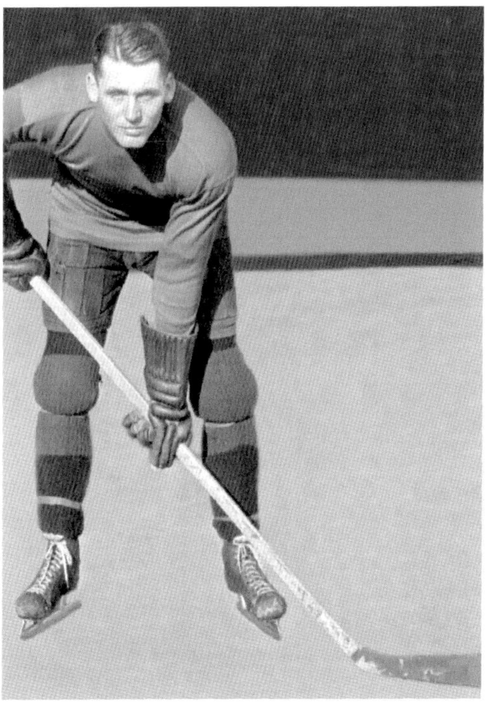

ARCHIE GRAY (DEFENSE). Gray garnered 7 points, 5 assists, and 38 PIM in 35 games with Portland in 1933–1934 and 1935–1936. The defenseman also skated in the WCHL/NWHL/PCHL with three other teams—Saskatoon in 1932–1933, league-champion Vancouver in 1934–1935, and Edmonton in 1935–1936.

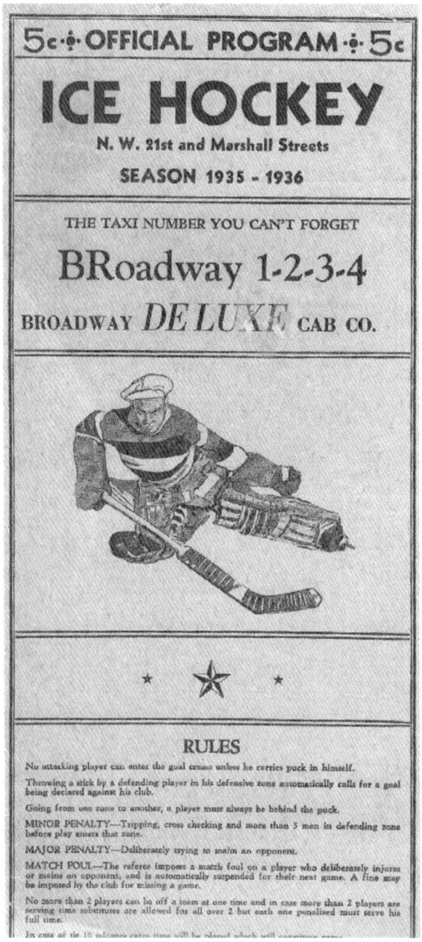

BUCKAROOS PROGRAM, 1935–1936. Eddie Ouelette is the WCHL/NWHL/PCHL Buckaroos' all-time leader in points (186), goals (96), and assists (90), while Ron Sutherland holds the all-time team record for the most games played (258) and most PIM (481). In net, Andy Aitkenhead holds all-time franchise records for career GAA (2.03), wins (116), shutouts (35), and games in goal (232).

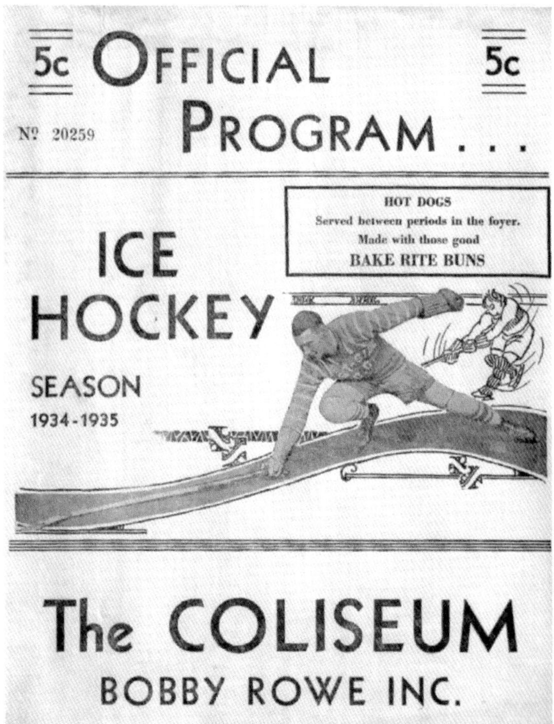

BUCKAROOS PROGRAM, 1934–1935. The Vancouver Lions hold the record for most playoff championships in WCHL/NWHL/PCHL history with four. The Portland Buckaroos have the second-most playoff championships in league history with two. The Calgary Tigers, Edmonton Eskimos, and Seattle Seahawks have one playoff championship each.

4

Hockey Returns after World War II

The Portland Eagles were inaugural members of the new Pacific Coast Hockey League (PCHL) in 1944–1945 and were coached by Jimmy Ward. Ward piloted the team through the 1949–1950 season. The Eagles finished in second place in the northern division with a 19-7-1 record in 1944–1945. In the postseason, Portland defeated the Seattle Stars in the division semifinal four games to three. The northern division finals series between Portland and the Seattle Ironmen suddenly turned into the PCHL championship finals midway in the series when San Francisco (winners of the central and southern division playoffs) announced that they were not going to compete in the PCHL finals. The Ironmen prevailed over the Eagles four games to two.

In 1945–1946, Portland had a 29-29-0 record with a second place divisional finish. The Eagles defeated the Seattle Ironmen two games to one in the division semifinals that season before losing in the division finals to Vancouver three games to two. The Eagles won the PCHL's Northern Division title in 1946–1947 with a 39-21-0 record. In the first two rounds of the playoffs, Portland defeated Vancouver three games to one and then the Seattle Ironmen four games to two to make it to the PCHL finals. In the finals, Los Angeles swept the Eagles in four games and captured the Philip Henderson Cup.

The next three seasons were not as fruitful for Portland. In 1947–1948, the Eagles had their first losing season (17-46-3), finished in last place in their division, and missed the playoffs for the first time. The PCHL owners decided to make the circuit a professional league in 1948–1949. The Eagles, who managed a winning record in 1948–1949 (32-31-7, fourth place), were swept in the first round of the postseason in three games against New Westminster. The Portland club changed its name to the Portland Penguins in 1949–1950 and finished with a 32-30-9 record (fifth place and out of the playoffs).

In 1950–1951, the name Eagles was brought back, and Portland named Tony Hemmerling coach. The club garnered a 30-32-8 record (fourth place) and lost in the opening playoff round in seven games against Victoria. The Eagles folded after the 1950–1951 season because of financial problems and an arena that was falling apart.

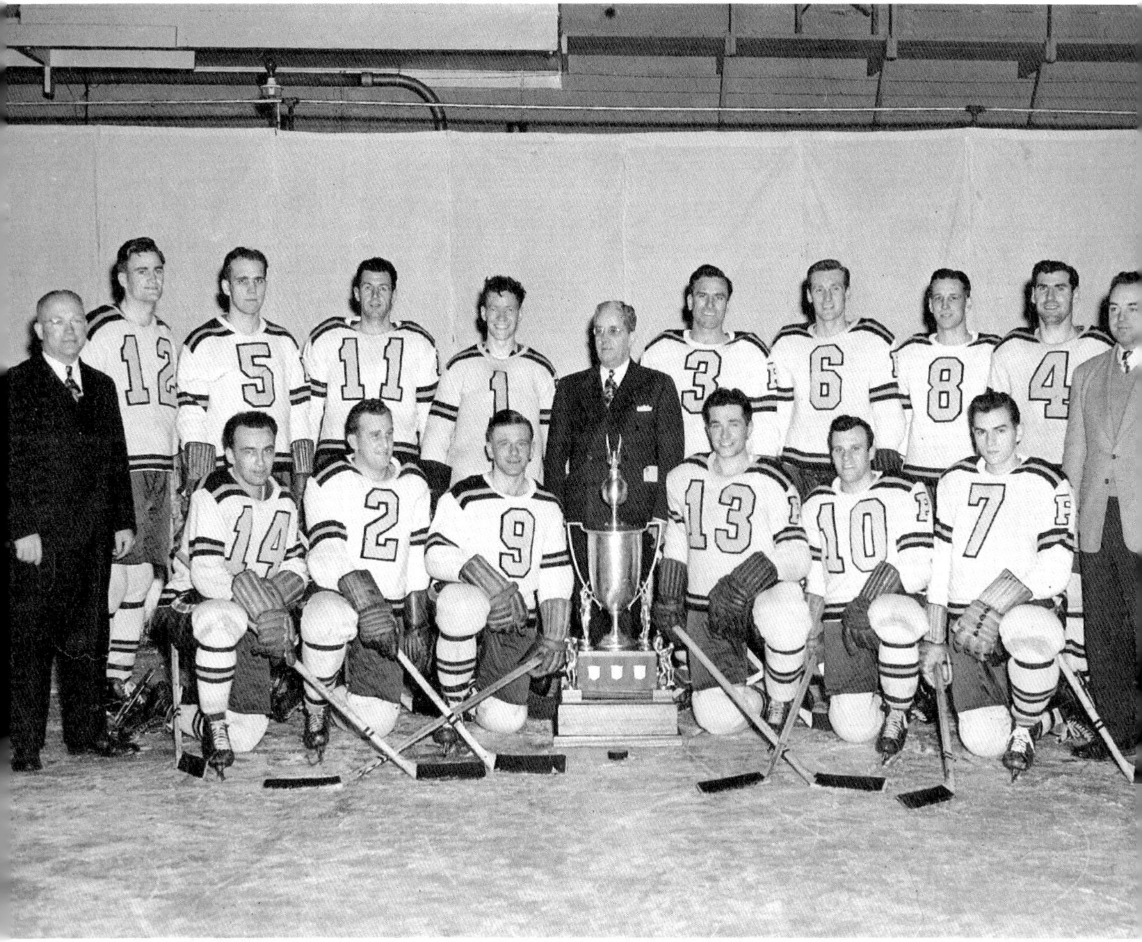

PCHL Northern Division Champion Eagles, 1946–1947. Pictured here from left to right are the following: (first row) Eddie Shamlock, Butch Marchant, Eddie Kullman, Phil Dalgleish, John Gauthier, and Joe Schmidt; (second row) Harold Regele (trainer), Larry Reardon, Jim Planche, Jack McDonald, Jerry Fodey, Harry Shipstad (manager), Hibbert Bean, Bill Kyle, Pat Desbiens, Bill Allan, and Jimmy Ward (coach). The trophy in the photograph is the Shipstad and Johnson Ice Follies Trophy, which was awarded annually to the winner of the Northern Division of the PCHL.

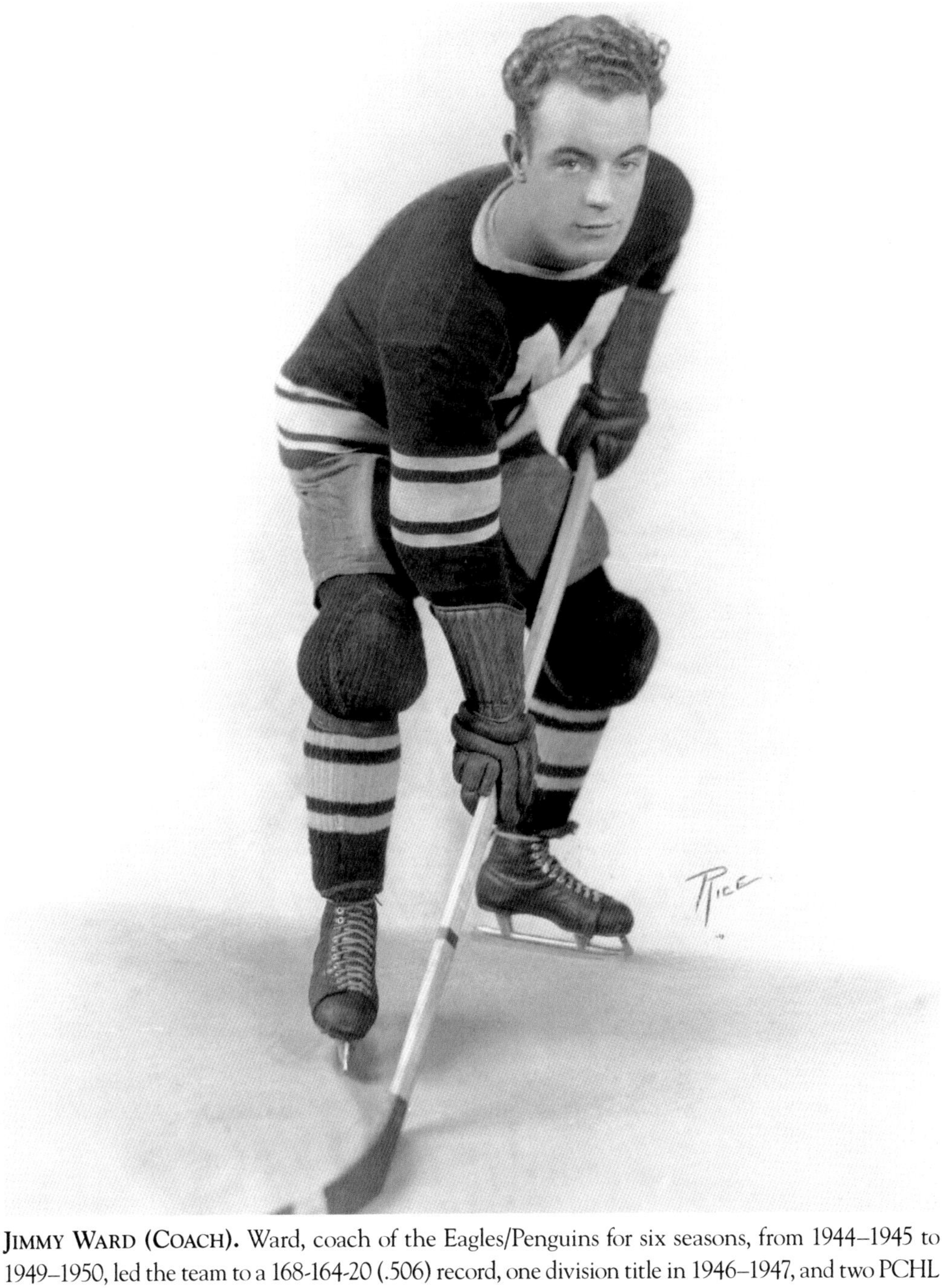

JIMMY WARD (COACH). Ward, coach of the Eagles/Penguins for six seasons, from 1944–1945 to 1949–1950, led the team to a 168-164-20 (.506) record, one division title in 1946–1947, and two PCHL finals appearances. Ward was a veteran of 12 NHL seasons, from 1927 to 1939, with the Maroons and Canadiens, garnering 274 points, 147 goals, and 455 PIM in 527 games. The right-winger won a Stanley Cup with the Maroons in 1934–1935. He got his start behind the bench with New Haven of the International American Hockey League (IAHL) as a player/coach in 1939–1940. The IAHL became known as the American Hockey League (AHL) starting with the 1940–1941 season.

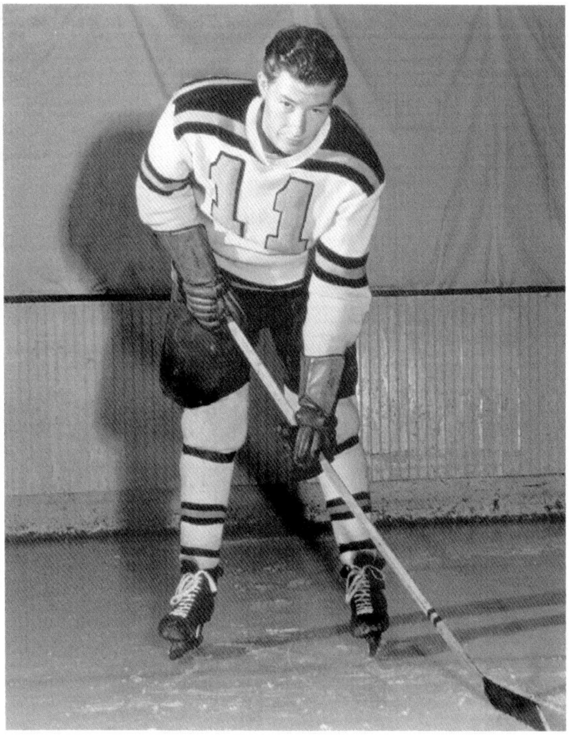

DOUG CARRIGAN (LEFT WING). The left-winger was with the Eagles from 1947 to 1949, garnering 62 points, 23 goals, and 112 PIM in 122 games. He also played in the PCHL with Tacoma and Vancouver during the 1946–1947 campaign. Carrigan spent time in the Eastern Amateur Hockey League (EAHL) from 1943 to 1946. The EAHL was known as the Eastern Hockey League (EHL) from 1954–1955 to 1972–1973.

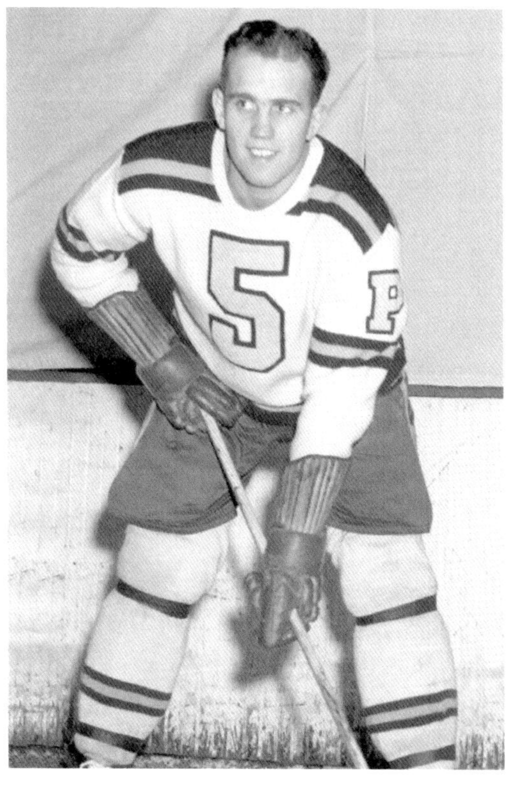

JIM PLANCHE (LEFT WING). Planche produced 148 points, 61 goals, and 31 PIM in 76 games during two campaigns with the Eagles in 1944–1945 and 1946–1947. He led the PCHL in points in 1946–1947. The left-winger played in two Memorial Cup tournaments with Montreal of the Quebec Senior Hockey League (QSHL) in 1940–1941 and 1941–1942, and one Allan Cup tournament with Sherbrooke (QSHL) in 1949–1950.

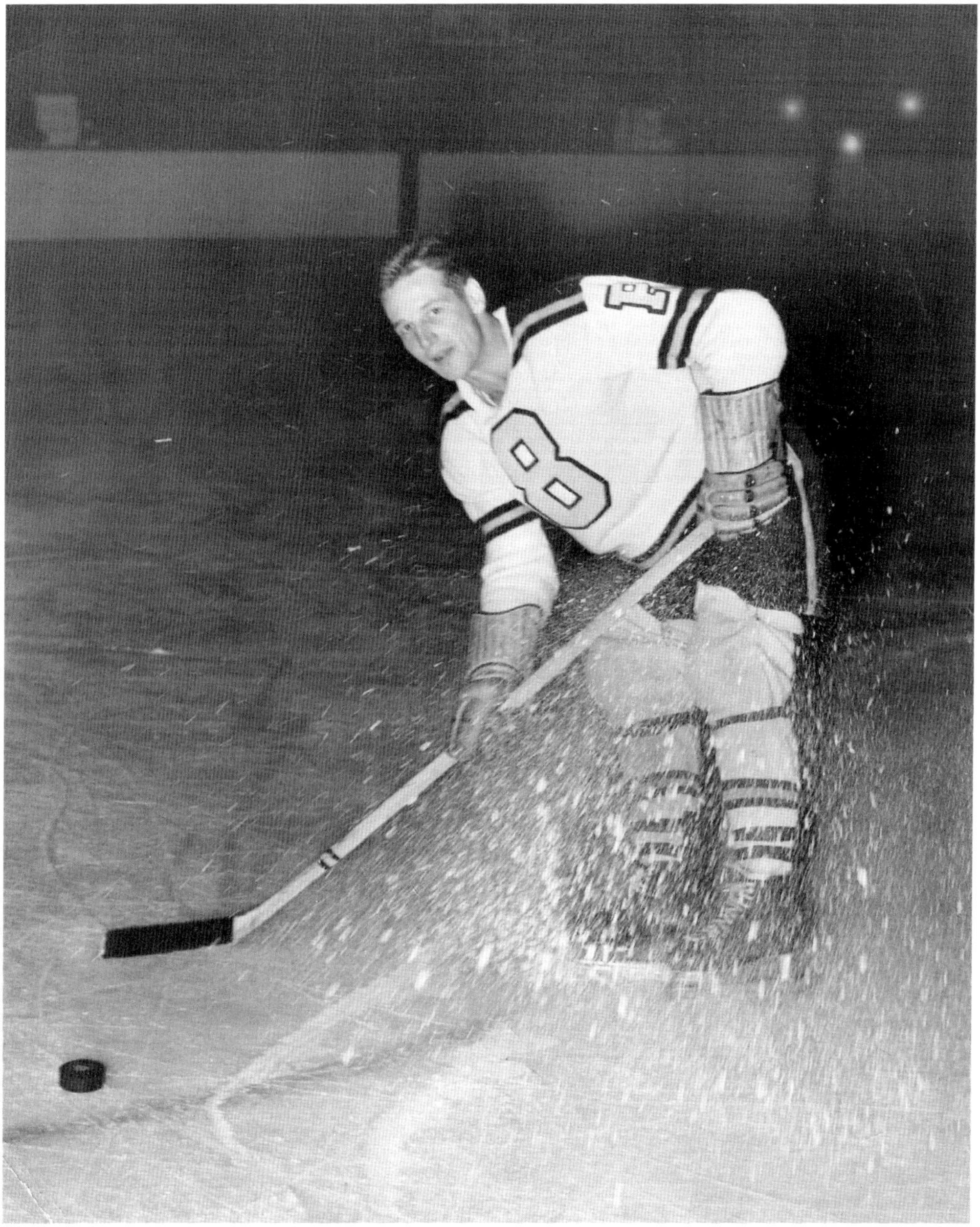

PAT DESBIENS (RIGHT WING). Desbiens is the Eagles'/Penguins' all-time leader in points (222) and goals (143). Overall, he ranks third in games played (251) and is tied for fourth in assists (79) in franchise history. The right-winger spent four seasons with Portland, from 1946 to 1950, and led the PCHL in goals twice. He shares the PCHL/WHL record for most goals in a game—five—and became the first player to score four goals in a period in PCHL/WHL history (both on November 24, 1948).

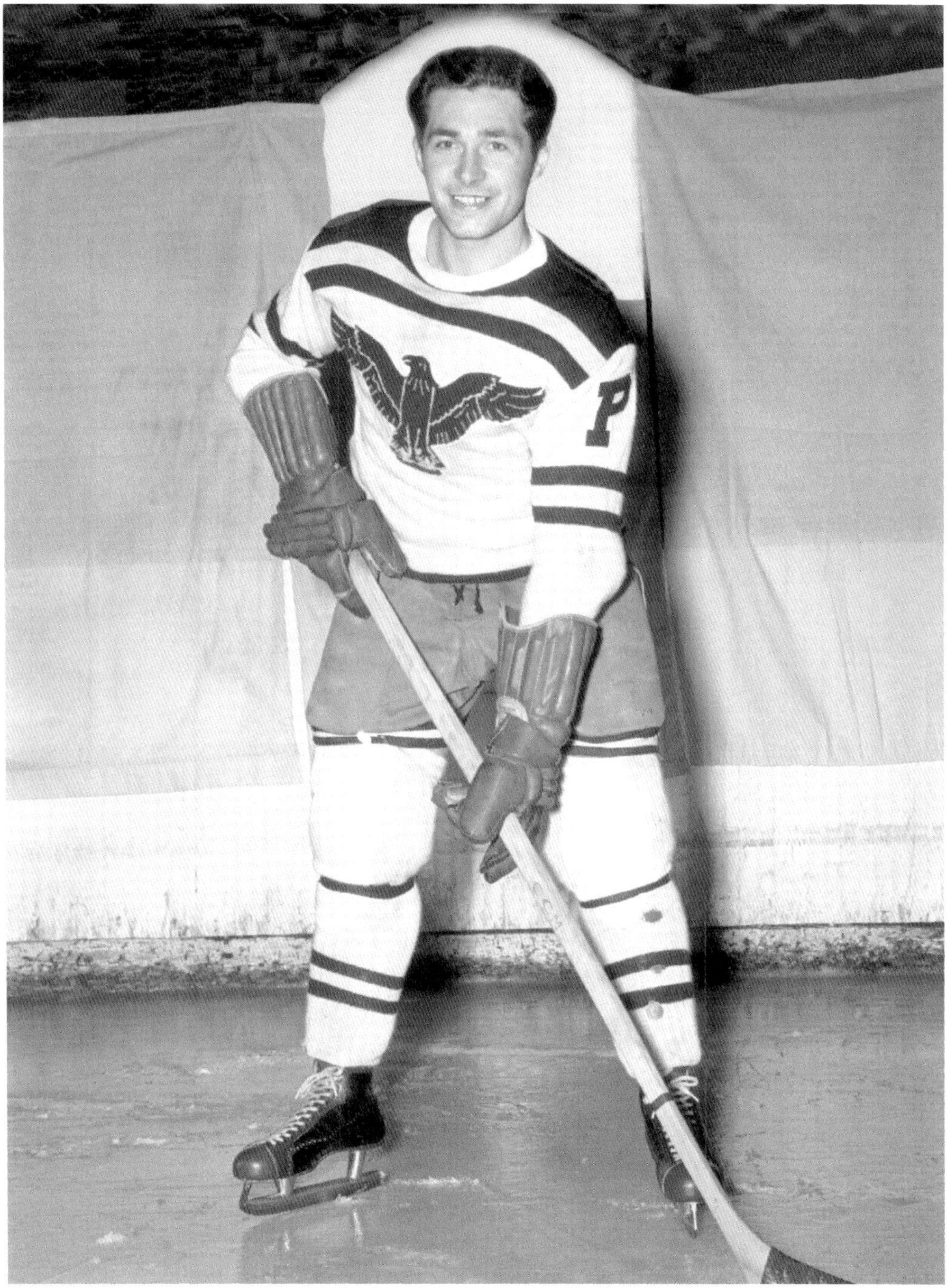

Phil Dalgleish (Defense). In Eagles'/Penguins' history, Dalgleish is first all time in assists (123), games played (314), and PIM (276) and second all time in points (221) and goals (98). The defenseman skated with Portland for five seasons, from 1945 to 1950. He also spent time in the Maritime Major Hockey League (MMHL) from 1950 to 1953 and played between 1953 and 1956 in the IHL (the league that was originally based in the Midwest and operated from 1945 to 2001).

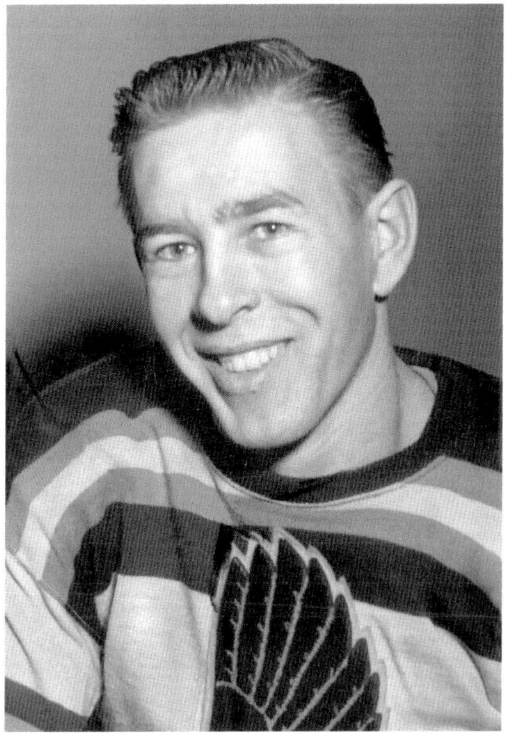

Joe Ciuman (Wing). Ciuman tallied 90 points, 47 goals, and 64 PIM in 117 games with Portland from 1949 to 1951. The winger also spent time in the EAHL from 1943 to 1947, the AHL from 1947 to 1949, and the United States Hockey League (USHL) in 1948–1949. He tied the PCHL/WHL record for most goals in a period with four (set on November 9, 1949).

Al Millar (Goalie). Millar earned a 3.39 GAA and a 15-10-3 record in 28 games with Portland in 1950–1951. In 1961–1962 and 1963–1964, he won the WHL Outstanding Goalkeeper Award and was named a WHL All-Star. Millar was a member of two Patrick Cup championship teams—Victoria in 1965–1966 and Vancouver in 1968–1969. The goaltender had a stint in the NHL in 1957–1958.

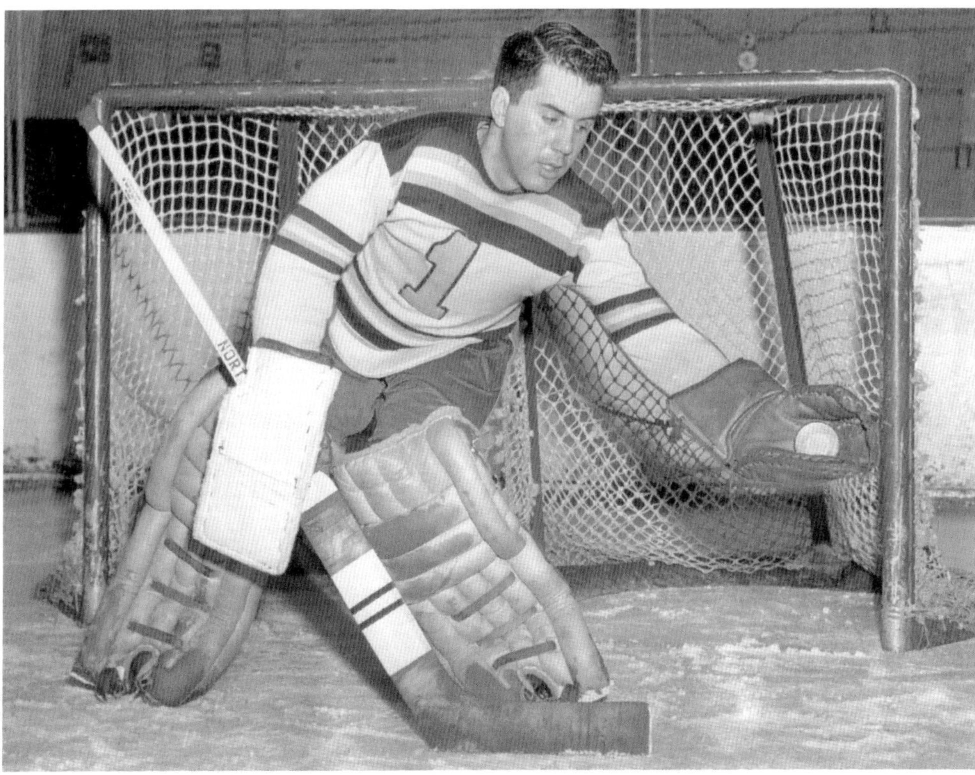

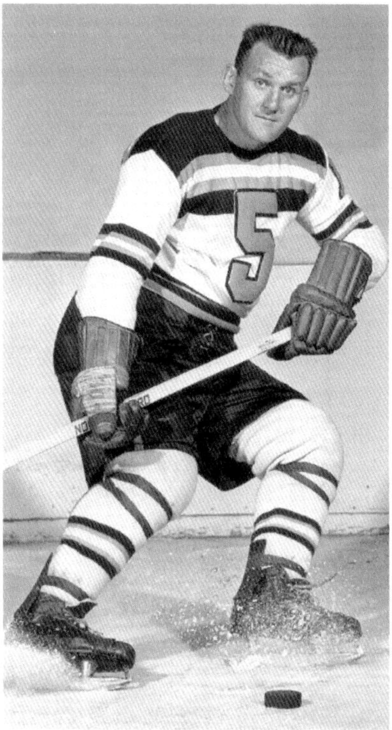

ALEX "SANDY" MILNE (DEFENSE). The defenseman totaled 51 points, 14 goals, and 141 PIM in 122 games with Portland from 1948 to 1950. Milne also played in the AHA in 1940–1941, spent several seasons in the AHL between 1941 and 1947, and skated in the USHL from 1946 to 1948.

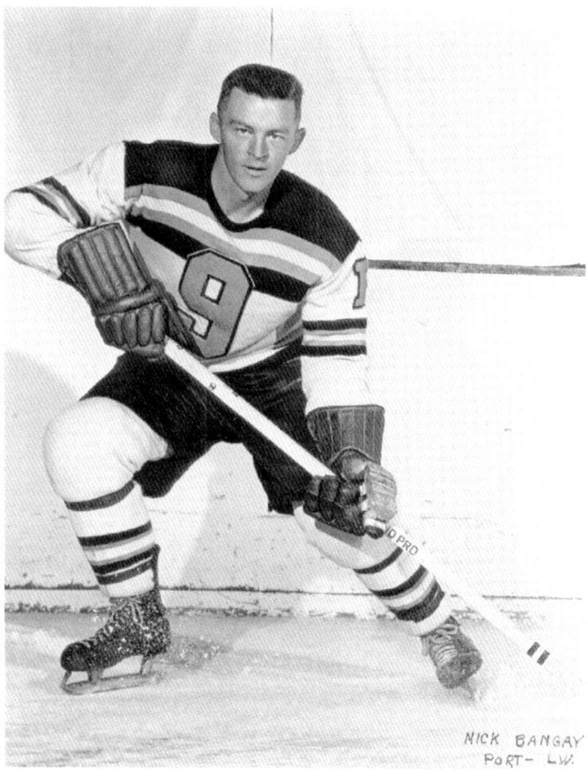

HAROLD "NICK" BANGAY (LEFT WING). In two seasons with Portland, from 1948 to 1950, the left-winger tallied 104 points, 49 goals, and 127 PIM in 140 games. He also played in the AHL with Philadelphia in 1947–1948.

AL SHEWCHUK (DEFENSE). In 1948–1949 with Portland, Shewchuk garnered 31 points, 23 assists, and 109 PIM in 65 games. The defenseman also played in the PCHL with San Francisco in 1949–1950, in the EAHL in 1945–1946, and in the AHL from 1946 to 1948.

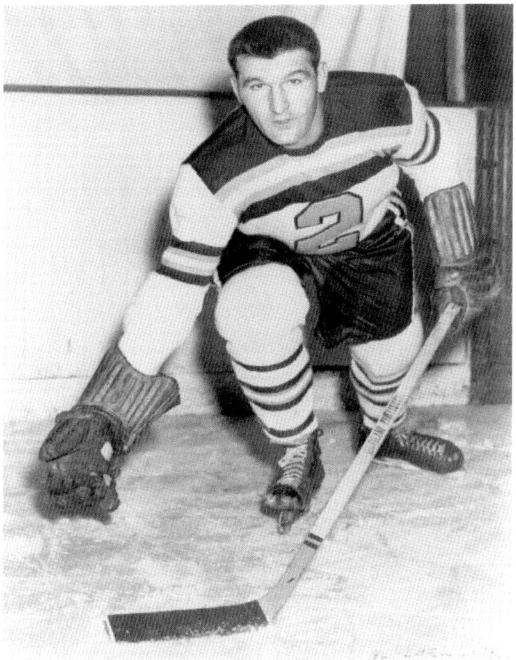

RUDY BOBROSKY (DEFENSE). Bobrosky produced 43 points and 15 goals in 122 games during two seasons with the Eagles, from 1947 to 1949. He also played in the PCHL with Seattle in 1947–1948.

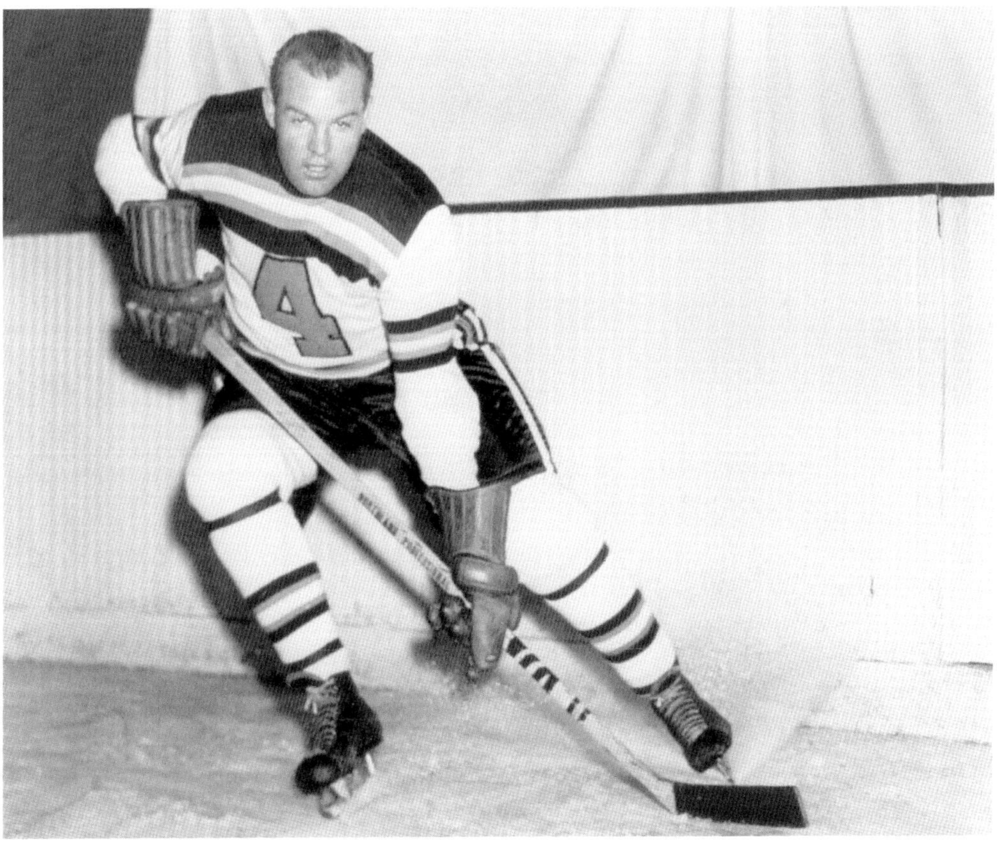

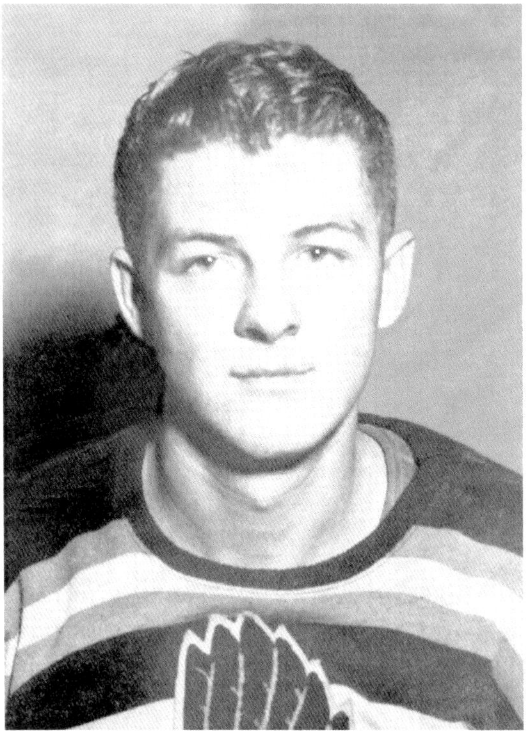

JOHN BAILEY (RIGHT WING). In 1950–1951, with the Eagles, Bailey had 13 points, 6 goals, and 10 PIM in 44 games. The right-winger also played in the PCHL/WHL with Seattle from 1951 to 1953, New Westminster in 1952–1953, and Saskatoon in 1953–1954. He also spent time in several other minor professional leagues and won back-to-back Turner Cups with St. Paul (IHL) in 1959–1960 and 1960–1961.

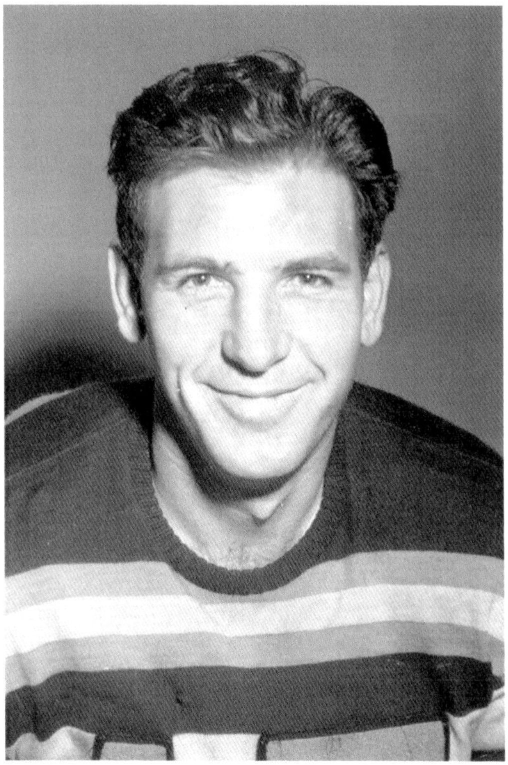

HUGH SUTHERLAND (DEFENSE). He ranks second all time in games played (272) and PIM (267) in Eagles'/Penguins' history. Sutherland also garnered 91 points and 29 goals during four seasons with Portland, from 1947 to 1951. The defenseman played in the PCHL with San Diego in 1946–1947 and with Seattle in 1947–1948.

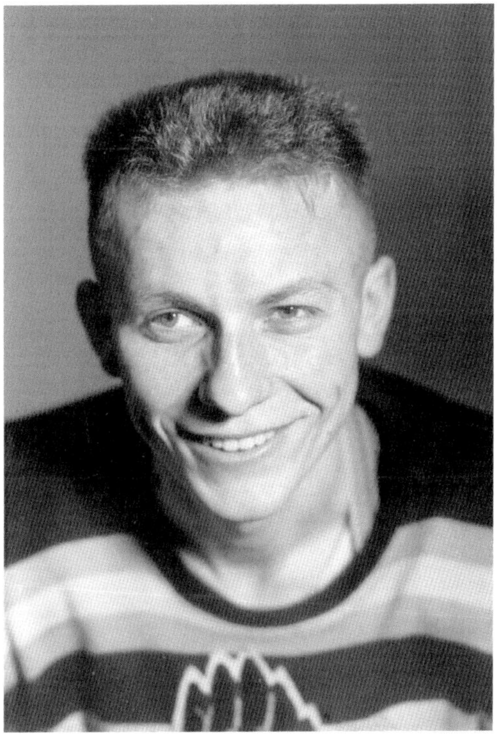

Frank Kubasek (Center). In 1950–1951, with the Eagles, Kubasek had 58 points, 23 goals, and 10 PIM in 65 games. The center also played in the PCHL/WHL with San Francisco in 1949–1950, Edmonton between 1951 and 1954, and Spokane in 1958–1959. He spent time in the AHL from 1952 to 1954, and played for two Calder Cup–winning teams in Cleveland (AHL) in 1952–1953 and 1953–1954.

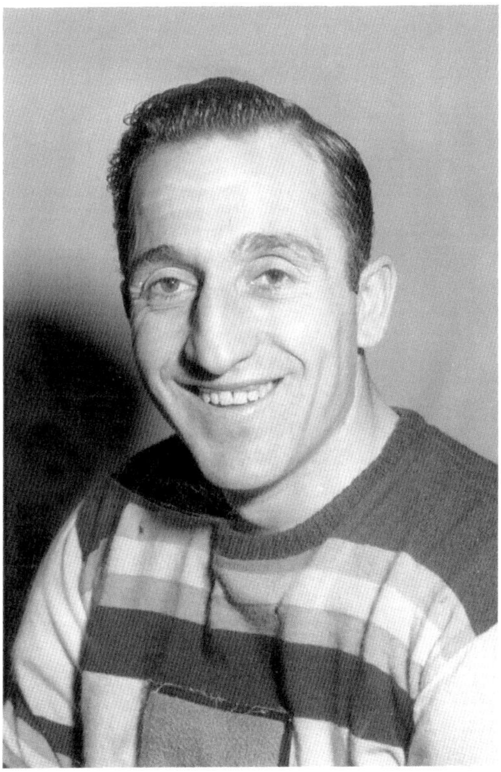

Larry Silvestri (Right Wing). Silvestri produced 70 points, 29 goals, and 6 PIM in 70 games with the Eagles in 1950–1951. The right-winger skated in the PCHL with Oakland in 1944–1945, San Francisco in 1949–1950, and Seattle in 1951–1952, and was also named a PCHL All-Star twice. He won back-to-back Loudon Trophies with Kansas City (USHL) in 1945–1946 and 1946–1947.

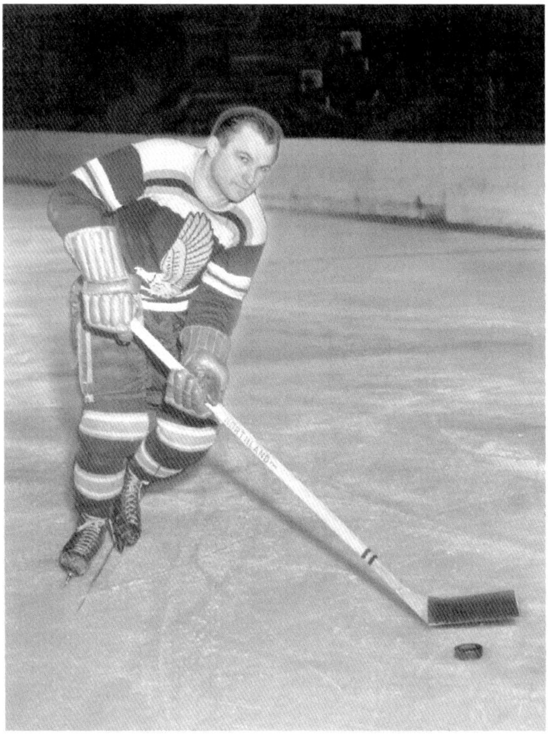

John Holota (Center). Holota produced 17 points and 6 goals in 18 games with Portland during the 1950–1951 season. The center played for Sinclair Trophy–winning Omaha (AHA) in 1941–1942, Stanley Cup–winning Detroit (NHL) in 1942–1943, and Calder Cup–winning Cleveland (AHL) in 1947–1948. He also had a stint with Detroit (NHL) in 1945–1946.

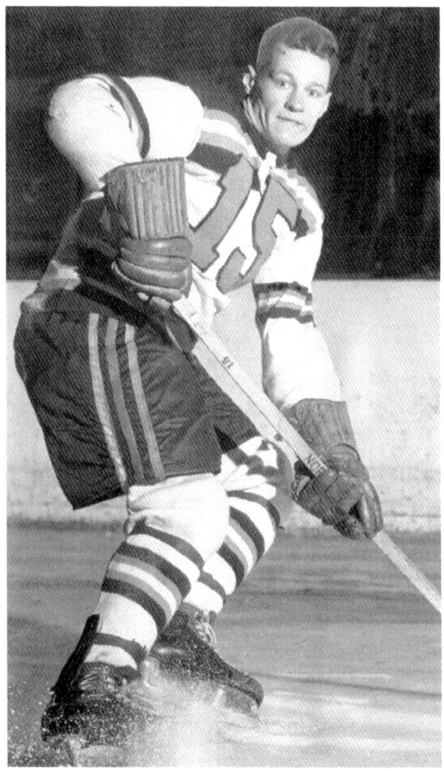

Hal Hopper (Center). In two campaigns with Portland, from 1949 to 1951, Hopper garnered 52 points, 24 goals, and 80 PIM in 91 games. He also played in the EAHL in 1949–1950 and in the USHL in 1950–1951.

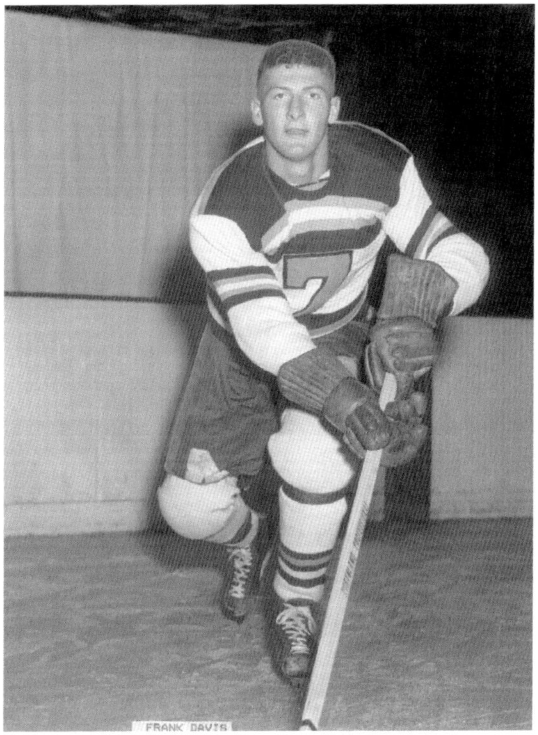

Frank Davis (Right Wing). In two seasons with Portland, from 1948 to 1950, the right-winger tallied 73 points, 36 goals, and 86 PIM in 136 games.

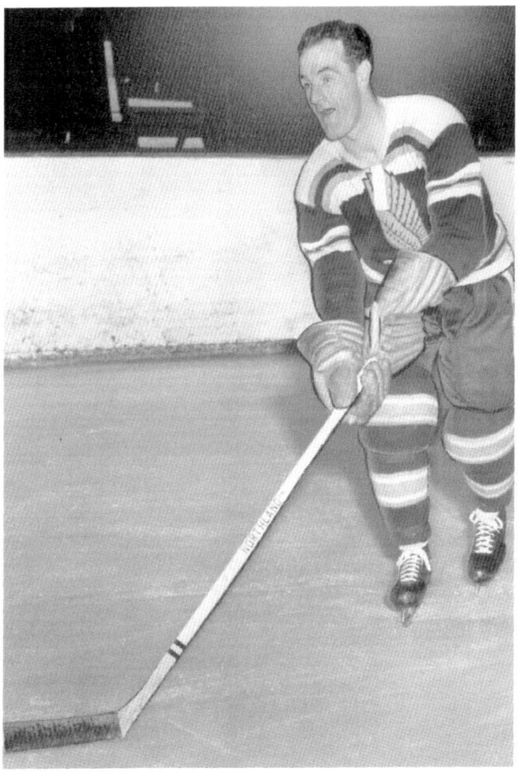

Bill Summerhill (Right Wing). The right-winger garnered 31 points, 15 goals, and 10 PIM in 40 games with the Eagles in 1950–1951. A veteran of three NHL regular-season campaigns (1938 to 1940 and in 1941–1942), Summerhill had 31 points, 14 goals, and 70 PIM in 72 games. He was a member of two Calder Cup–winning teams with Cleveland (AHL) in 1940–1941 and Buffalo (AHL) in 1942–1943.

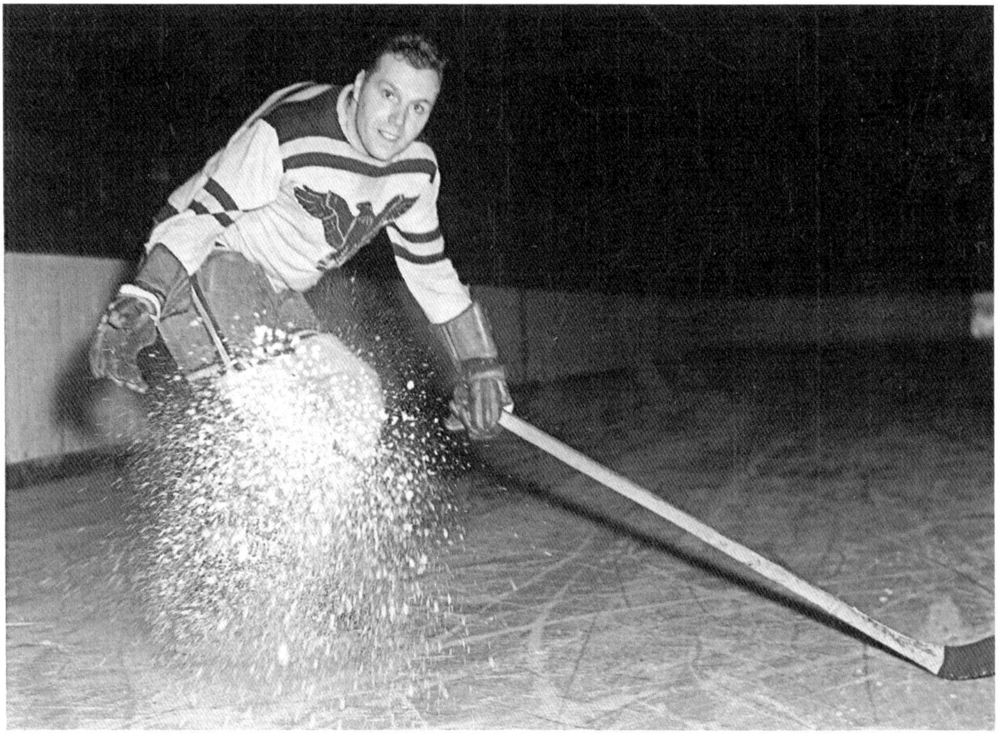

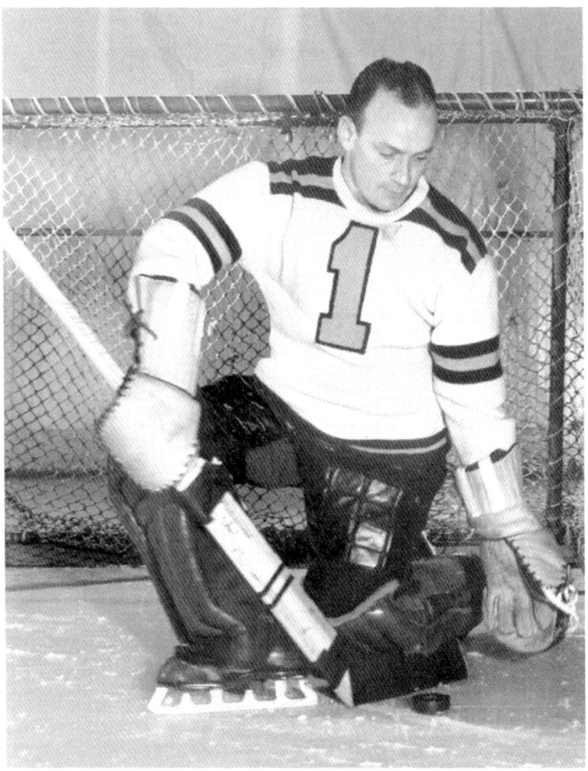

Aubrey Webster (Right Wing). The right-winger played for the Eagles from 1944 to 1946 and collected 44 points, 16 goals, and 44 PIM in 76 games. Webster also played for the WCHL/NWHL/PCHL Buckaroos from 1938 to 1940 and produced 49 points, 28 goals, and 35 PIM in 62 games. He was a member of Portland's 1938–1939 championship team.

Craig McClelland (Goalie). McClelland compiled a 5.16 GAA in 30 games with the Eagles in 1947–1948. The goaltender also played in the PCHL with Tacoma in 1946–1947.

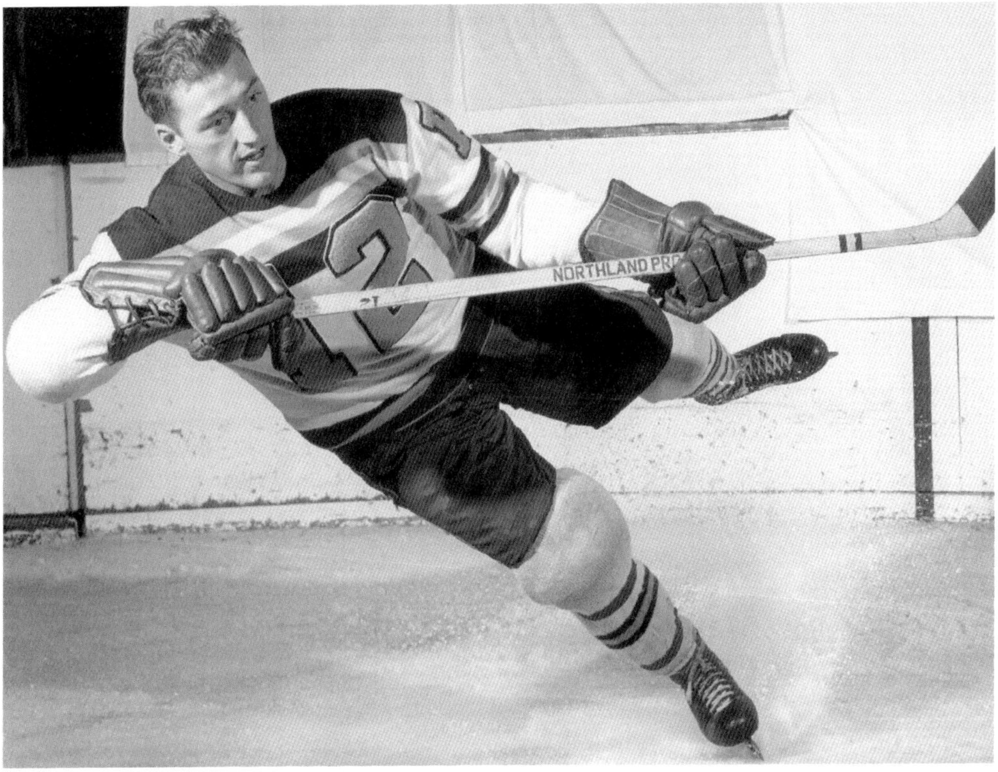

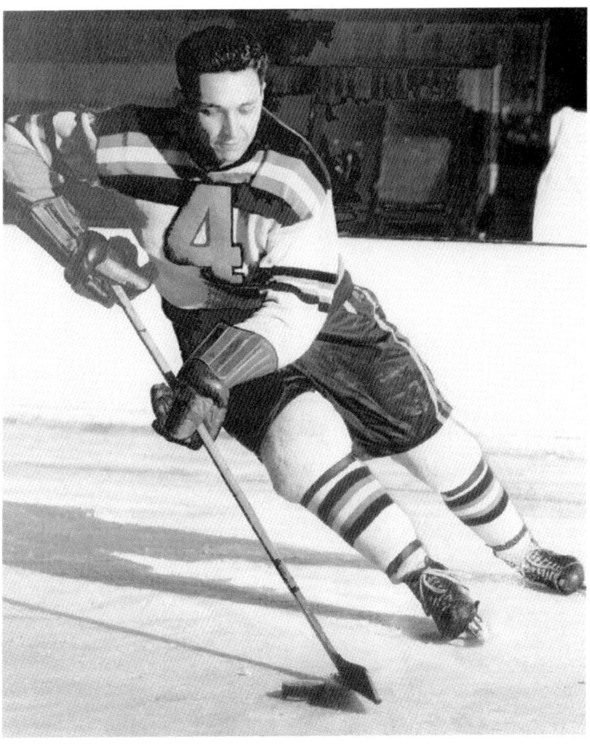

ART STROBEL (LEFT WING). In 1949–1950, with the Penguins, the left-winger produced 43 points, 20 goals, and 28 PIM in 71 games. Strobel had a stint in the NHL with New York in 1943–1944. He also spent time in the EAHL in 1943–1944, the AHL from 1944 to 1946, and the USHL from 1945 to 1949.

NICK TOMIUK (LEFT WING). In 1949–1950, with the Penguins, the left-winger produced 39 points, 10 goals, and 20 PIM in 47 games. Tomiuk also played in the PCHL with Seattle in 1951–1952. He spent time in the USHL from 1946 to 1951 and the AHL in 1950–1951. Tomiuk won a Loudon Trophy with Minneapolis (USHL) in 1949–1950.

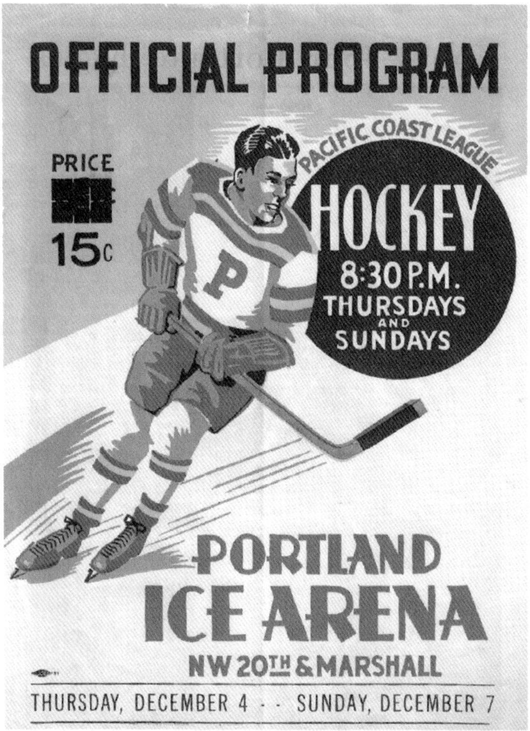

EAGLES PROGRAM, 1947–1948. Portland finished with an all-time record of 198-196-28 (.502) from 1944–1945 to 1950–1951. The Eagles/Penguins had a 94-93-24 (.502) during the club's professional years from 1948–1949 to 1950–1951. Pat Desbiens is the Eagles'/Penguins' all-time leader in points (222) and goals (143), and Phil Dalgleish holds the franchise's all-time records for assists (123), PIM (276), and games played (314).

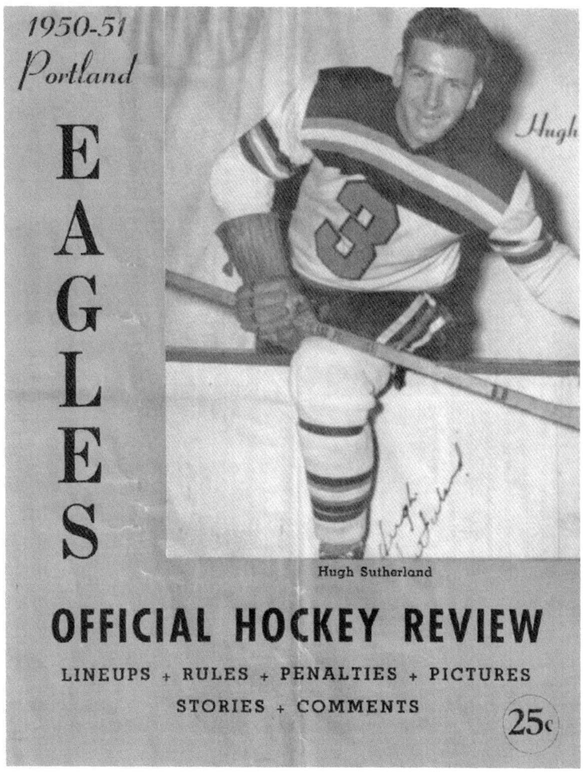

EAGLES PROGRAM FEATURING HUGH SUTHERLAND, 1950–1951. The number of teams in the PCHL dropped by over half from the start of the 1949–1950 season to shortly after the 1950–1951 season, declining from 11 to 5 franchises. For the 1951–1952 campaign, three teams from the Western Canada Major Hockey League (WCMHL)—Calgary Stampeders, Edmonton Flyers, and Saskatoon Quakers—joined the PCHL and increased the loop's membership to eight teams.

EAGLES PROGRAM FEATURING AL SHEWCHUK, 1948–1949. Eddie Shore's minor league hockey empire extended to the PCHL as owner of the Oakland Oaks. At one time or another, Shore also owned and/or operated the Buffalo Bisons (AHL), Fort Worth Rangers (USHL), New Haven Eagles (AHL), Syracuse Warriors (AHL), and two Springfield Indians franchises (the AHL team and the EAHL/Quebec Hockey League [QHL] team).

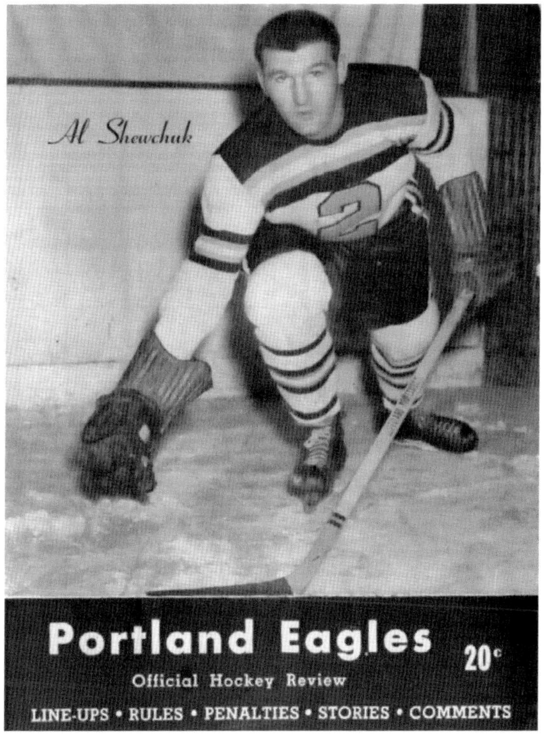

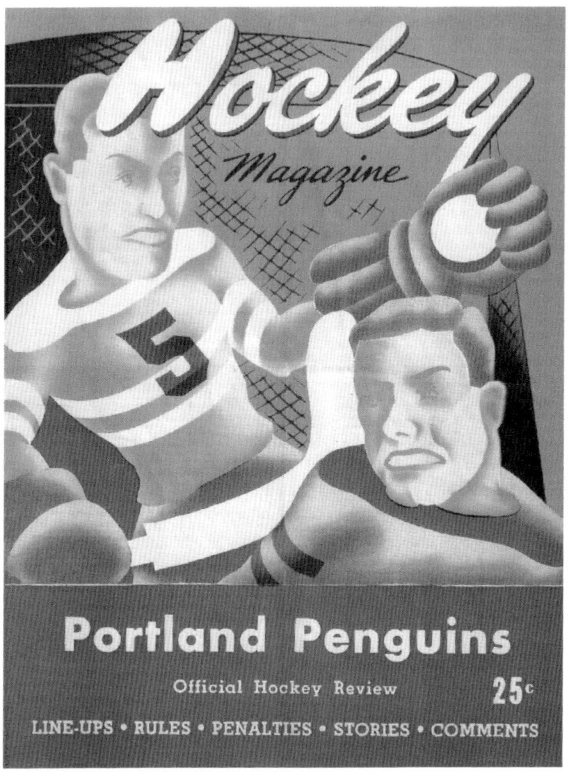

PENGUINS PROGRAM, 1949–1950. The Portland Penguins had a live penguin mascot that made an appearance before the start of each of the club's games during the 1949–1950 season. Unfortunately the penguin's foot was run over by a player's skate, and the mascot was permanently sidelined. The team changed its name back to the Eagles for the 1950–1951 season.

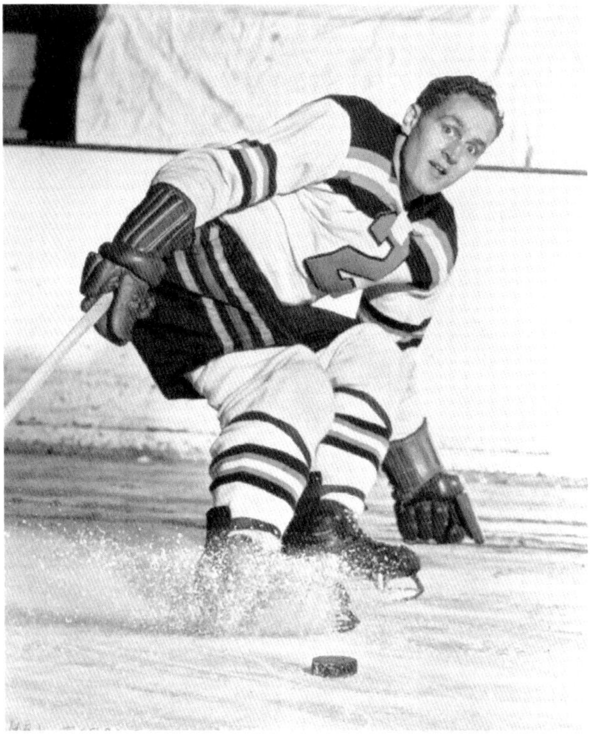

HAL TARALA (DEFENSE). Tarala produced 59 points, 42 assists, and 81 PIM in 110 games during two seasons with Portland, from 1949 to 1951. He also spent time in the PCHL/WHL with Vancouver in 1951–1952, Tacoma in 1952–1953, and New Westminster in 1955–1956. The defenseman also played in the USHL from 1947 to 1950, the QHL in 1953–1954, and the AHL in 1953–1954.

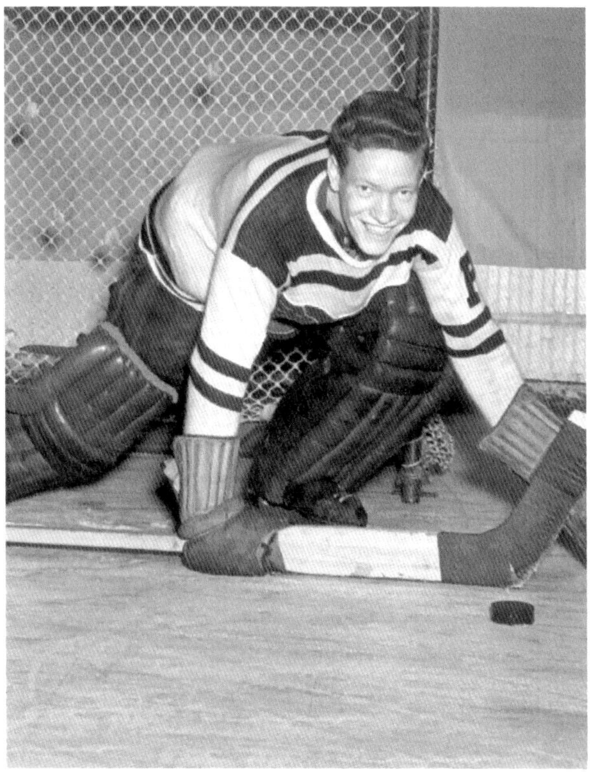

JERRY FODEY (GOALIE). In three seasons with the Eagles, from 1945 to 1948, Fodey compiled a 4.12 GAA and three shutouts in 139 games. The goaltender also played in the PCHL with Seattle in 1948–1949 and with Victoria in 1949–1950.

TOM KARAKAS (GOALIE). Karakas played the most games between the pipes (182) in Eagles'/Penguins' history. The goaltender earned a 3.39 GAA, had six shutouts, and was named to the PCHL All-Star Team twice during three seasons with Portland, from 1948 to 1951. He also spent two seasons in the USHL between 1947 and 1951.

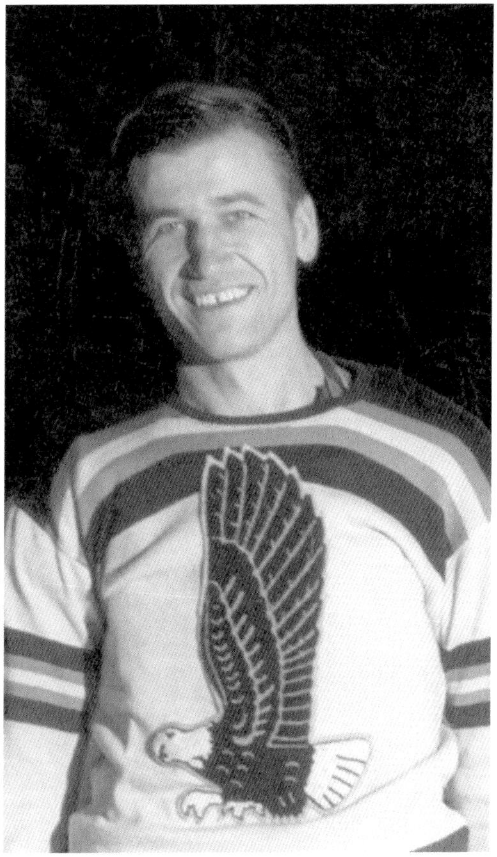

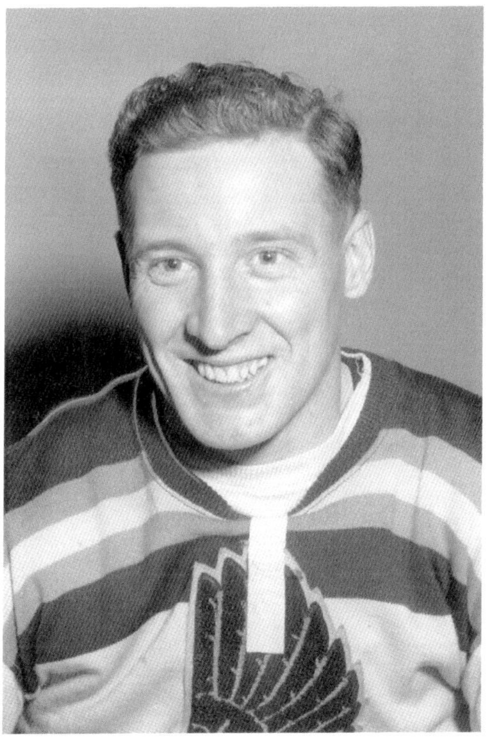

JIM FAIRBURN (RIGHT WING). Fairburn played in all 70 Eagles' games during the 1950–1951 campaign and did not have any penalty minutes. He had 62 points and 29 goals that season with Portland. Fairburn also skated in the PCHL/WHL with San Francisco from 1948 to 1950, Seattle in 1951–1952, Victoria in 1952–1953, and New Westminster in 1953–1954.

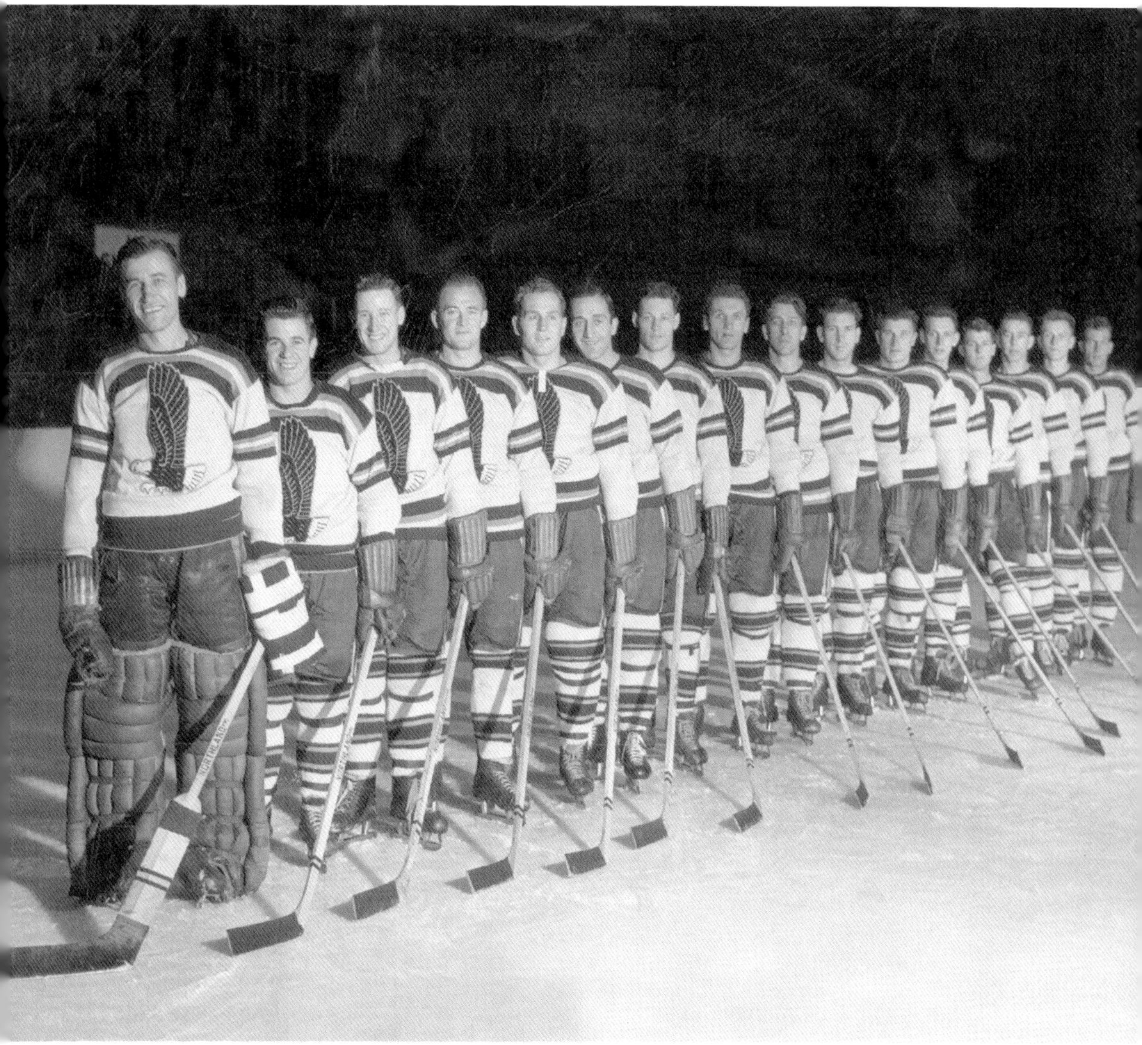

PORTLAND EAGLES, 1950–1951. Pictured here from left to right are Tom Karakas, Nelson Boyce, Jim Fairburn, George Homenuke, Hal Tarala, Larry Silvestri, Hal Hopper, Walter Samanski, Rudy Brodeur, Hugh Sutherland, Walter Bak, Bill Hartsburg, John Bailey, Joe Ciuman, Frank Kubasek, and Jack "Danny" Nixon.

5

The Buckaroos Win the Patrick Cup in their Inaugural Season

The Portland Buckaroos became members of the Western Hockey League (WHL) in 1960–1961 as a transfer franchise from New Westminster (WHL). The New Westminster Royals last season was in 1958–1959, but the team could not relocate to Portland until the completion of the 10,500-seat Portland Memorial Coliseum. Portland was granted a one-year leave of absence for the 1959–1960 season, and their players were loaned to the Victoria Cougars (WHL) while the club awaited the construction of their home rink in Portland. The Buckaroos were coached by Hal Laycoe starting in 1960–1961, and he would pilot the team through the 1968–1969 season. Harry Glickman was the team's general manager in 1960–1961 and 1961–1962 and returned as general manager in 1969–1970. Laycoe was general manager from the 1962–1963 season to the 1968–1969 season.

The Buckaroos won the Patrick Cup championship in their inaugural season, 1960–1961. Portland finished the regular season in second place with a 38-23-9 record. In the postseason, the Buckaroos won the first two playoff rounds by three-games-to-one counts against the Spokane Comets in the opening rounds and the Vancouver Canucks in the semifinals, respectfully. In the first All-America team finals since the league went professional in 1948–1949, the Buckaroos defeated the Seattle Totems four games to two. The Buckaroos were also a success at the gate during their first campaign, drawing 265,327 fans and breaking the previous WHL single-season attendance record of 187,793, set by Calgary seven years earlier. Portland also set the WHL record for highest single-game attendance with 10,334 fans on April 30, 1961, in a game against Seattle. (Both attendance records were later surpassed by other teams).

Prior to the 1960–1961 campaign, the WHL playoff championship trophy, the President's Cup, was renamed the Lester Patrick Cup in memory of Lester Patrick, who passed away on June 1, 1960. The President's Cup had been awarded to the circuit's postseason champion since the 1951–1952 season, when the WCMHL teams joined the loop and one year before the league changed its name from PCHL to WHL. From 1944–1945 to 1950–1951, PCHL playoff winners earned the Philip Henderson Cup.

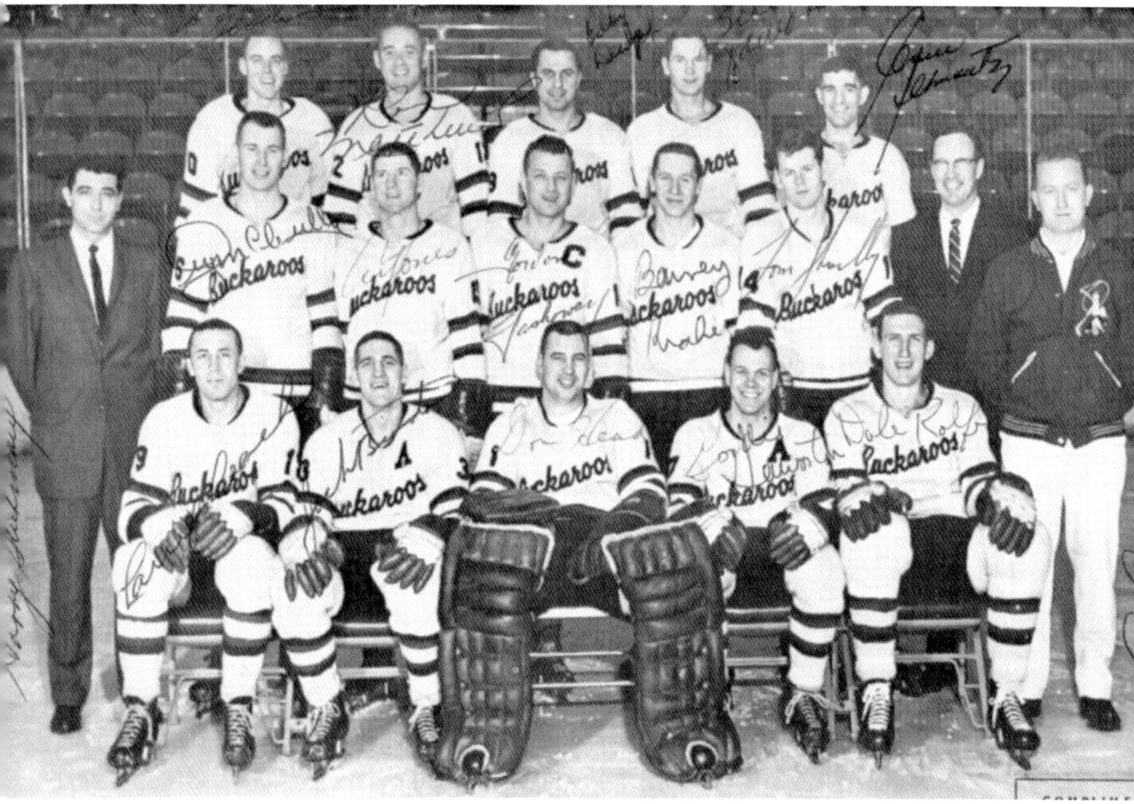

PATRICK CUP CHAMPION BUCKAROOS, 1960–1961. Pictured here from left to right are the following: (first row) Larry Leach, Jack Bionda, Don Head, Gordon Haworth, and Dale Rolfe; (second row) Harry Glickman (manager), Bill McCulley, Art Jones, Gordon Fashoway, Barney Krake, Pat Ginnell, Hal Laycoe (coach), and Berlyn Hodges (trainer); (third row) Arlo Goodwin, Ron Matthews, Eddie Dudych, Bill Davidson, and Arnie Schmautz.

BUCKAROOS PROGRAM FEATURING THE OFFICIAL BUCKAROO LOGO, 1960–1961. The Buckaroos won the Patrick Cup title in 1960–1961 and became only the third team to win the league playoff championship in its inaugural season since the loop turned professional in 1948–1949. The 1951–1952 Saskatoon Quakers and the 1955–1956 Winnipeg Warriors were the other two teams who took the postseason title in their first year in the league.

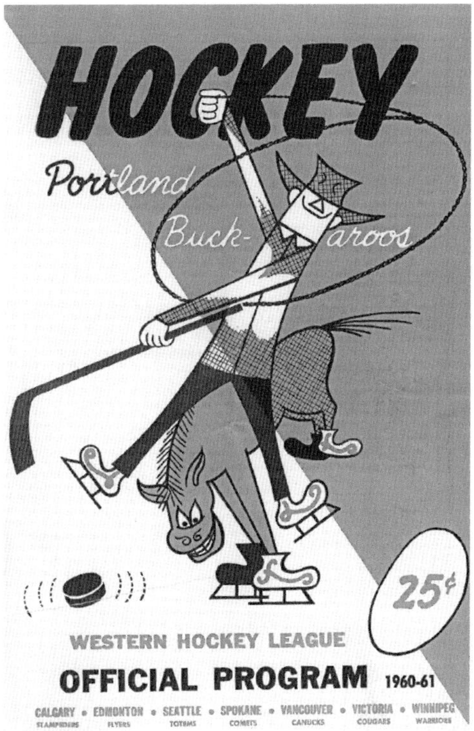

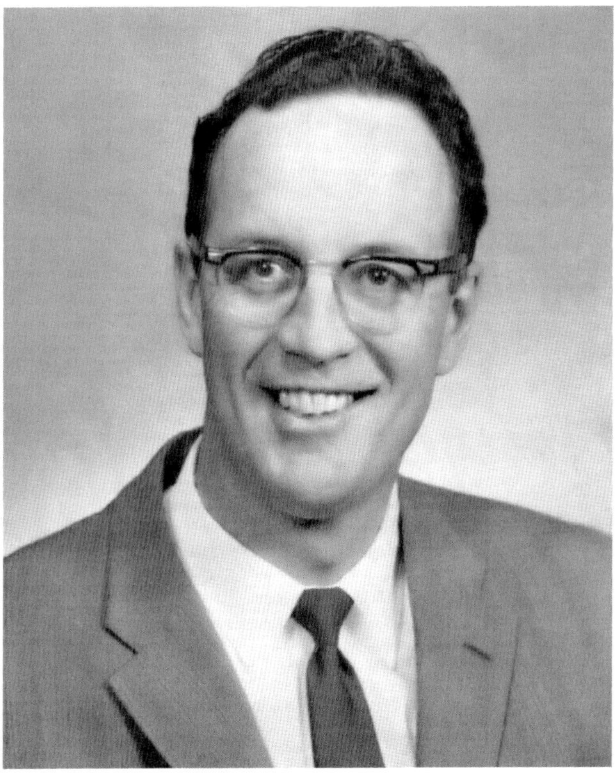

HAL LAYCOE (GENERAL MANAGER/COACH). Laycoe is one of the greatest coaches in minor league hockey history. He piloted the Buckaroos to a 362-212-66 (.617) record from 1960–1961 to 1968–1969 and led the club to two Patrick Cups and seven WHL regular-season titles. Laycoe was general manager of the Buckaroos from 1962–1963 to 1968–1969. He coached in the NHL from 1969 to 1972, compiling a 49-114-17 (.319) record.

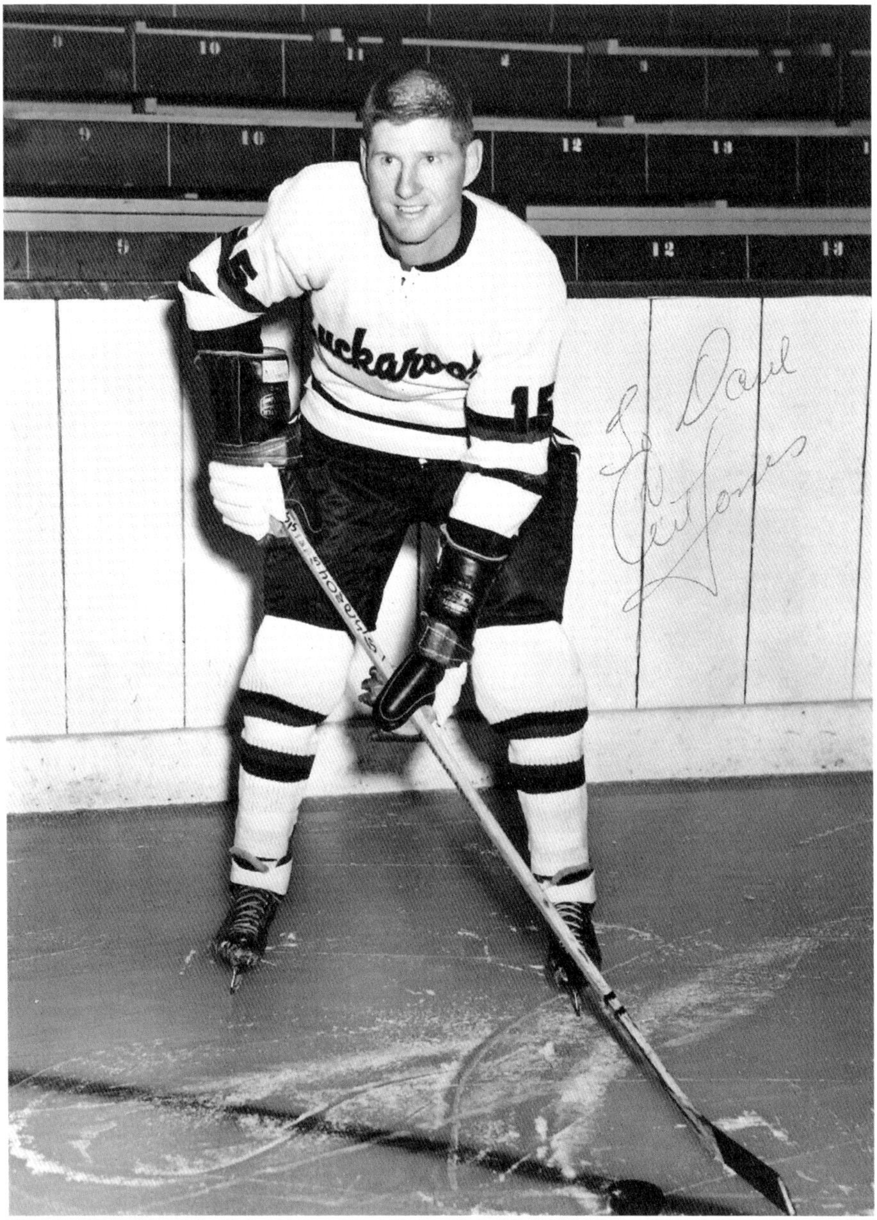

ART JONES (CENTER). "Mr. Buckaroo" is the only player to appear in all 14 Buckaroos seasons, from 1960 to 1974. He led the team in points during 12 of those campaigns and was a member of all three Portland Patrick Cup championship teams (1960–1961, 1964–1965, and 1970–1971). He is the franchise's all-time leader in points (1,361), goals (492), assists (869), and games played (981). Jones won the WHL Leading Scorer Award (most regular-season points) six times, won the Leader Cup (WHL MVP) twice, and was named a WHL All-Star eight times. The center is one of the WHL's all-time greatest players, ranking first overall in goals (578) and second overall in points (1,580), assists (1,002), and games played (1,180) in league history. Jones holds the WHL all-time, single-season point mark of 127, set in 1969–1970.

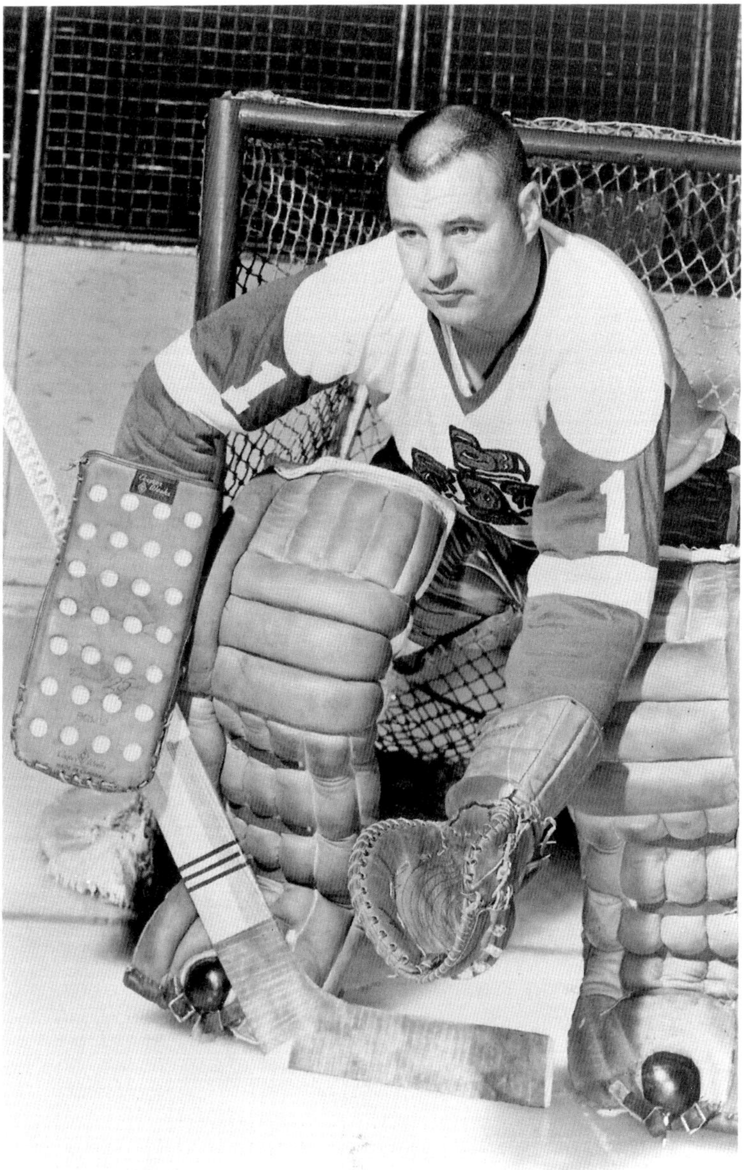

DON HEAD (GOALIE). Head compiled the most shutouts (21) and wins (162) in Buckaroos' history and ranks second in career GAA (2.77) and games in goal (292) on Portland's all-time list. The goaltender spent seven seasons with the Buckaroos from 1960 to 1967 and tallied a 162-99-29 record (.609). Head holds the WHL all-time record for career GAA (2.87) and was named to the WHL All-Star team more than any other netminder (five times). He also won the WHL Outstanding Goalkeeper Award three times (1960–1961, 1962–1963, and 1965–1966) and the WHL Rookie Award (for oustanding rookie) in 1960–1961. Head was a member of two Portland Patrick Cup teams in 1960–1961 and 1964–1965, and won a Patrick Cup with Seattle in 1967–1968. In his only NHL season, in 1961–1962, the goaltender earned a 4.24 GAA and a 9-26-3 record, and had two shutouts in 38 games.

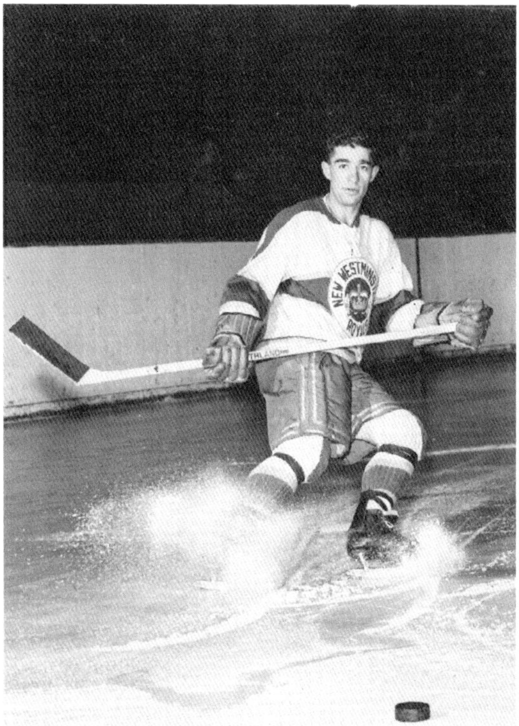

ARNIE SCHMAUTZ (RIGHT WING). Schmautz ranks sixth overall in goals (159), seventh in points (390) and games played (556), and eighth in assists (231) in Buckaroos' history. The right-winger spent eight seasons with Portland, from 1960 to 1968, and was a member of two Buckaroos' Patrick Cup winning teams (1960–1961 and 1964–1965). He also played in the WHL with New Westminster from 1955 to 1959 and with Victoria in 1959–1960.

RON MATTHEWS (DEFENSE). From 1960 to 1962, with Portland, Matthews tallied 105 points, 76 assists, and 44 PIM in 140 games. He was a member of the Buckaroos' 1960–1961 Patrick Cup–winning team. The defenseman ranks ninth all time in games played (947) in WHL history and was named a WHL All-Star four times. Matthews played 14 seasons in the PCHL/WHL—in 1948–1949 and from 1953 to 1966.

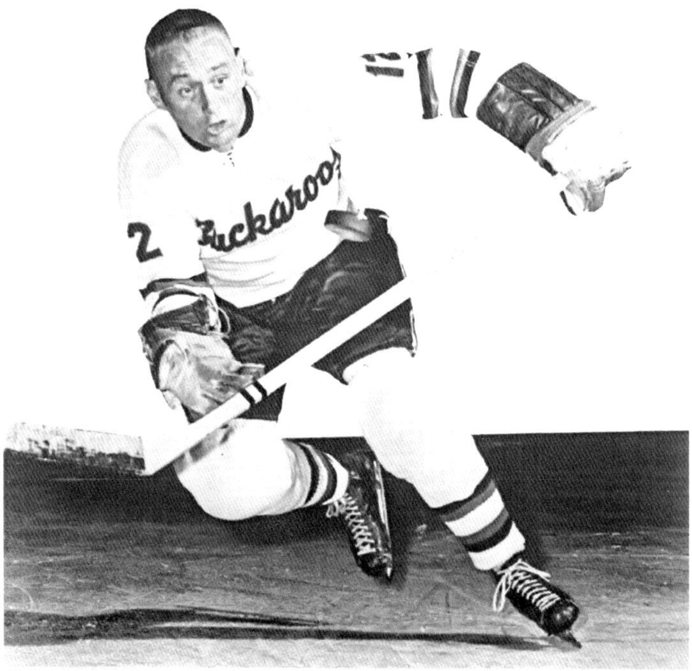

JACK BIONDA (DEFENSE). Bionda won two Patrick Cup titles with the Buckaroos in 1960–1961 and 1964–1965. In seven seasons with Portland, from 1960 to 1967, the defenseman had 161 points, 130 assists, and 560 PIM in 401 games. A veteran of four NHL campaigns from 1955 to 1959, Bionda garnered 12 points, 9 assists, and 113 PIM in 93 games. He is considered Canada's greatest lacrosse player of all time.

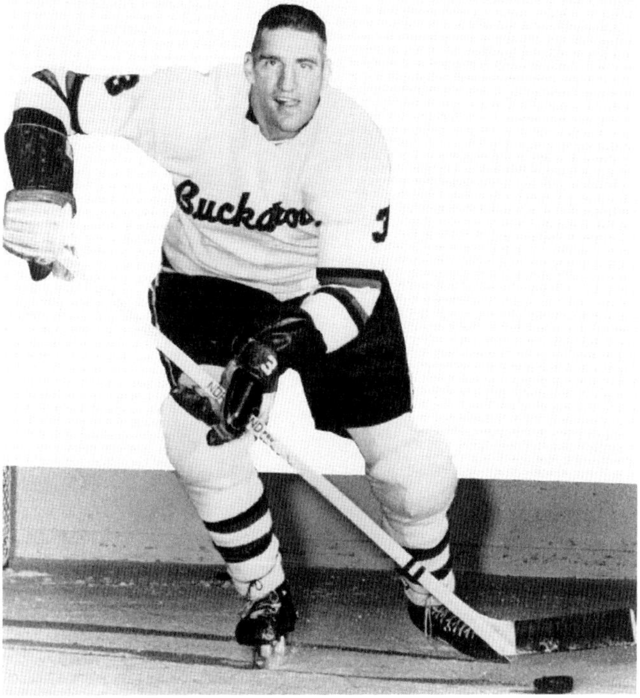

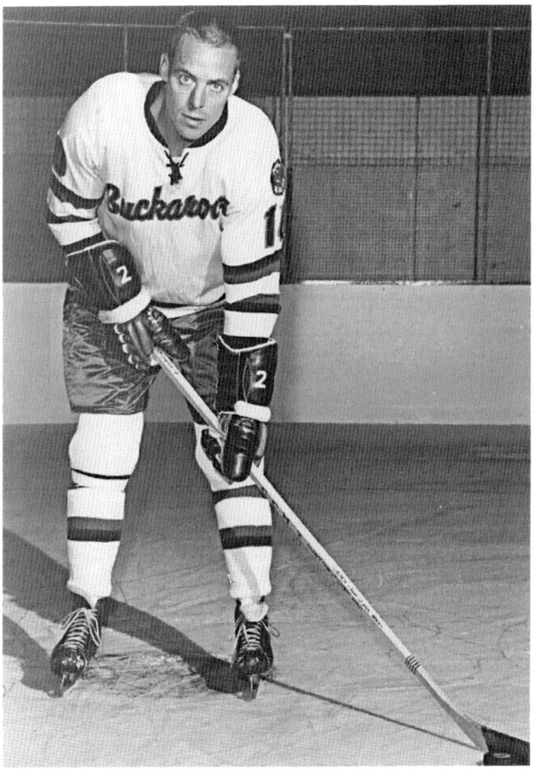

ARLO GOODWIN (CENTER). Goodwin skated for seven seasons with Portland, from 1960 to 1964 and from 1965 to 1968, producing 157 points, 101 assists, and 136 PIM in 394 games. Goodwin was a member of the Buckaroos' 1960–1961 Patrick Cup–winning team. The center also played in the WHL with New Westminster from 1955 to 1959 and with Victoria in 1959–1960.

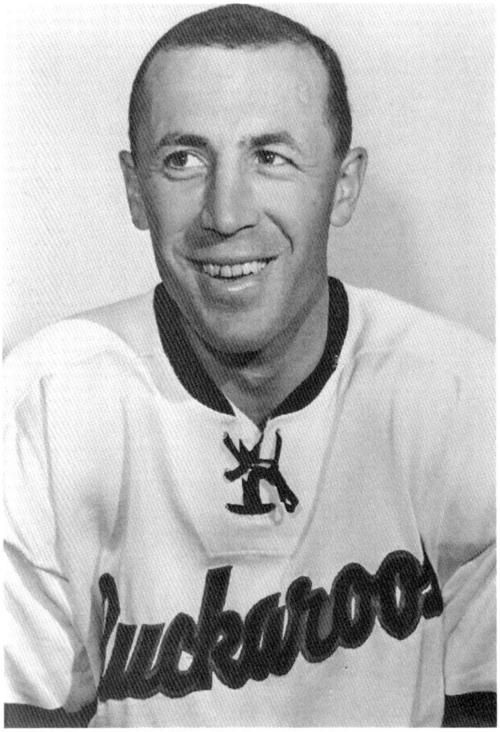

LARRY LEACH (CENTER). Leach was a member of all three Buckaroo Patrick Cup–winning teams (1960–1961, 1964–1965, and 1970–1971). In Buckaroos' history, he ranks fourth all time in games played (649). The center also had 288 points, 117 goals, and 472 PIM during 10 seasons with Portland (in 1960–1961 and from 1964 to 1973). Leach tallied 42 points in 126 NHL games between 1958 and 1962.

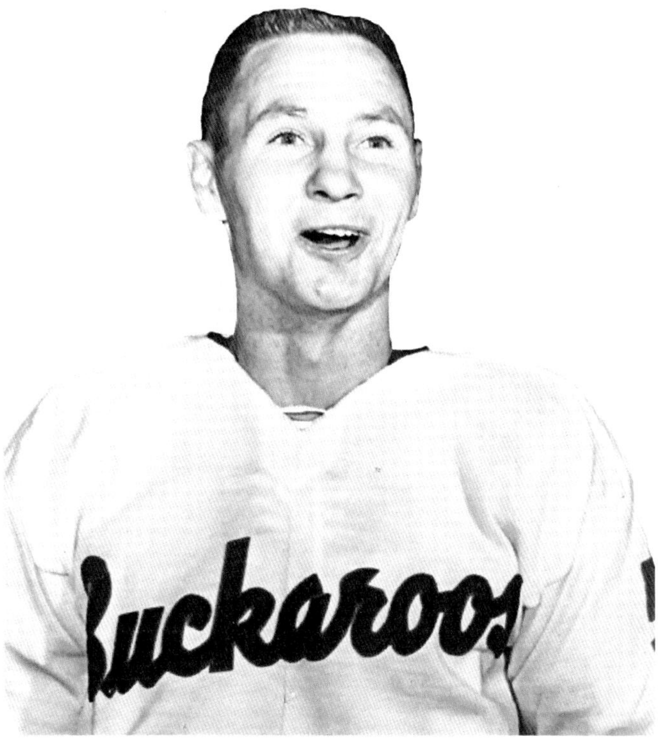

BILL DAVIDSON (DEFENSE). He spent three seasons with Portland, from 1960 to 1963, garnering 71 points, 55 assists, and 88 PIM in 192 games, and won a Patrick Cup with the Buckaroos in 1960–1961. Davidson also skated in the PCHL/WHL with Tacoma from 1951 to 1953; Seattle in 1953–1954 and from 1957 to 1961; and Victoria from 1954 to 1957, winning a Patrick Cup with Seattle in 1958–1959.

6

Back-to-Back WHL Regular-Season Championships

The Buckaroos had the best regular-season record in the WHL in 1961–1962 and 1962–1963 and captured the WHL Southern Division title in both seasons. During the 1961–1962 and 1962–1963 postseasons, however, Portland was upset in the division finals round (the Buckaroos earned a first round bye). The Buckaroos achieved a 42-23-5 record in 1961–1962 and lost in the division finals against the Spokane Comets four games to three. In 1962–1963, Portland posted a 43-21-6 record but did not advance in the postseason, losing in the division finals against the San Francisco Seals four games to three.

The Portland Memorial Coliseum was host to the fifth annual WHL All-Star Game on January 8, 1962, which was held during the 1961–1962 season. The midseason contest was played between all-stars from the WHL's Northern and Southern Divisions as chosen by vote of the coaches in each division. Eight Buckaroo players made the Southern Division All-Star team: goalie Bruce Gamble; defensemen Ron Matthews and Dale Rolfe; and forwards Art Jones, Arnie Schmautz, Bill Saunders, Gordon Fashoway, and Doug Macauley. Hal Laycoe was named coach of the Southern Division All-Stars. The Northern Division All-Stars won the game 7-3, and player of the game honors when to Northern Division All-Star defenseman Doug Barkley of Calgary. Macauley was the only Buckaroo that scored in the game, and Gamble (who played the entire game) had 32 saves for the Southern Division All-Stars. Former Eagles/Penguins players Pat Desbiens and Hal Tarala were linesmen in the game.

In the other two WHL All-Star games played during the Buckaroos existence, in 1960–1961 and 1962–1963 at Vancouver, Portland was represented by Art Jones and Arnie Schmautz in 1960–1961 and Don Head, Bill Saunders, and Dallas Smith in 1962–1963.

In 1963–1964, the WHL went to a single-division format and the Buckaroos finished in second place out of six teams with a 33-30-7 mark. San Francisco ended the Buckaroos' playoff run early with a four-games-to-one series win in the semifinals.

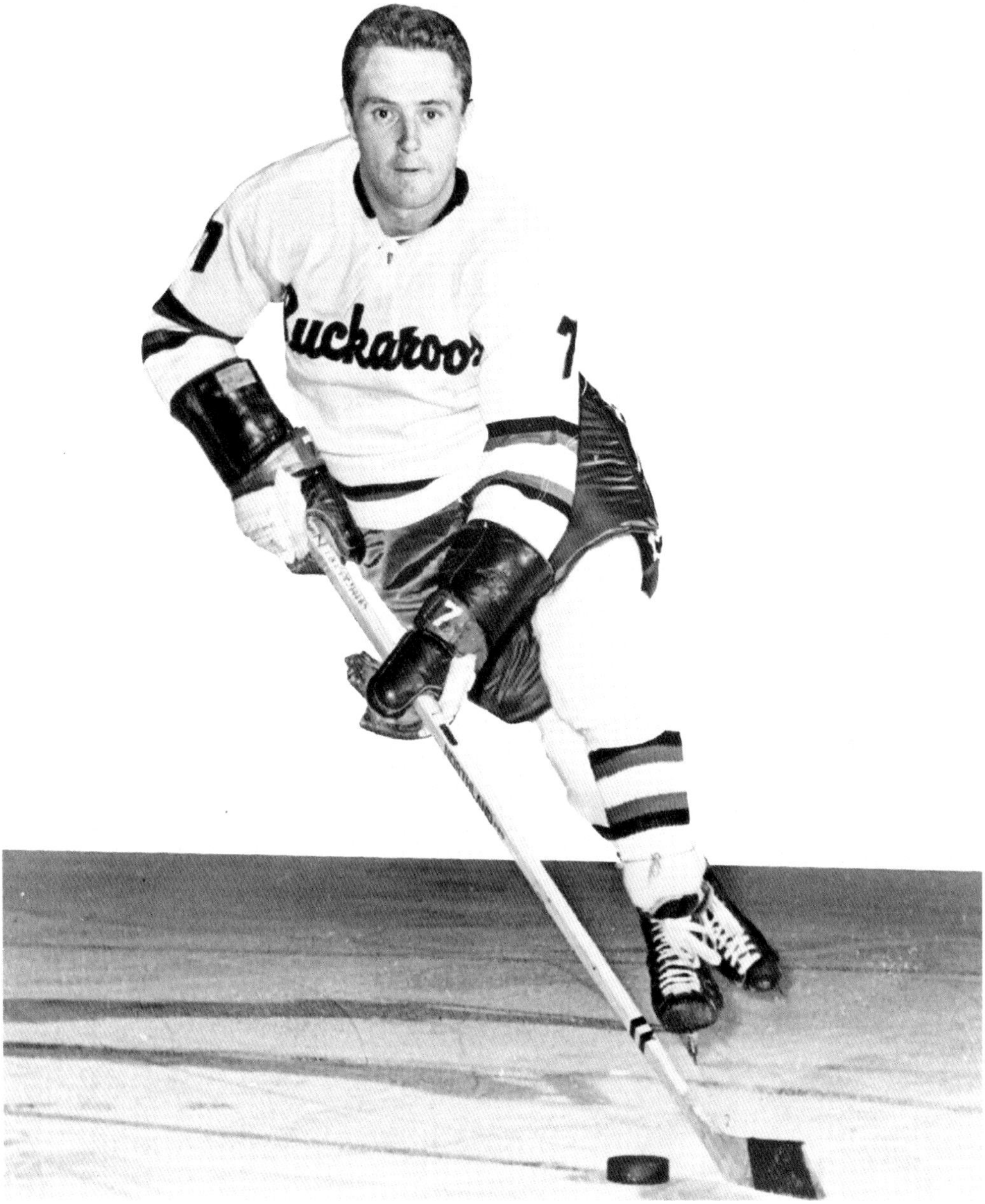

BILL SAUNDERS (FORWARD). In the Buckaroos' record book, Saunders ranks second all time in points (856), goals (392), assists (464), and games played (836), and is tied for second in seasons played (12). He won two Patrick Cups with Portland in 1964–1965 and 1970–1971 and registered 352 PIM during his dozen seasons with the club, from 1961 to 1973. In WHL history, Saunders is tied for third all time in goals (425), is sixth all time in points (932), and ninth all time in assists (507). The forward was named to the WHL All-Star Team four times.

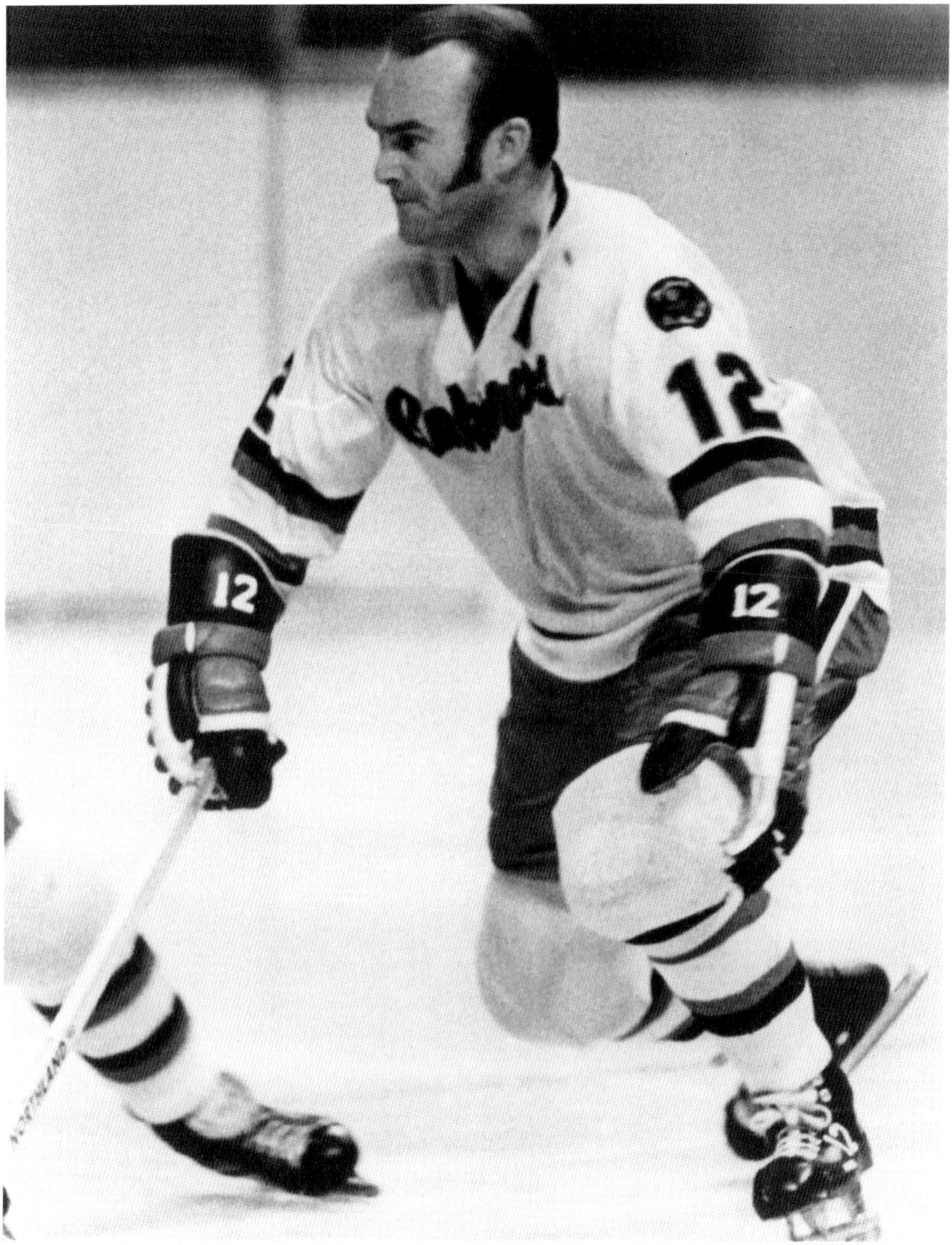

MIKE DONALDSON (DEFENSE). Donaldson ranks second overall in Buckaroos' history for PIM (1,146), is tied for second in seasons played (12), and ranks third in games played (816). The defenseman also compiled 174 points and 151 assists with Portland from 1962 to 1974. He was a member of two Buckaroo Patrick Cup–winning teams in 1964–1965 and 1970–1971.

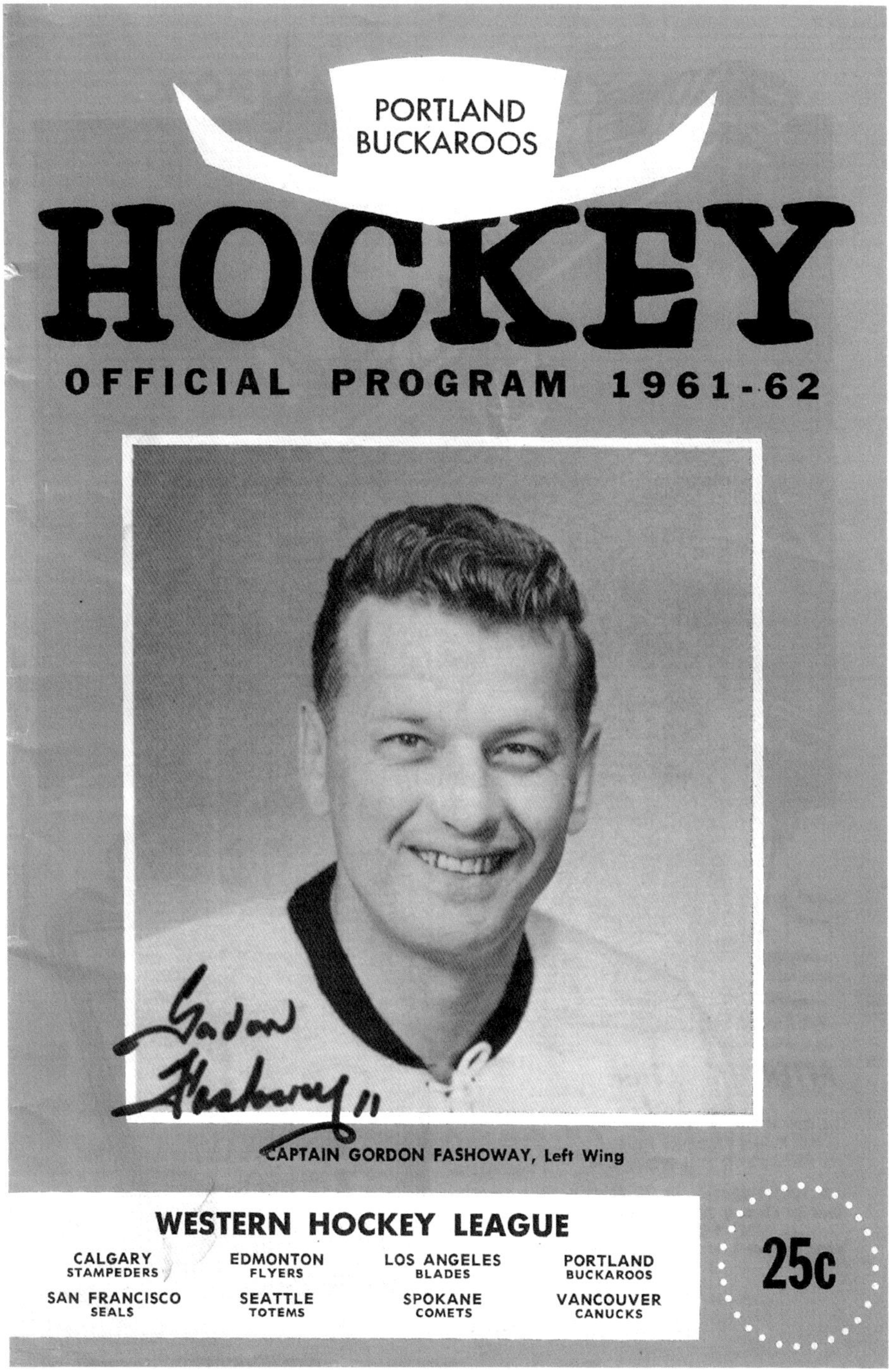

BUCKAROOS PROGRAM FEATURING GORDON FASHOWAY, 1961–1962. The Most Valuable Player award in the WHL was called the Leader Cup. George "Al" Leader was president of the league from the 1947–1948 season to the 1969–1970 season. He remained active in the affairs of the league as president emeritus. Leader was elected to the Hockey Hall of Fame in 1969 as a builder.

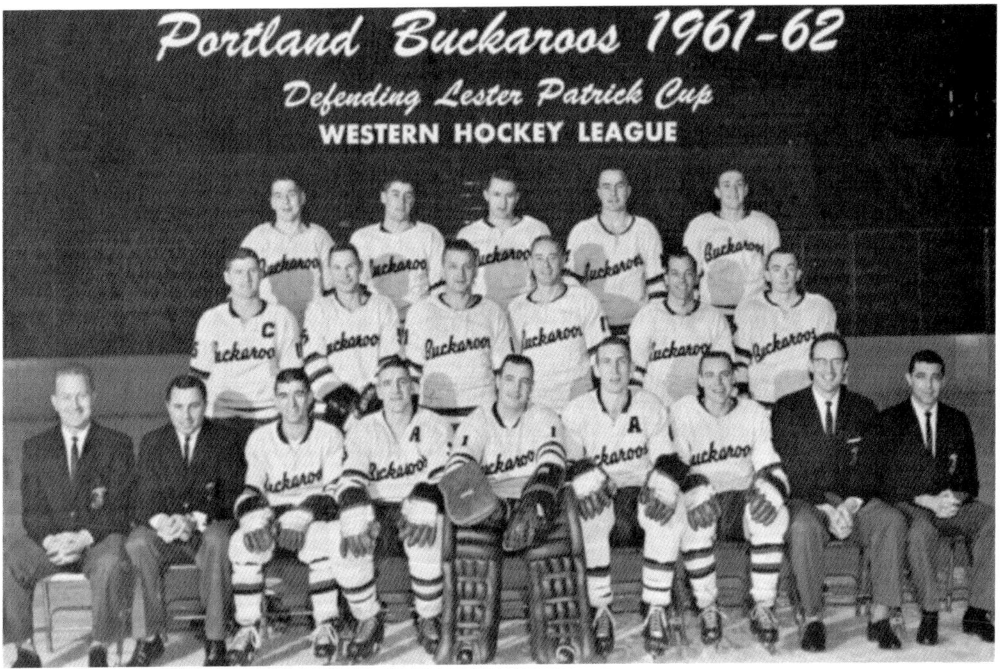

PORTLAND BUCKAROOS, 1961–1962. Pictured here from left to right are the following: (first row) Berlyn Hodges (trainer), Eddie Dudych, Arnie Schmautz, Jack Bionda, Don Head, Dale Rolfe, Arlo Goodwin, Hal Laycoe (coach), and Harry Glickman (general manager); (second row) Art Jones, Bill Davidson, Gordon Fashoway, Ron Matthews, Doug Anderson, and Doug Macauley; (third row) Tom McVie, Ed Lawson, Bill Saunders, Gene Achtymichuk, and George Knipelberg.

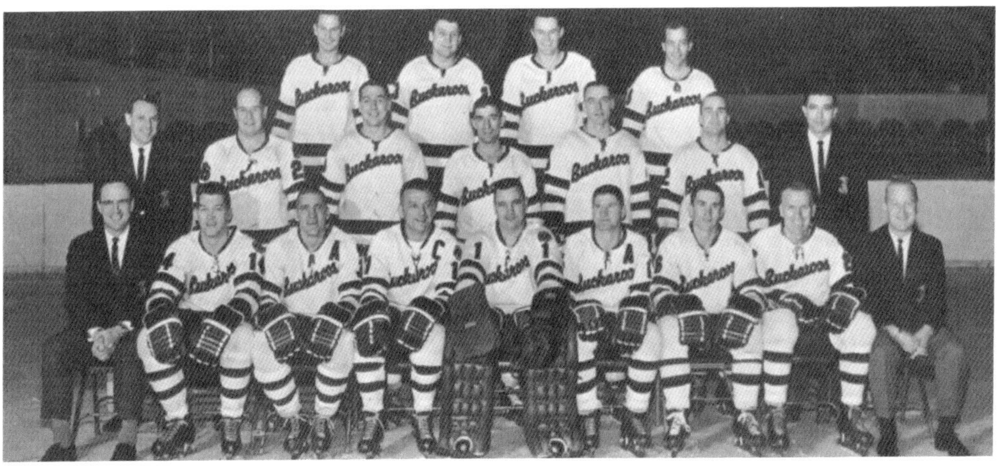

PORTLAND BUCKAROOS, 1962–1963. Pictured are, from left to right, the following: (first row) Hal Laycoe (general manager/coach), Tom McCarthy, Jack Bionda, Gordon Fashoway, Don Head, Art Jones, Dallas Smith, Gerry Goyer, and Berlyn Hodges (trainer); (second row) George Rickles (business manager), Orval Tessier, Tom McVie, Arnie Schmautz, Arlo Goodwin, Mike Donaldson, and Harry Glickman (managing director); (third row) Bill Davidson, Ken Laufman, Bill Saunders, and Doug Anderson.

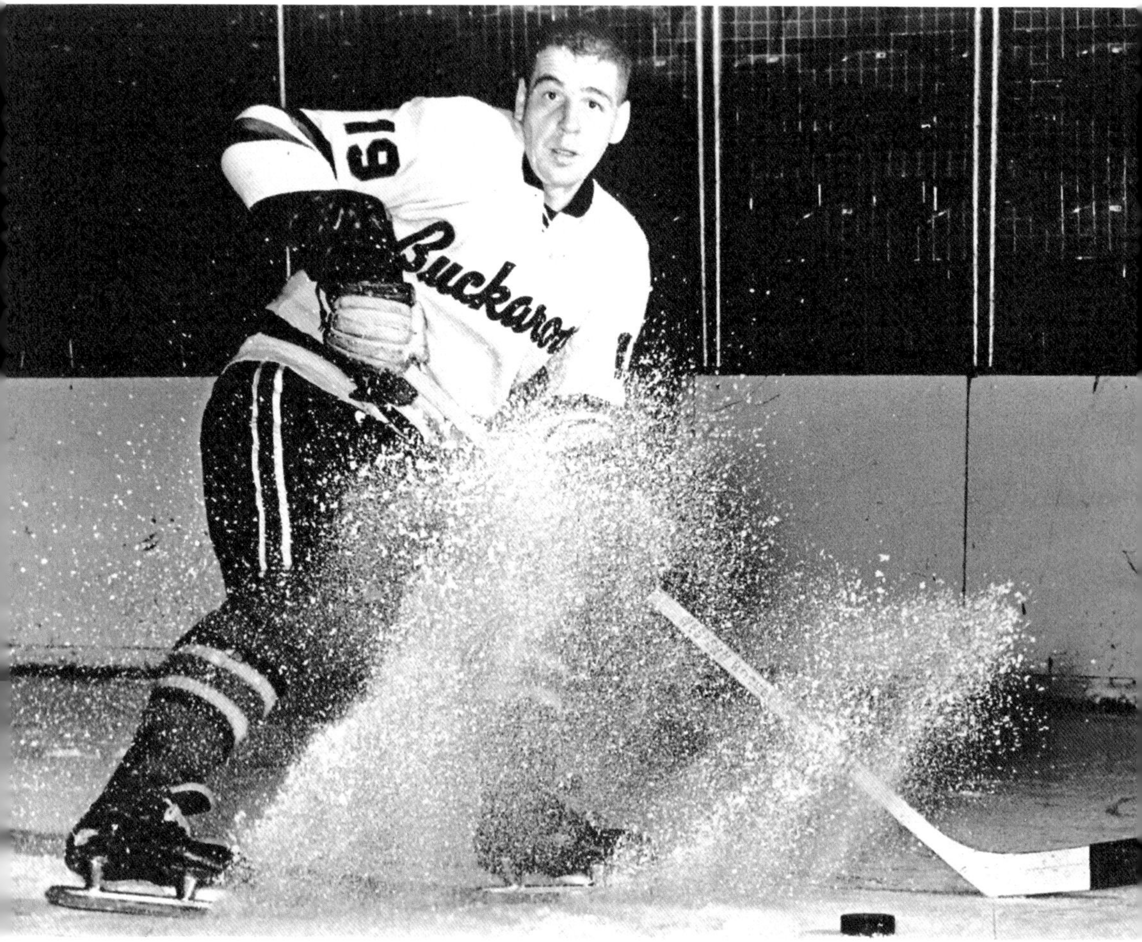

TOM "DOBIE" MCVIE (LEFT WING). In Buckaroos' history, McVie ranks fifth all time in goals (168) and 10th all time in points (321). The left-winger also tallied 153 assists and 251 PIM in 310 games with Portland from 1961 to 1966 and in 1972–1973. He was a member of the Buckaroos' 1964–1965 Patrick Cup–winning team. McVie ranks ninth overall in goals (362) in WHL history, was named a WHL All-Star three times, and won a Patrick Cup with Seattle in 1958–1959. McVie shares the WHL record for most goals in a game with five (set on December 10, 1961). After his playing days were over, he coached in the NHL and WHA.

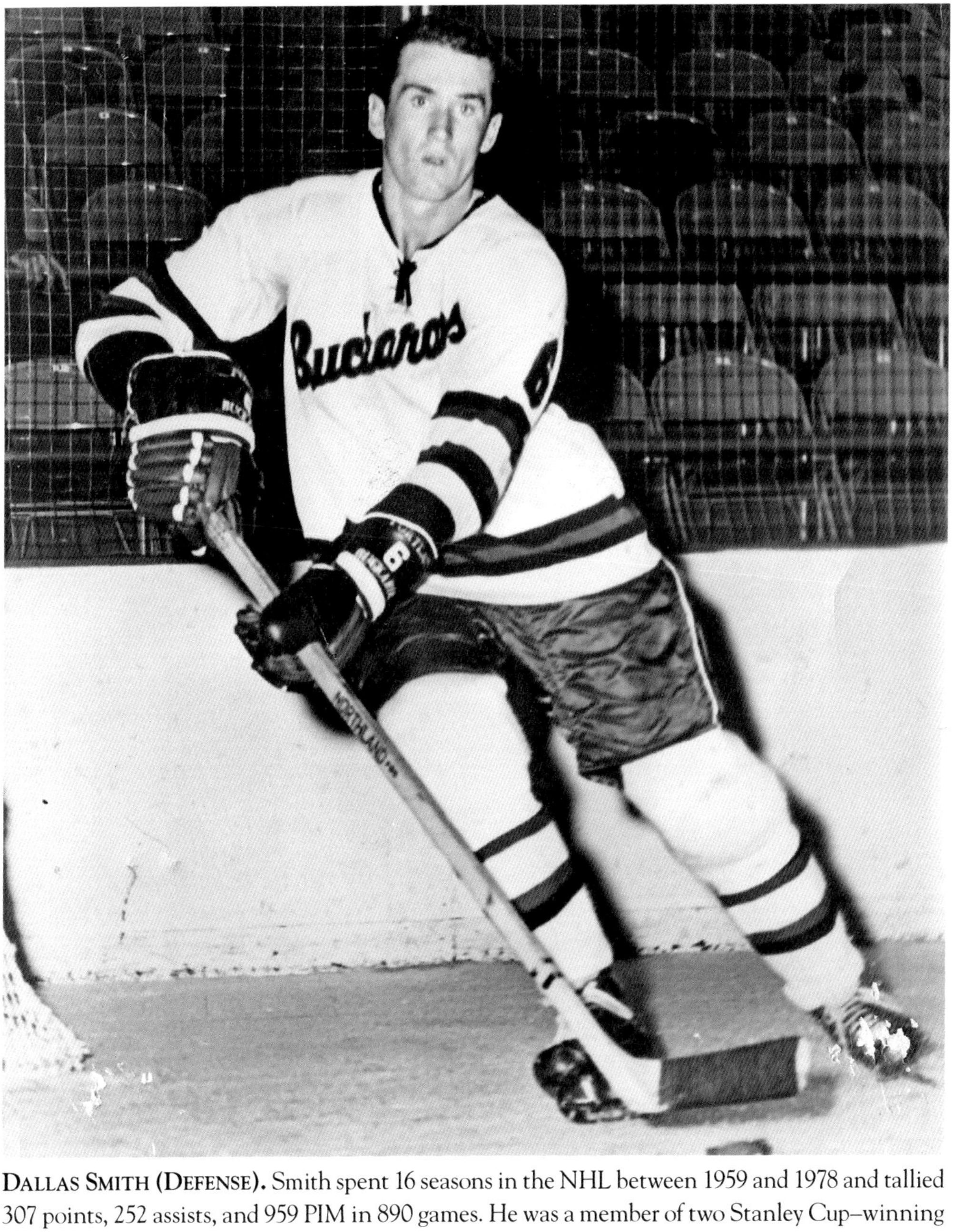

DALLAS SMITH (DEFENSE). Smith spent 16 seasons in the NHL between 1959 and 1978 and tallied 307 points, 252 assists, and 959 PIM in 890 games. He was a member of two Stanley Cup–winning teams with Boston in 1969–1970 and 1971–1972. In two campaigns with Portland, from 1962 to 1964, Smith garnered 40 points, 32 assists, and 121 PIM in 132 games. He also won two Adams Cups with Oklahoma City of the Central Professional Hockey League (CPHL) in 1965–1966 and 1966–1967. The CPHL was later known as the Central Hockey League beginning with the 1968–1969 season.

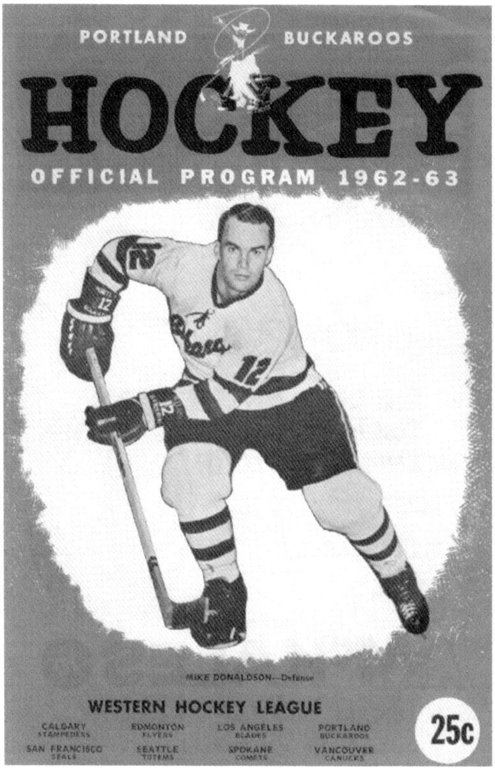

BUCKAROOS PROGRAM FEATURING MIKE DONALDSON, 1962–1963. The WHL held an annual all-star game for six seasons from 1957–1958 to 1962–1963. The sites of the all-star games were as follows: Calgary (1957–1958), Edmonton (1959–1960), Portland (1961–1962), and Vancouver (1958–1959, 1960–1961, and 1962–1963). Every WHL All-Star game involved intra-league teams, except in 1962–1963 when the Toronto Maple Leafs blanked the WHL All-Stars 3-0.

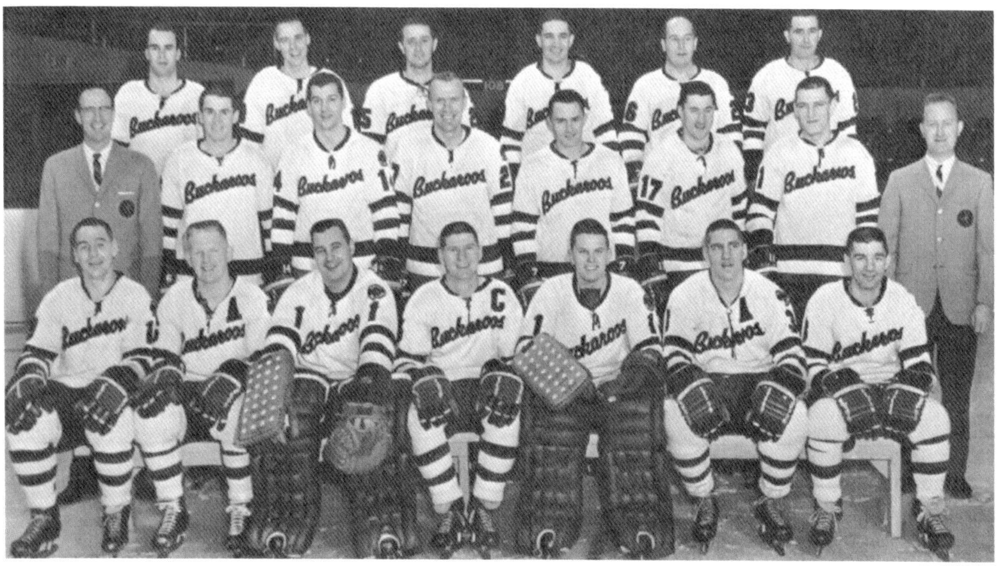

PORTLAND BUCKAROOS, 1963–1964. Pictured here from left to right are the following: (first row) Tom McVie, Pat Stapleton, Don Head, Art Jones, Dave Kelly, Jack Bionda, and Arnie Schmautz; (second row) Hal Laycoe (general manager/coach), Dallas Smith, Tom McCarthy, Gerry Goyer, Bill Saunders, Sid Finney, Doug Messier, and Berlyn Hodges (trainer); (third row) Mike Donaldson, Arlo Goodwin, Bob Ertel, Cliff Schmautz, Orval Tessier, and Dick Van Impe.

DOUG ANDERSON (CENTER). Anderson played his last two professional seasons in Portland from 1961 to 1963 and produced 37 points, 28 assists, and 2 PIM in 114 games. He also played in the PCHL/WHL with Victoria from 1951 to 1961, and he spent time in the AHL with Buffalo in 1953–1954. Anderson had a stint in the NHL during the 1952–1953 Stanley Cup playoffs.

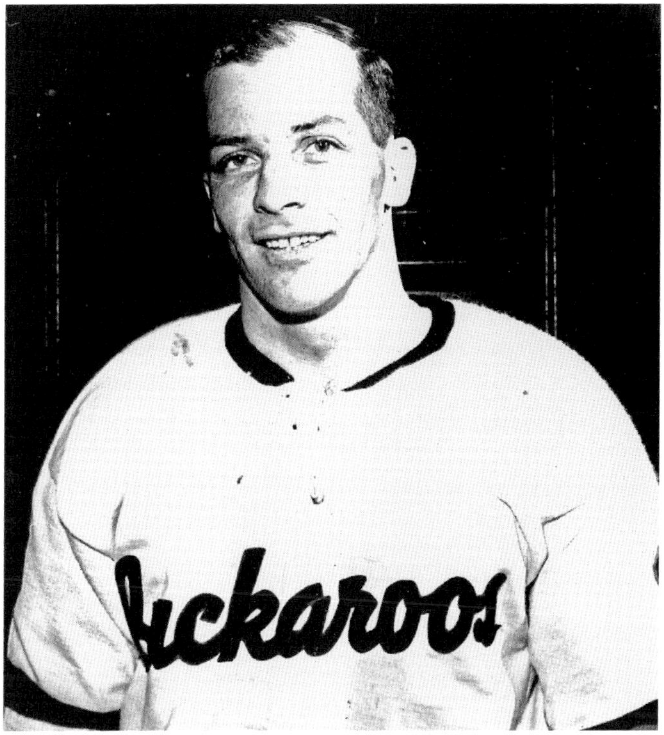

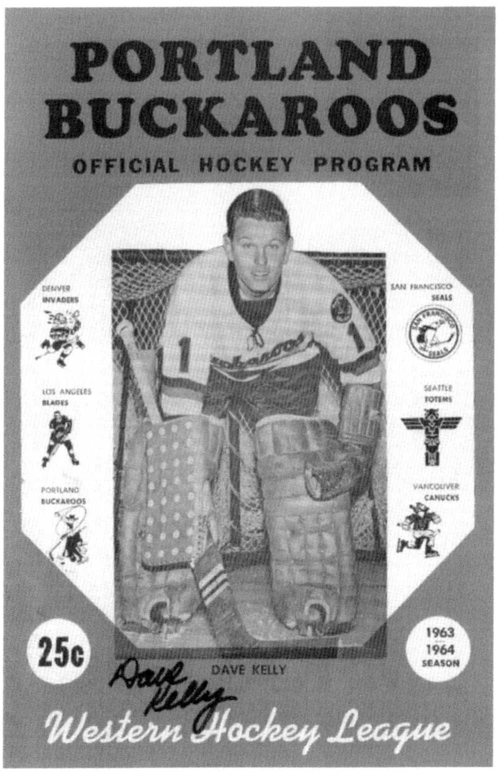

BUCKAROOS PROGRAM FEATURING DAVE KELLY, 1963–1964. In 1963–1964, the San Francisco Seals became the first WHL team to win consecutive playoff championships (also won in 1962–1963). The Seattle Totems (1966–1967 and 1967–1968), the Vancouver Canucks (1968–1969 and 1969–1970), and the Phoenix Roadrunners (1972–1973 and 1973–1974) later achieved back-to-back postseason titles. Phoenix is the only team in WHL history to win consecutive regular-season and playoff championships (1972–1973 and 1973–1974).

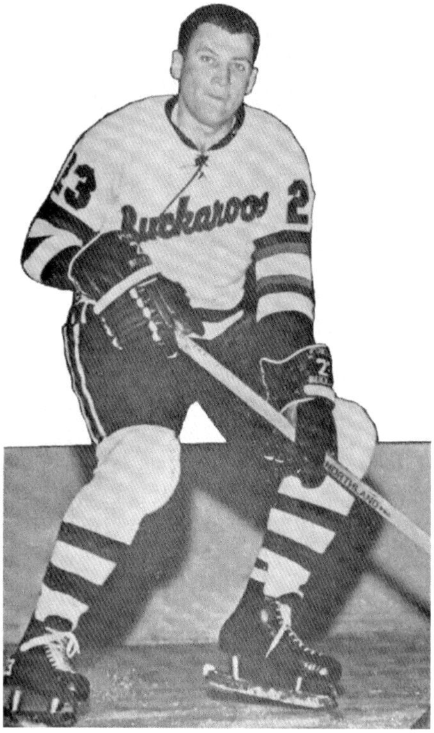

Ken Laufman (Center). Laufman tallied 69 points, 52 assists, and 24 PIM in 83 games with the Buckaroos from 1962 to 1964. Laufman, a center, was a member of two Atlantic City Boardwalk Trophy championship teams with Johnstown (EHL) in 1960–1961 and 1961–1962. He also spent time in the Eastern Professional Hockey League (EPHL) in 1959–1960 and the CPHL in 1963–1964.

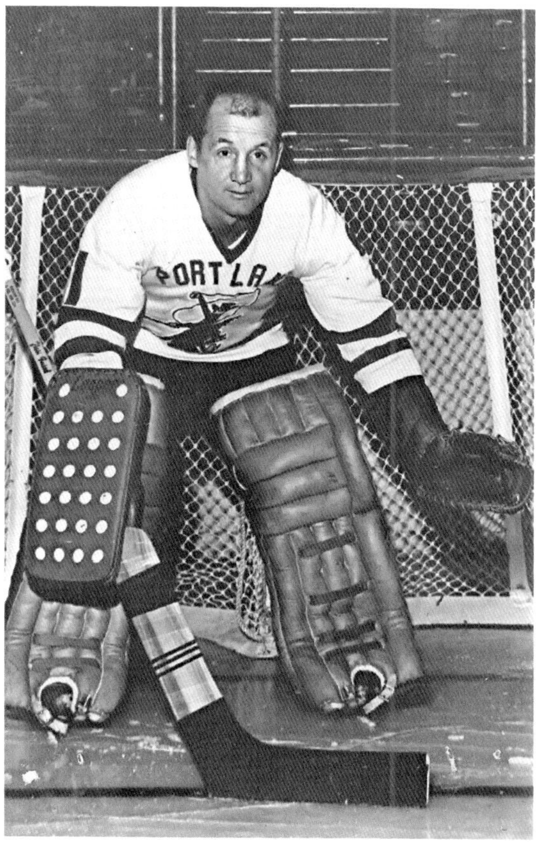

Marv Edwards (Goalie). In 1967–1968, with Portland, Edwards won the WHL Outstanding Goalkeeper Award and compiled a 2.36 GAA, a 21-16-2 record, and four shutouts in 40 games. He spent most of his professional career in the EHL, from 1960 to 1967, and was a member of five EHL playoff championship teams. In the NHL between 1968 and 1974, Edwards earned a 3.77 GAA, a 15-34-7 record, and two shutouts in 61 games.

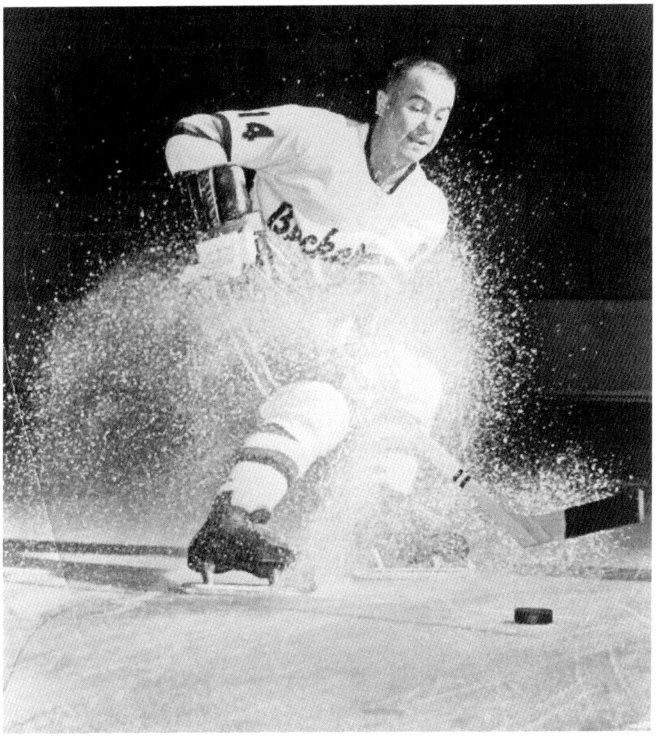

Gene Achtymichuk (Center). With Portland, in 1961–1962, Achtymichuk garnered 73 points, 56 assists, and 10 PIM in 68 games. He also played with the Buckaroos during the 1965–1966 Patrick Cup playoffs. A veteran of four NHL campaigns between 1951 and 1959, the center had eight points in 32 NHL games. Achtymichuk was a member of O'Connell Trophy–winning Quebec (QHL) in 1956–1957 and Walker Cup–winning Long Island (EHL) in 1964–1965.

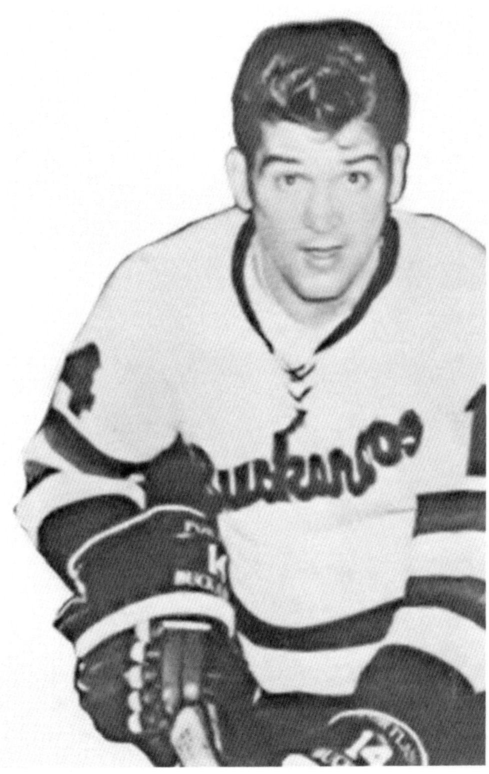

Tom McCarthy (Left Wing). In two seasons with Portland, from 1962 to 1964, the left-winger tallied 98 points, 60 assists, and 92 PIM in 121 games. A veteran of four NHL seasons between 1956 and 1961, McCarthy produced 17 points, 8 goals, and 8 PIM in 60 games. He played with five WHL teams. He was a member of Calder Cup–winning Hershey (AHL) in 1958–1959.

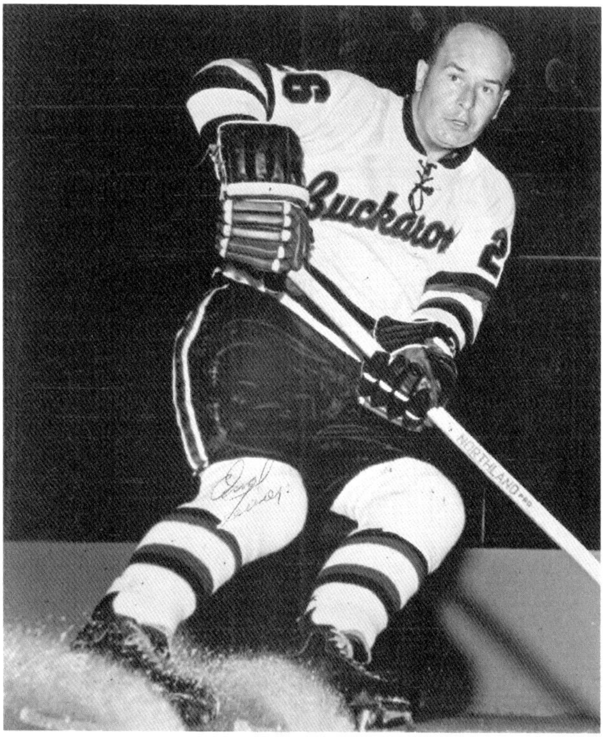

ORVAL TESSIER (CENTER). Tessier skated with Portland from 1962 to 1964 and collected 84 points, 55 assists, and 13 PIM in 102 games. The center spent three seasons in the NHL between 1954 and 1961, garnering 12 points, 7 assists, and 6 PIM in 59 games. He won an O'Connell Trophy with Quebec (QHL) in 1956–1957. Tessier later coached in the NHL from 1982 to 1985 and compiled a 99-93-21 (.514) record.

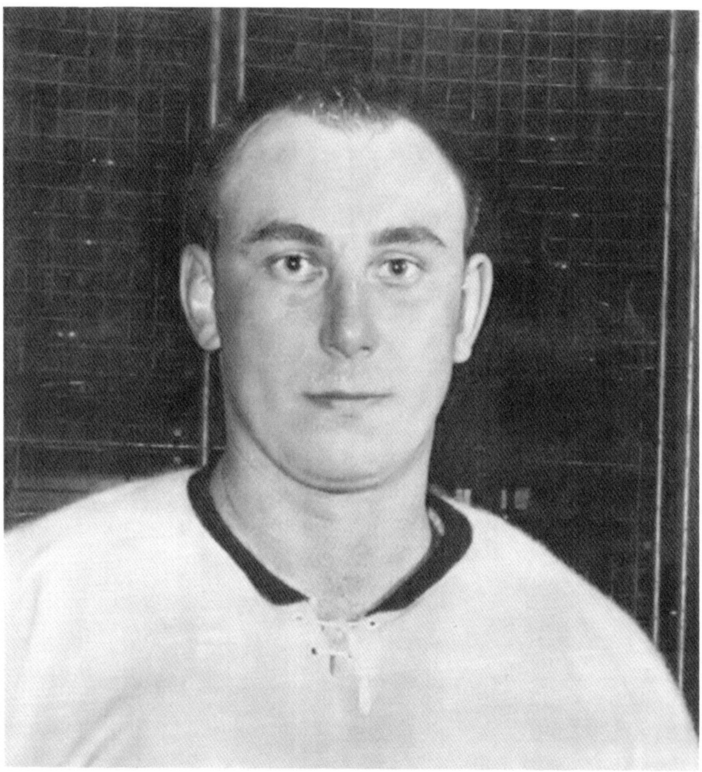

BRUCE GAMBLE (GOALIE). Gamble earned a 3.21 GAA, a 110-150-46 record, and 22 shutouts in 327 games during 10 NHL seasons between 1958 and 1972. With Portland in 1961–1962, the goalie compiled a 2.62 GAA, a 28-11-2 record, and two shutouts in 41 games. Gamble was named of the WHL Coast Division Outstanding Rookie in 1958–1959.

7

The Buckaroos Establish All-Time WHL Records

The Buckaroos captured a WHL record of five consecutive regular-season titles from 1964–1965 to 1968–1969. During these five seasons, the club compiled a 206-115-39 (.626) regular-season record and added a second Patrick Cup title in 1964–1965. In 1964–1965, the Buckaroos had the WHL's best regular-season record (42-23-5) and skated through the playoffs, defeating the Vancouver Canucks four games to one in the semifinals and beating the Victoria Maple Leafs four games to one in the finals.

Portland achieved a WHL all-time record sixth consecutive winning season in 1965–1966 with a first-place, 43-24-5 finish. The Buckaroos faced the same two teams in the playoffs as the year before, but this time each series went seven games. Laycoe's team edged Vancouver in the semifinals but fell short against Victoria in the finals.

In 1966–1967, the Buckaroos earned a 41-24-7 mark and captured the WHL regular-season crown. Portland, however, was swept in the semifinals against Vancouver in four games.

Portland outperformed the rest of the league once again in 1967–1968, attaining a 40-26-6 record and earning another first-place finish. In the playoffs that season, the Buckaroos started another WHL all-time record streak. The Buckaroos won their first of five semifinals series in a row and became the only team in WHL history to appear in five consecutive Patrick Cup finals. In 1967–1968, Portland defeated the San Diego Gulls four games to three in the semifinals. The Seattle Totems downed the Buckaroos in the finals four games to one.

In Hal Laycoe's last season as Buckaroos general manager/coach in 1968–1969, the locals compiled a 40-18-16 mark and were again on top of the regular-season standings for a WHL all-time record fifth consecutive season. Portland's Jim McLeod established the all-time WHL single-season GAA record that year (2.29). For the second season in a row, Portland knocked off San Diego in the semifinals in seven games but was swept in the finals by Vancouver four games to none.

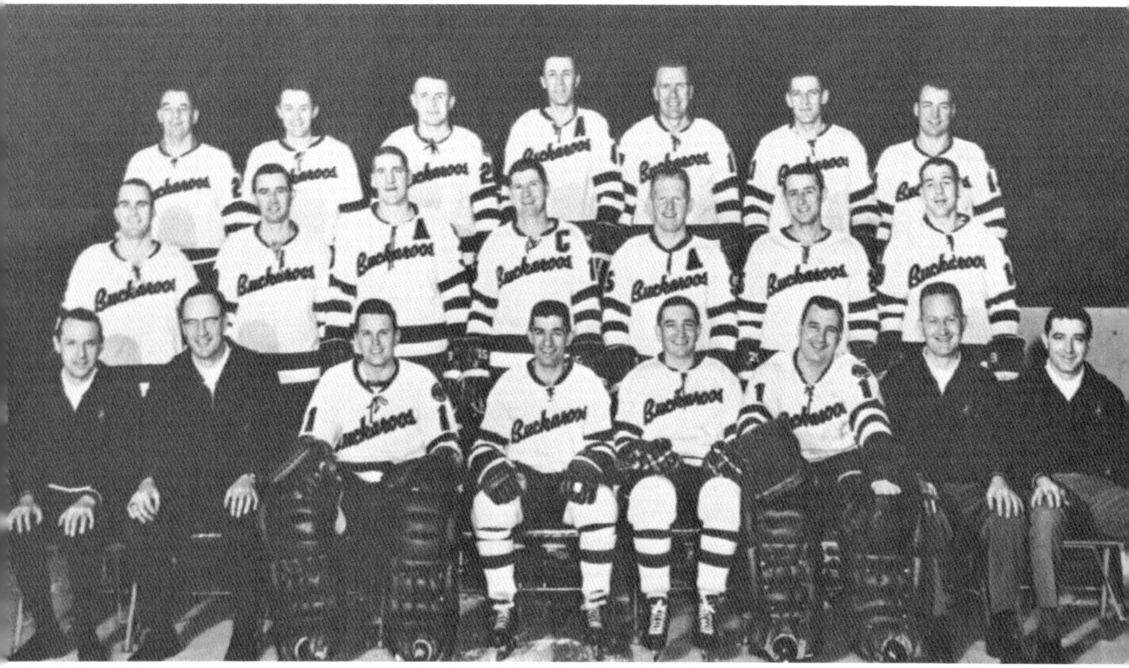

PATRICK CUP CHAMPION BUCKAROOS, 1964–1965. Pictured here from left to right are the following: (first row) George Rickles (business manager), Hal Laycoe (general manager/coach), Dave Kelly, Arnie Schmautz, Cliff Schmautz, Don Head, Berlyn Hodges (trainer), and Harry Glickman (managing director); (second row) Mike Donaldson, Dick Van Impe, Jack Bionda, Art Jones, Pat Stapleton, Bob Ertel, and Tom McVie; (third row) Connie Madigan, Bill Saunders, Jim Hay, Larry Leach, Gerry Goyer, Doug Messier, and Andy Hebenton.

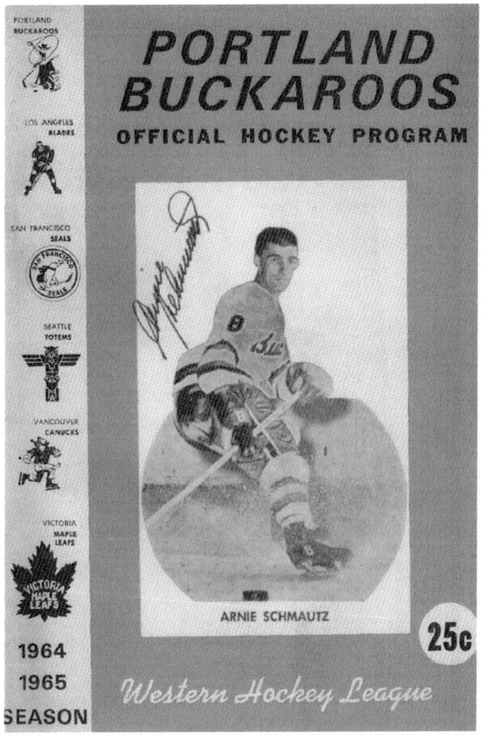

BUCKAROOS PROGRAM FEATURING ARNIE SCHMAUTZ, 1964–1965. For the 1964–1965 season, the WHL began presenting an annual award to the league's outstanding defenseman. For the 1965–1966 season, the award was renamed the Hal Laycoe Cup after longtime Buckaroo general manager/coach Hal Laycoe. Laycoe is noted as one of the prime movers in gaining an outstanding pension plan for the players of the WHL.

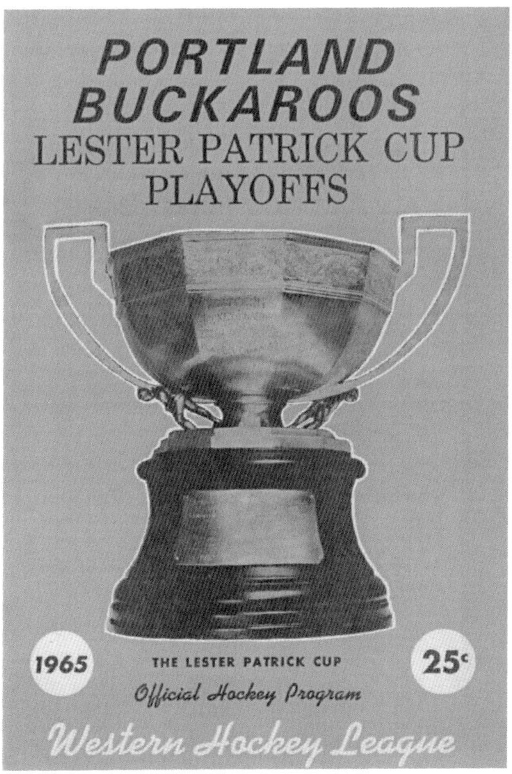

PATRICK CUP FINALS PROGRAM: BUCKAROOS VERSUS THE VICTORIA MAPLE LEAFS, 1964–1965. Portland defeated Victoria four games to one in the 1964–1965 Patrick Cup finals to win their second WHL postseason title. The Buckaroos outscored the Maple Leafs 17-8 in the series.

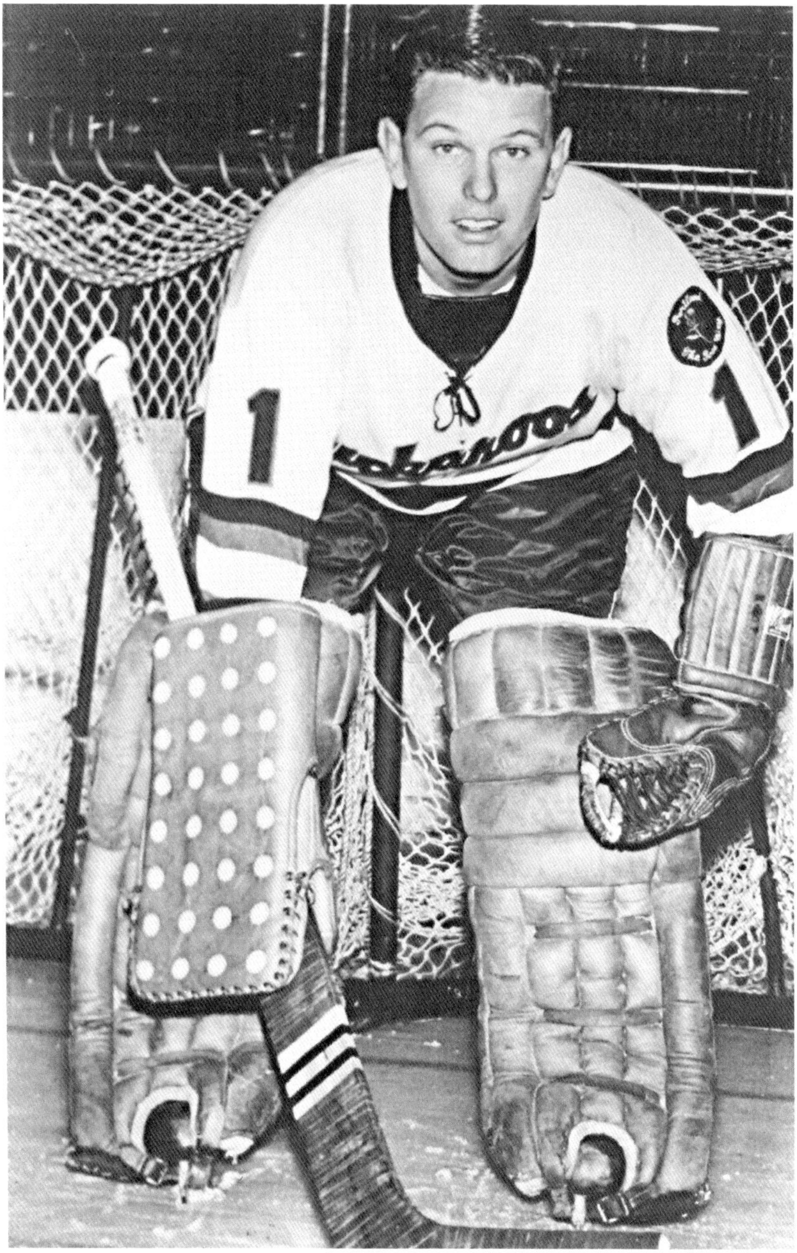

Dave Kelly (Goalie). Kelly spent more seasons (9) and games (319) between the pipes for the Buckaroos than any other goaltender. He posted the second-most shutouts (16) and wins (statistic unavailable) in Buckaroos' history and compiled a 3.40 GAA with Portland from 1963 to 1966 and from 1968 to 1974. Kelly was a member of Buckaroos' Patrick Cup championship teams in 1964–1965 and 1970–1971. He was named WHL Outstanding Rookie in 1963–1964 and shared the WHL Outstanding Goalkeeper Award twice with teammate Jim McLeod in 1968–1969 and 1970–1971. The netminder also played in the WHL with Los Angeles (1966–1967) and with San Diego (1967–1968 and 1973–1974).

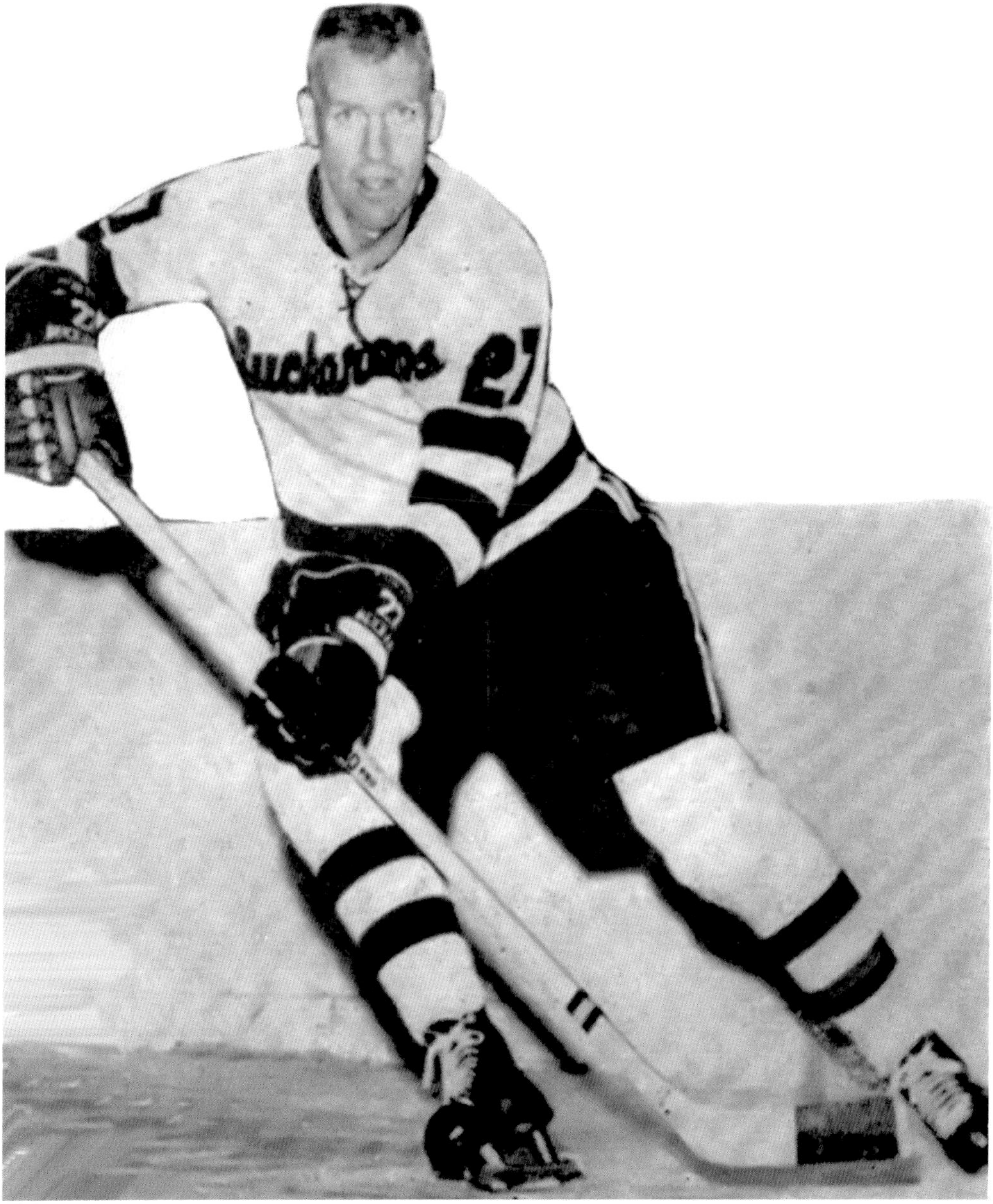

GERRY GOYER (CENTER). Goyer ranks sixth all time in points (392), seventh all time in assists (254), eighth all time in goals (138), and 10th all time in games played (418) in Buckaroos' history. He also accumulated 113 PIM during seven seasons with Portland, from 1962 to 1967 and from 1968 to 1970. He led the Buckaroos in points during the 1962–1963 campaign. The center was a member of three Patrick Cup championship teams—Seattle in 1958–1959, Portland in 1964–1965, and Vancouver in 1969–1970. Goyer is fourth all time in assists (619), fifth all time in points (948), and eighth all time in games played (951) in WHL history.

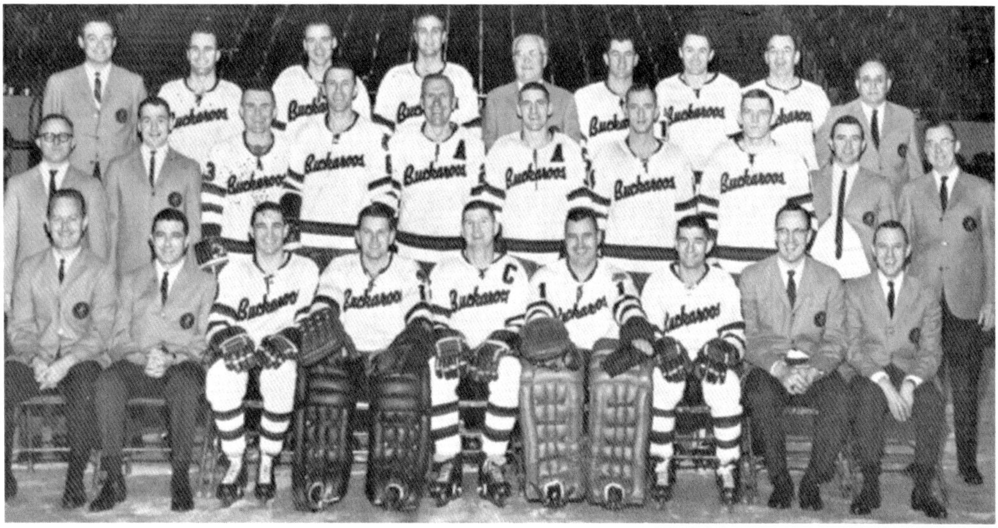

PORTLAND BUCKAROOS, 1965–1966. Pictured from left to right are the following: (first row) Berlyn Hodges (trainer), Harry Glickman (managing director), Cliff Schmautz, Dave Kelly, Art Jones, Don Head, Arnie Schmautz, Hal Laycoe (general manager/coach), and George Rickles (business manager); (second row) Dr. Irving Puziss (team physician), Tom McVie, Jim Hay, Larry Leach, Gerry Goyer, Jack Bionda, Chuck Holmes, Doug Messier, Dick Van Impe, and Dr. Frank Smith (team physician); (third row) Dr. Larry Mudrick (team dentist), Mike Donaldson, Arlo Goodwin, Fred Hilts, C. Howard Lane (board chairman), Len Ronson, Bill Saunders, Connie Madigan, and Moe Tonkon (secretary).

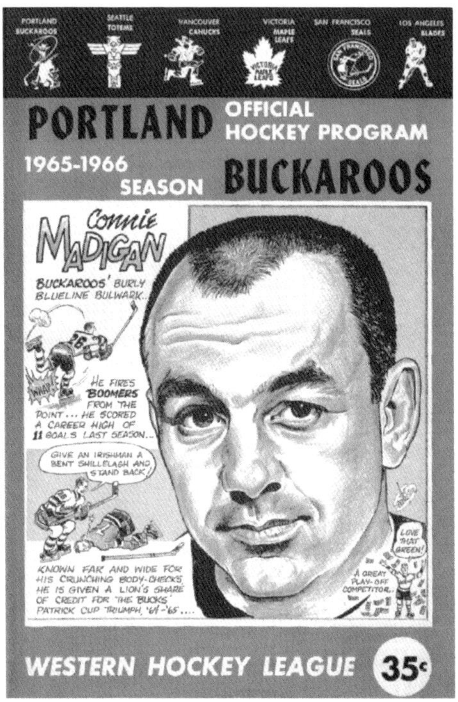

BUCKAROOS PROGRAM FEATURING CONNIE MADIGAN, 1965–1966. Connie Madigan had a cameo appearance in the classic 1977 film *Slap Shot* starring Paul Newman. Madigan played the character Ross "Mad Dog" Madison, a player on the fictitious Syracuse Bulldogs team who was lured out of retirement for the league championship game.

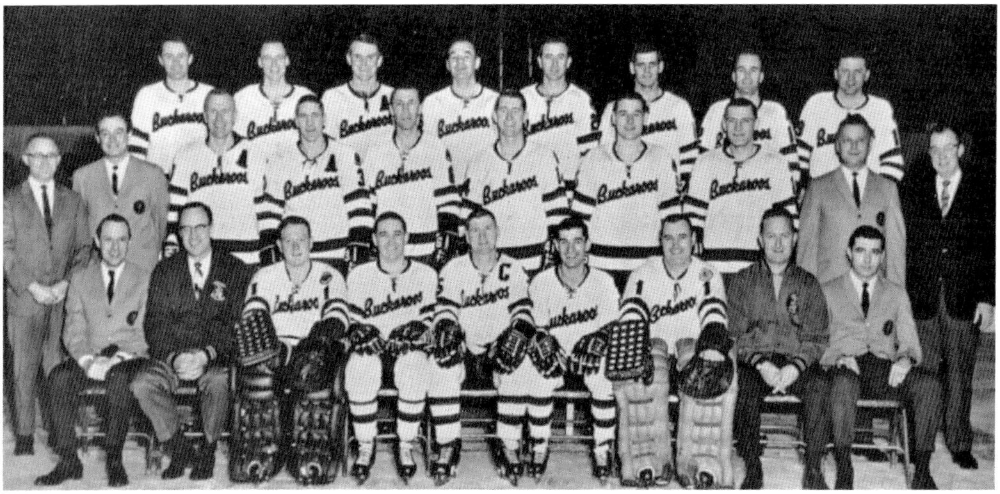

PORTLAND BUCKAROOS, 1966–1967. Pictured from left to right are the following: (first row) George Rickles (business manager), Hal Laycoe (general manager/coach), Rick Charron, Cliff Schmautz, Art Jones, Arnie Schmautz, Don Head, Berlyn Hodges (trainer), and Harry Glickman (president); (second row) Dr. Irving Puziss (team doctor), Dr. Larry Mudrick (team dentist), Gerry Goyer, Jack Bionda, Larry Leach, Len Lunde, Tracy Pratt, Doug Messier, Gordon Fashoway (scout), and Dr. Frank Smith (team doctor); (third row) Bill Saunders, Arlo Goodwin, Jim Hay, Connie Madigan, Dick Van Impe, Alain Caron, Mike Donaldson, and Wally Boyer.

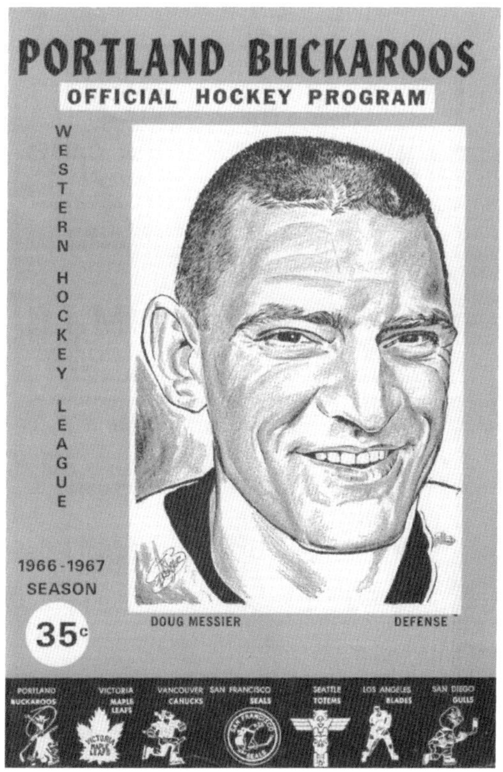

BUCKAROOS PROGRAM FEATURING DOUG MESSIER, 1966–1967. The WHL and QHL playoff champions played each other in a best-of-nine series from 1953–1954 to 1956–1957 for the Duke of Edinburgh Trophy. Winners of the series were as follows: Calgary Stampeders (WHL), 1953–1954; Shawinigan Cataracts (QHL), 1954–1955; Winnipeg Warriors (WHL), 1955–1956; and Quebec Aces (QHL), 1956–1957.

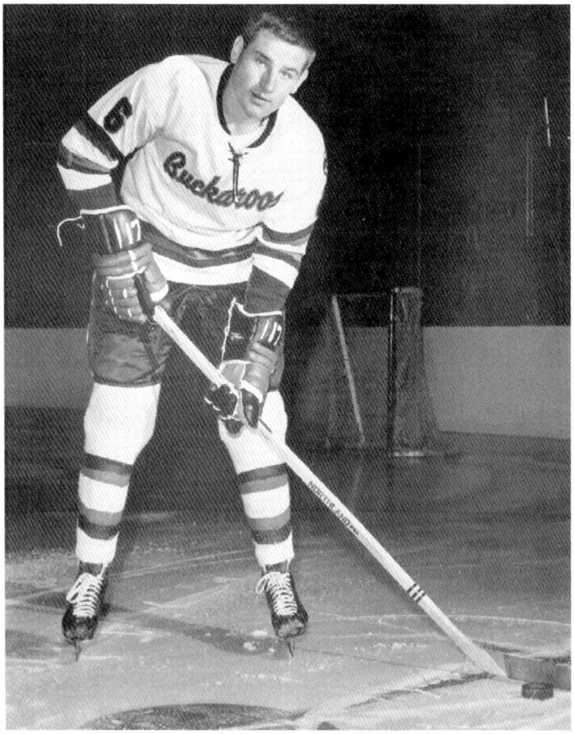

Tracy Pratt (Defense). In the NHL from 1967 to 1977, Pratt accumulated 114 points, 97 assists, and 1,026 PIM in 580 games. During the 1966–1967 season with the Buckaroos, the defenseman garnered 10 points and had 92 PIM in 63 games. He also spent time in the WHL with Vancouver from 1967 to 1969, winning a Patrick Cup with the club in 1968–1969. Hockey Hall of Famer Walter "Babe" Pratt is his father.

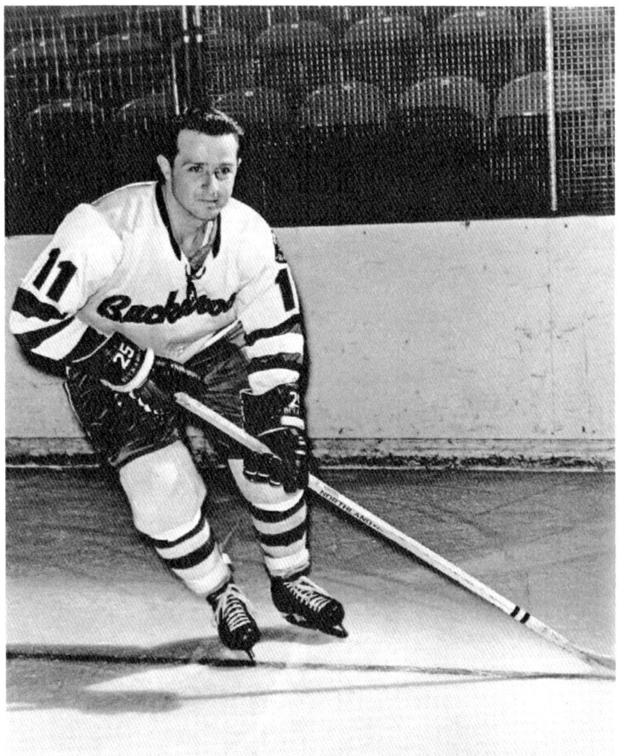

Bob Ertel (Right Wing). In two seasons with Portland, from 1963 to 1965, Ertel tallied 24 points, 14 assists, and 60 PIM in 117 games. Ertel won a Patrick Cup championship with the Buckaroos in 1964–1965. His other minor professional experience included playing four seasons in the EHL from 1960 to 1964.

CHARLIE HOLMES (RIGHT WING). Holmes was a member of four WHL playoff championship teams with Edmonton (1954–1955 and 1961–1962) and Seattle (1966–1967 and 1967–1968). The right-winger played with Portland in 1965–1966 and tallied 30 points, 20 assists, and 20 PIM in 71 games. Holmes played 16 seasons in the WHL between 1954 and 1971.

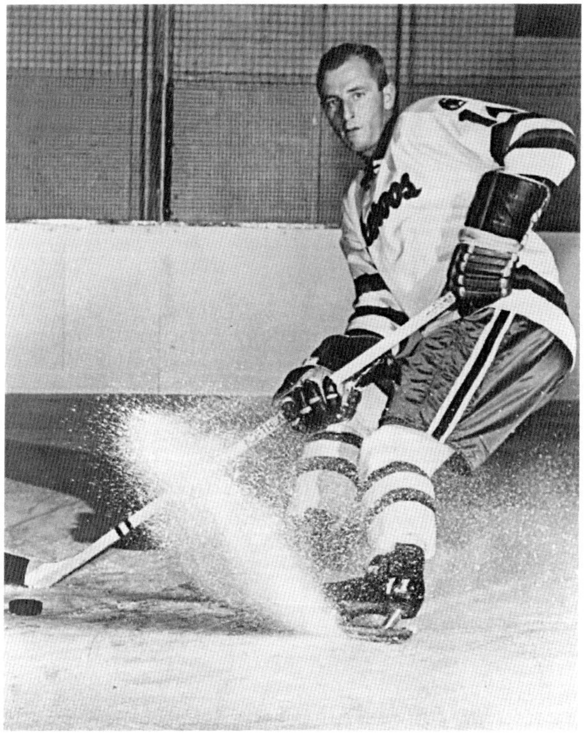

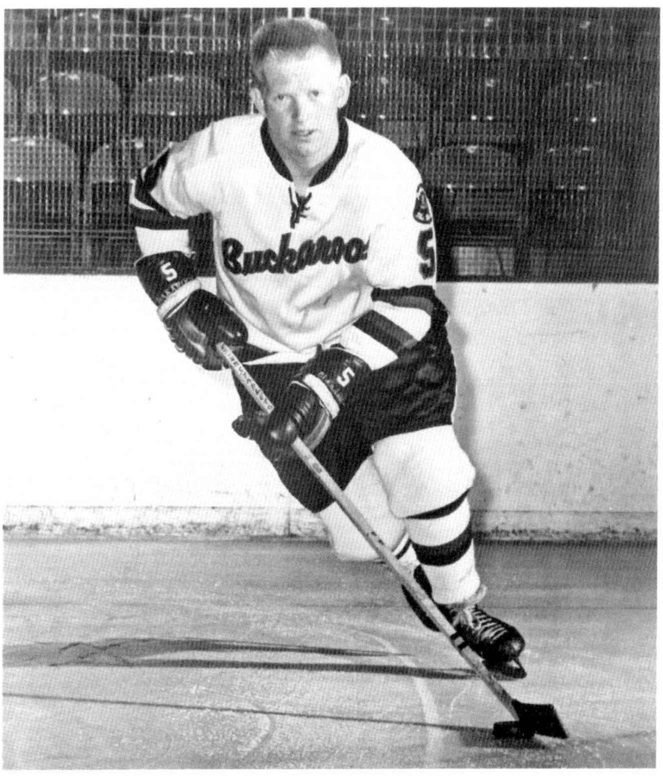

PAT STAPLETON (DEFENSE). In two seasons with the Buckaroos, from 1963 to 1965, Stapleton tallied 135 points, 101 assists, and 141 PIM in 140 games. He was named WHL Outstanding Defenseman in 1964–1965 with Patrick Cup–champion Portland and was named to the WHL All-Star Team twice. A veteran of 10 NHL campaigns between 1961 and 1973, Stapleton produced 337 points, 294 assists, and 353 PIM in 635 games.

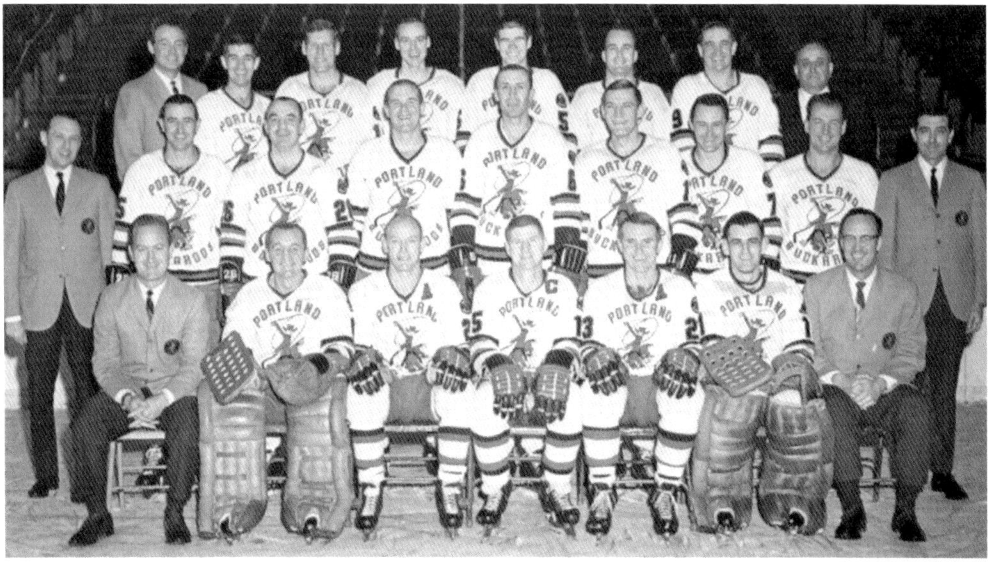

PORTLAND BUCKAROOS, 1967–1968. Pictured from left to right are the following: (first row) Berlyn Hodges (trainer), Marv Edwards, Norm Johnson, Art Jones, Jim Hay, Jim McLeod, and Hal Laycoe (general manager/coach); (second row) George Rickles (business manager), Dick Van Impe, Connie Madigan, Wayne Smith, Larry Leach, Doug Messier, Bill Saunders, Andy Hebenton, and Harry Glickman (president); (third row) Dr. Larry Mudrick (team dentist), Arnie Schmautz, Mel Pearson, Arlo Goodwin, Dennis Kearns, Mike Donaldson, Cliff Schmautz, and Moe Tonkon (secretary).

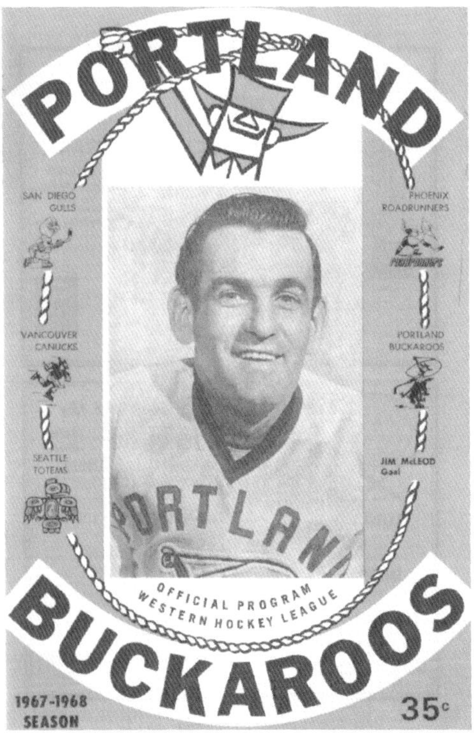

BUCKAROOS PROGRAM FEATURING JIM McLEOD, 1967–1968. The WHL played an interlocking regular-season schedule with the AHL in 1965–1966 and 1967–1968. The WHL won the overall series 81-62-9. The WHL also played an interleague regular-season schedule with the CHL during the 1972–1973 campaign (48 games overall) because the CHL operated with only four teams that season.

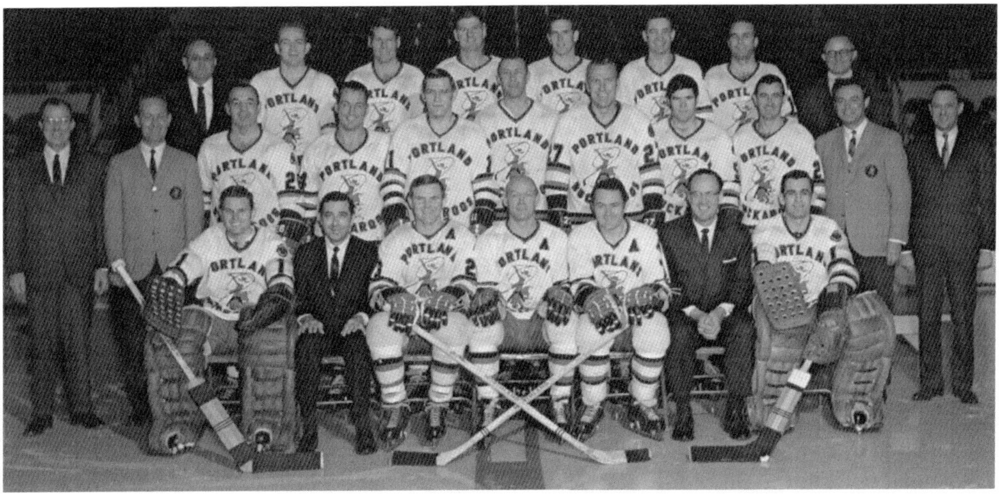

PORTLAND BUCKAROOS, 1968–1969. Pictured from left to right are the following: (first row) Dave Kelly, Harry Glickman (president), Jim Hay, Norm Johnson, Bill Saunders, Hal Laycoe (general manager/coach), and Jim McLeod; (second row) Dr. Frank Smith (team physician), Berlyn Hodges (trainer), Connie Madigan, Andy Hebenton, Doug Messier, Larry Leach, Gerry Goyer, Dennis Kearns, Dick Van Impe, Dr. Larry Mudrick (team dentist), and George Rickles (business manager); (third row) Moe Tonkon (secretary), Ken Campbell, Mel Pearson, Art Jones, Roger Bellerive, Cliff Schmautz, Mike Donaldson, and Dr. Irving Puziss (team physician).

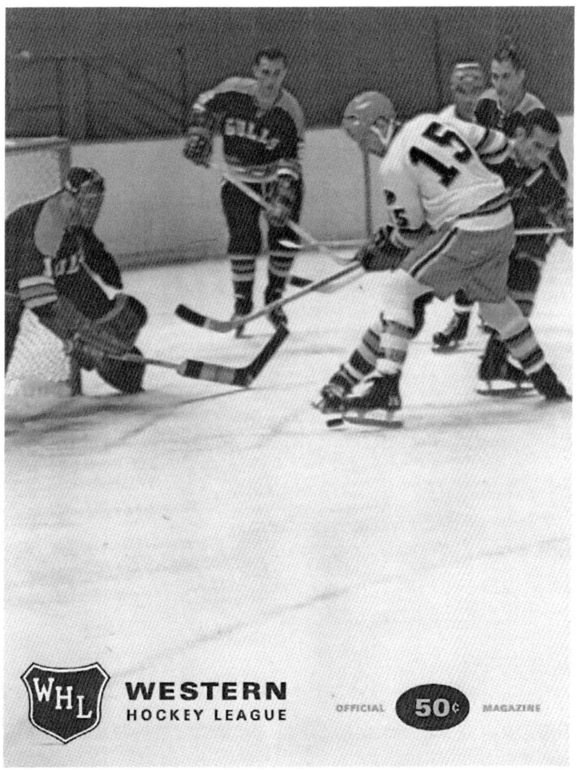

BUCKAROOS PROGRAM FEATURING ART JONES (NO. 15) ATTEMPTING TO SCORE AGAINST SAN DIEGO, 1968–1969. From 1960–1961 to 1973–1974, the Fred J. Hume Cup was awarded to the WHL's most gentlemanly player. Hume was owner of the New Westminster Royals and was regarded as one of the outstanding gentlemen of hockey throughout the West. Hume was elected to the Hockey Hall of Fame in 1962 as a builder.

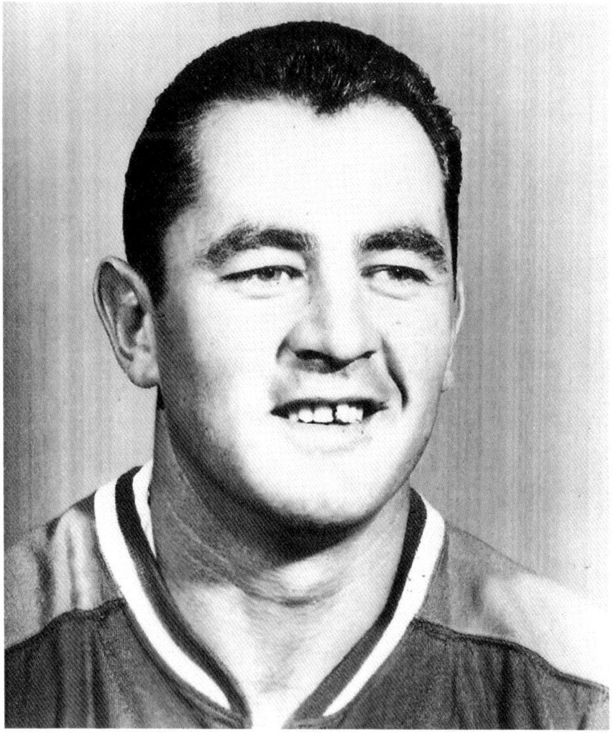

Len Ronson (Left Wing). In 1965–1966, with the Buckaroos, the left-winger tallied 31 points, 18 goals, and 6 PIM in 68 games. The left-winger was selected to the WHL All-Star Team twice. He spent two seasons in the NHL between 1960 and 1969, collecting 3 points and 10 PIM in 18 games. Ronson won an Adams Cup with Omaha (CPHL) in 1963–1964.

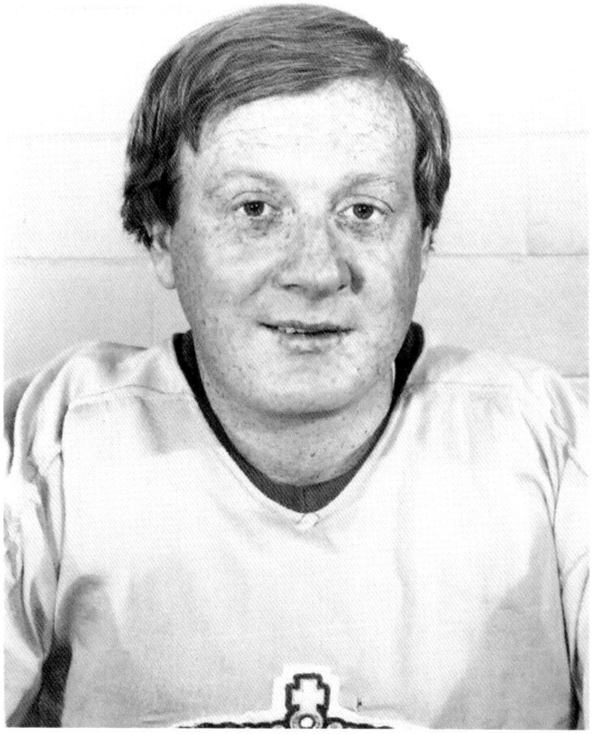

Rick Charron (Goalie). Charron spent three seasons with Portland in 1964–1965, 1966–1967, and 1973–1974. He was also with the Buckaroos during the 1965–1966 postseason. With the Buckaroos, in 1973–1974, Charron earned a 2.63 GAA, a 30-14-3 record, posted 3 shutouts in 48 games, and won the WHL Outstanding Goalkeeper Award. The goalie also played in the WHL with Phoenix from 1967 to 1970 and with Salt Lake City in 1970–1971.

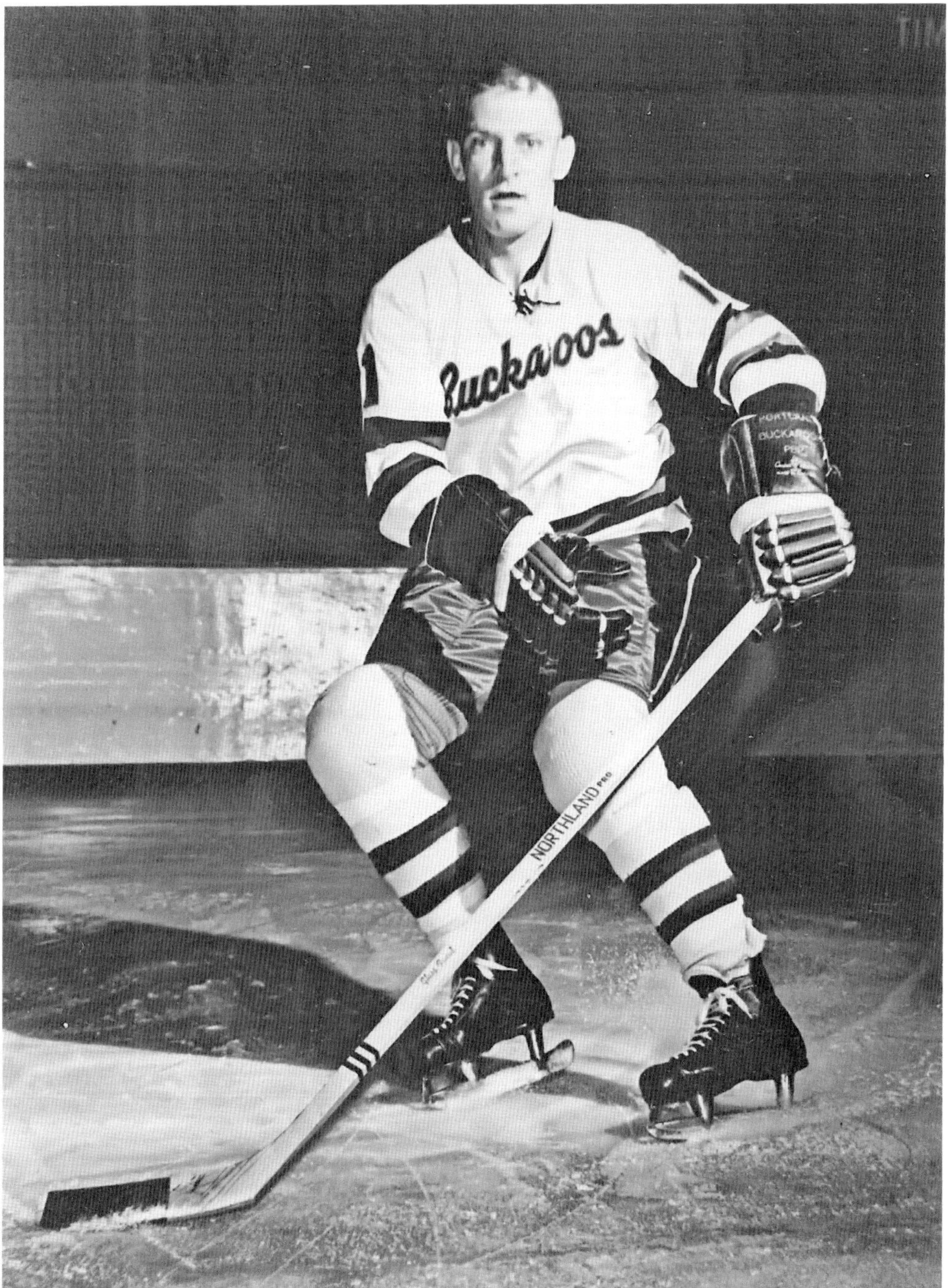

Doug Messier (Defense). Messier was a member of Portland's 1964–1965 Patrick Cup championship team. The defenseman accumulated 186 points, 146 assists, and 658 PIM in 363 games from 1963 to 1969. Messier also played in the WHL with Seattle in 1960–1961 and with Edmonton from 1961 to 1963. He won a Patrick Cup with Edmonton in 1961–1962. He is the father of NHL legend Mark Messier.

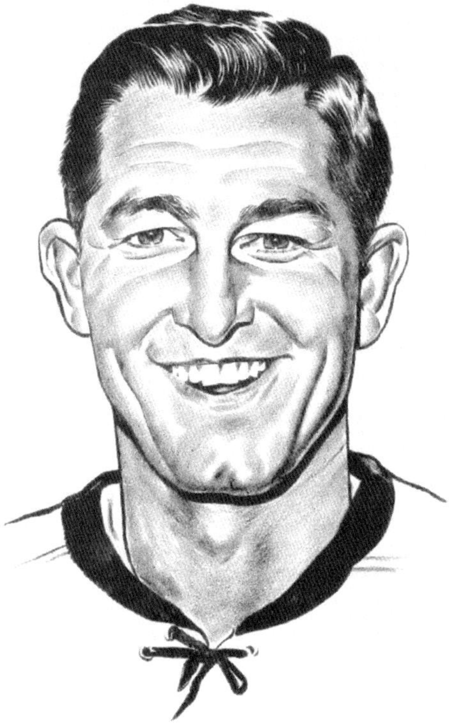

Len Lunde (Left Wing). Lunde was a member of three Patrick Cup–winning teams—Edmonton (1961–1962) and Vancouver (1968–1969 and 1969–1970). With Portland, in 1966–1967, the left-winger garnered 59 points, 26 goals, and 16 PIM in 72 games. He spent eight seasons in the NHL between 1958 and 1971, producing 122 points, 83 assists, and 75 PIM in 321 games.

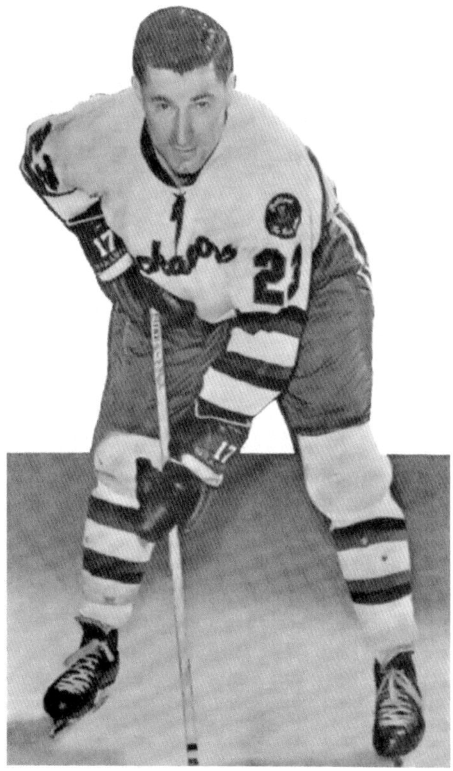

Sid Finney (Center). In 1963–1964, Finney had 19 points, 10 assists, and 2 PIM in 39 games with Portland. He also played in the WHL with Calgary from 1952 to 1962 and with Edmonton in 1962–1963. The center won a President's Cup with Calgary in 1953–1954, was a three-time WHL All-Star, and was selected WHL MVP in 1957–1958. In the NHL, from 1951 to 1954, he garnered 17 points in 59 games.

8

Gordon Fashoway Takes the Coaching Reins

Gordon Fashoway was named coach of the Buckaroos prior to the 1969–1970 campaign. Harry Glickman became the team's new general manager, but Fashoway would fill that role from 1970–1971 to 1972–1973. The Buckaroos clinched their 10th consecutive regular-season winning record in 1969–1970 but were edged out of the first-place spot for the first time in six seasons by Vancouver. Portland finished in second place with a 42-23-7 record. In the semifinals, the locals defeated Seattle four games to two, but in the finals, Vancouver again took the spoils away from the Buckaroos with a four-games-to-one series victory.

In 1970–1971, the Buckaroos had the greatest single season in the history of the WHL and in the process won a WHL all-time record eighth regular-season championship and a third Patrick Cup title. Portland's 48-17-7 (.715) record that season earned the club the highest single-season regular-season winning percentage in league history since the loop turned professional in 1948–1949. In the Patrick Cup playoffs, the Buckaroos defeated the San Diego Gulls in the semifinals four games to two and beat Phoenix in the finals four games to one.

Portland posted its 12th consecutive regular-season winning record (38-31-3)—an all-time WHL record—and reached the league finals for a fifth consecutive year in 1971–1972— an all-time record. The Buckaroos' third-place finish that season marked the first time in franchise history that the club placed lower than second place. In the postseason, Portland downed Phoenix four games to two in the semifinals but lost to the Denver Spurs in the finals four games to one.

In 1972–1973, the Buckaroos had their first losing regular-season record ever (21-39-12), finished in last place, and missed the postseason for the only time. During the season, Berlyn Hodges (16-26-11 record) replaced Fashoway behind the bench, and Larry Regan replaced Fashoway as the team's general manager. The Buckaroos also suffered financially, and the WHL took over ownership of the Portland franchise midseason.

Buckaroos hockey was in doubt for the 1973–1974 season until the Los Angeles Kings (NHL), the Buckaroos' parent team, announced that it would operate the Portland franchise. The WHL still maintained ownership of the team. Ron Stewart was named team coach, and Larry Regan stayed on as general manager. The team got back on track with a 39-33-6 record (fourth place) and a playoff berth. The locals returned to the Patrick Cup finals by defeating Salt Lake City four games to one in the semifinals. Portland lost in the finals to Phoenix four games to one.

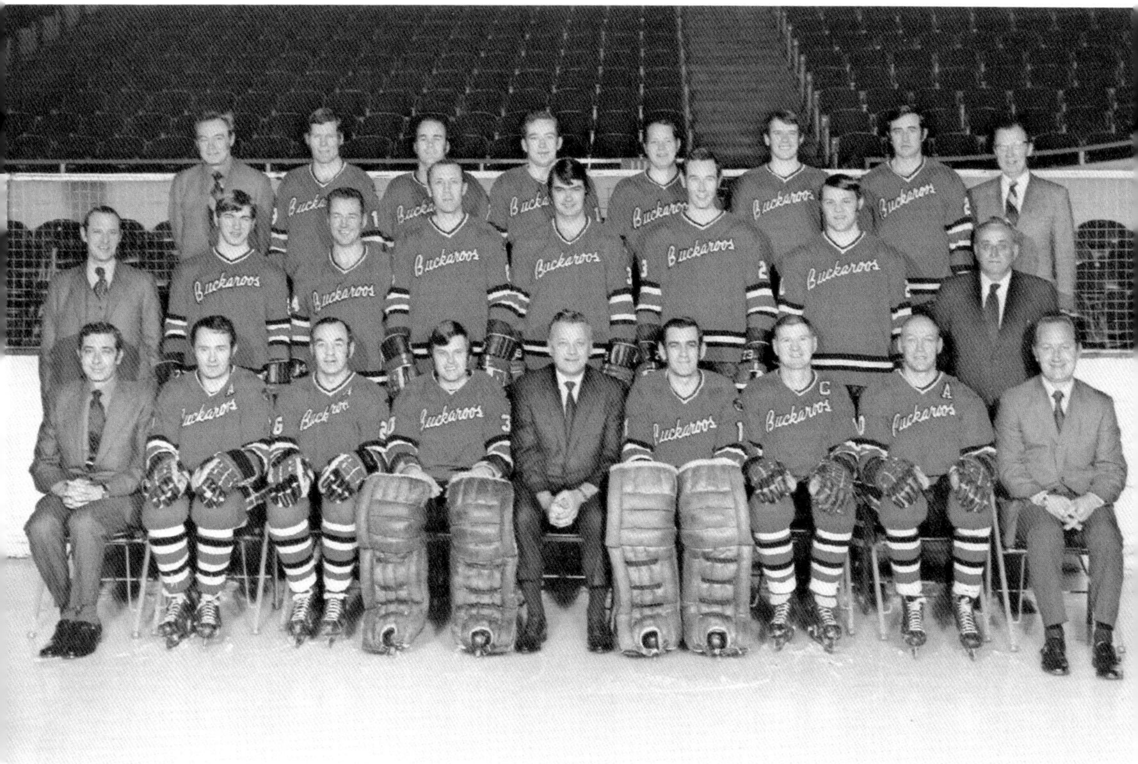

PATRICK CUP CHAMPION BUCKAROOS, 1970–1971. Pictured from left to right are the following: (first row) Harry Glickman (president), Bill Saunders, Connie Madigan, Dave Kelly, Gordon Fashoway (coach), Jim McLeod, Art Jones, Norm Johnson, and Berlyn Hodges (trainer); (second row) George Rickles (business manager), Barry Cummins, Andy Hebenton, Larry Leach, Rick Foley, Ray McKay, John Barber, and Moe Tonkon (secretary); (third row) Dr. Larry Mudrick (team dentist), Mel Pearson, Mike Donaldson, Ken Campbell, Oscar Gaudet, Roger Bellerive, Dick Van Impe, and Dr. Frank Smith (team physician).

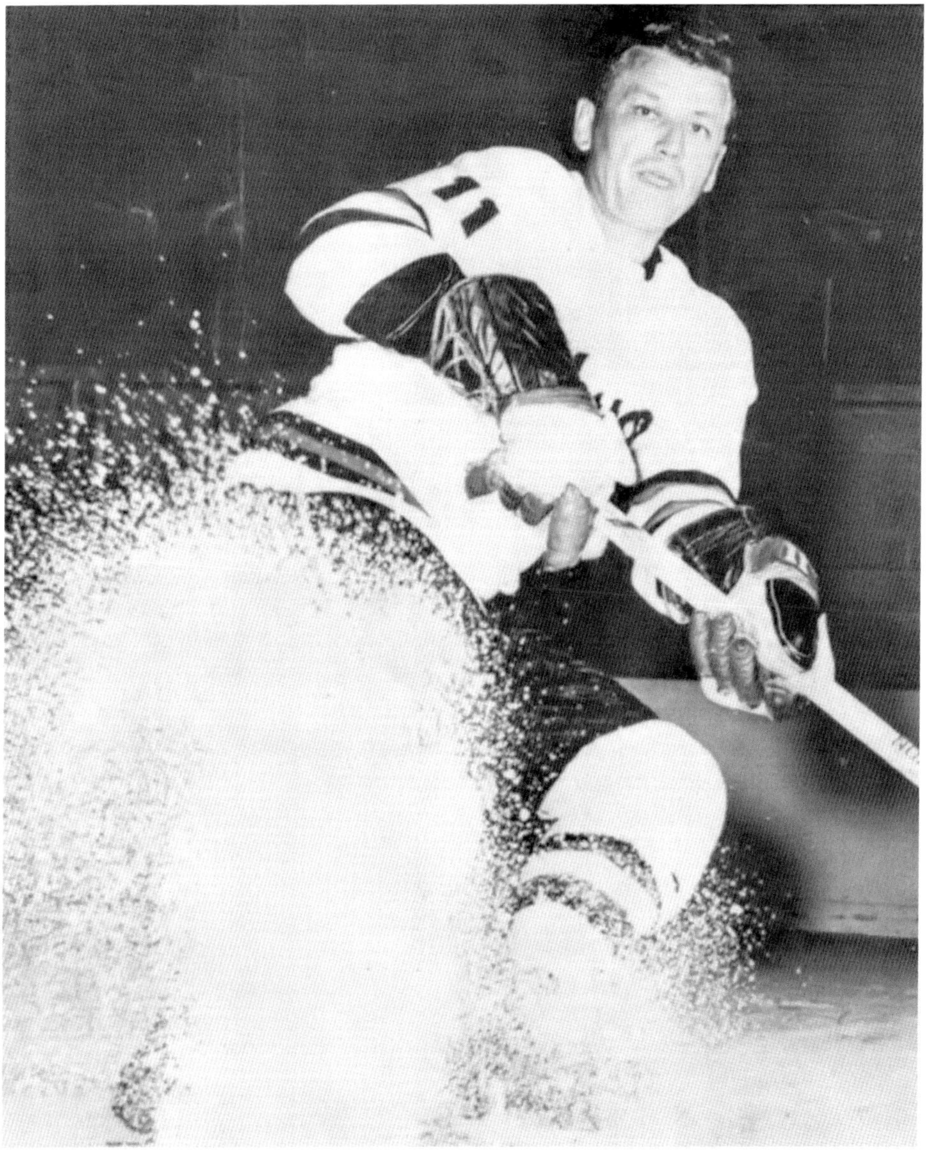

GORDON FASHOWAY (GENERAL MANAGER/COACH/LEFT WING). Fashoway piloted Portland during four seasons from 1969–1970 to 1972–1973 and compiled a 133-84-18 (.604) record. He led the Buckaroos to a Patrick Cup title in 1970–1971. Fashoway was also general manager of Portland from 1970–1971 to 1971–1973. Fashoway played for the Buckaroos from 1960 to 1964, tallying 186 points, 107 goals, and 30 PIM in 188 games. The left-winger was a member of Portland's 1960–1961 Patrick Cup–winning team. He ranks second all time in goals (485) and ninth all time in points (844) in WHL history. Fashoway was a five-time PCHL/WHL All-Star (professional years) and a one-time PCHL All-Star (amateur years). He was named WHL's most gentlemanly player in 1960–1961. He also played in the PCHL/WHL with New Westminster in 1947–1948 and from 1950 to 1959 and with Victoria in 1959–1960. The left-winger had a stint in the NHL in 1950–1951 with Chicago.

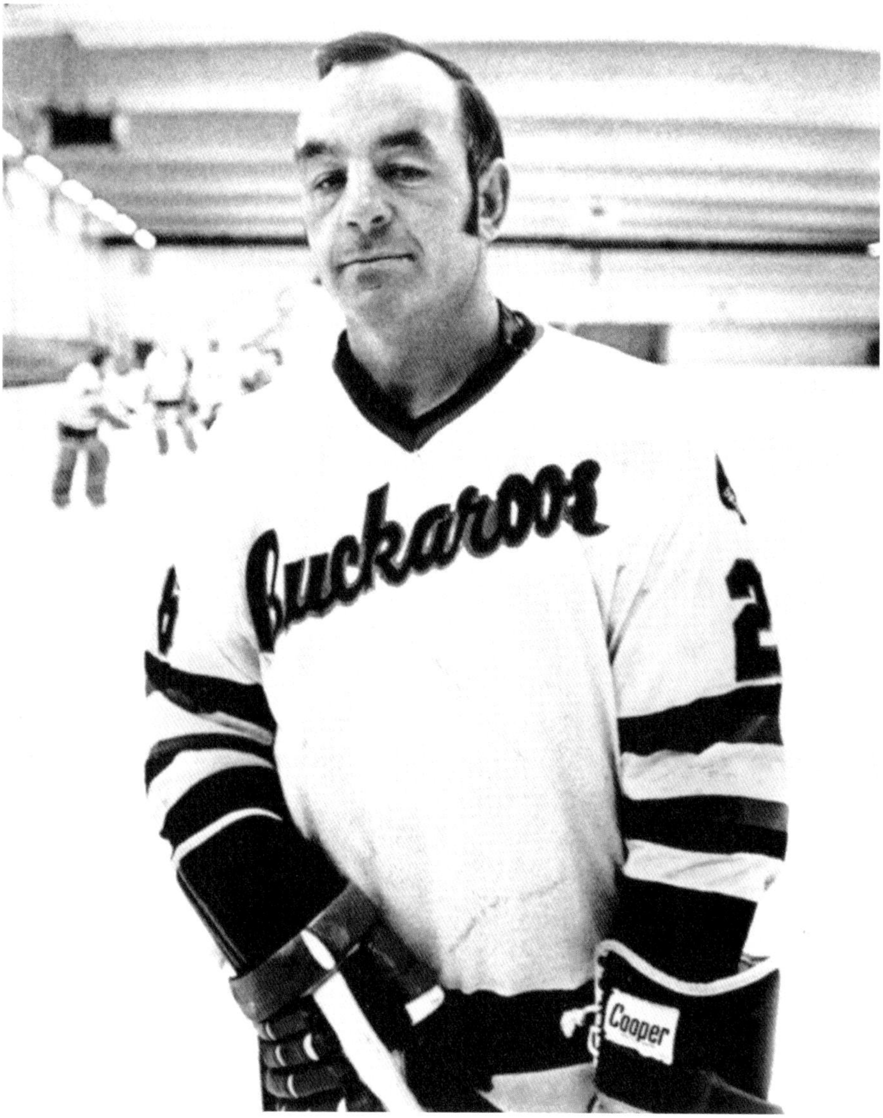

CONNIE "MAD DOG" MADIGAN (DEFENSE). Madigan is the Buckaroos' all-time leader in PIM (1,350). He also ranks fourth in assists (316), fifth in games played (585), and eighth in points (383) in Buckaroos' history. The defenseman tallied 67 goals during 10 seasons with Portland, from 1964 to 1974, and was a member of two Buckaroo Patrick Cup teams—1964–1965 and 1970–1971. Madigan was named to the WHL All-Star Team seven times and was named WHL Outstanding Defenseman in 1965–1966. Madigan is the WHL's all-time penalty minutes king with 1,846 PIM and holds the WHL record for PIM in a game with 37 (set on November 18, 1964). He established the WHL record for assists by a defenseman in a single season with 59 (set in 1970–1971). The blueliner also played in the WHL with Spokane in 1958–1959 and from 1961 to 1963; Denver in 1963–1964; Los Angeles in 1963–1964; and San Diego in 1973–1974. Madigan became the NHL's oldest rookie of all time at age 38 in 1972–1973 with St. Louis; he played 20 games with the club that season.

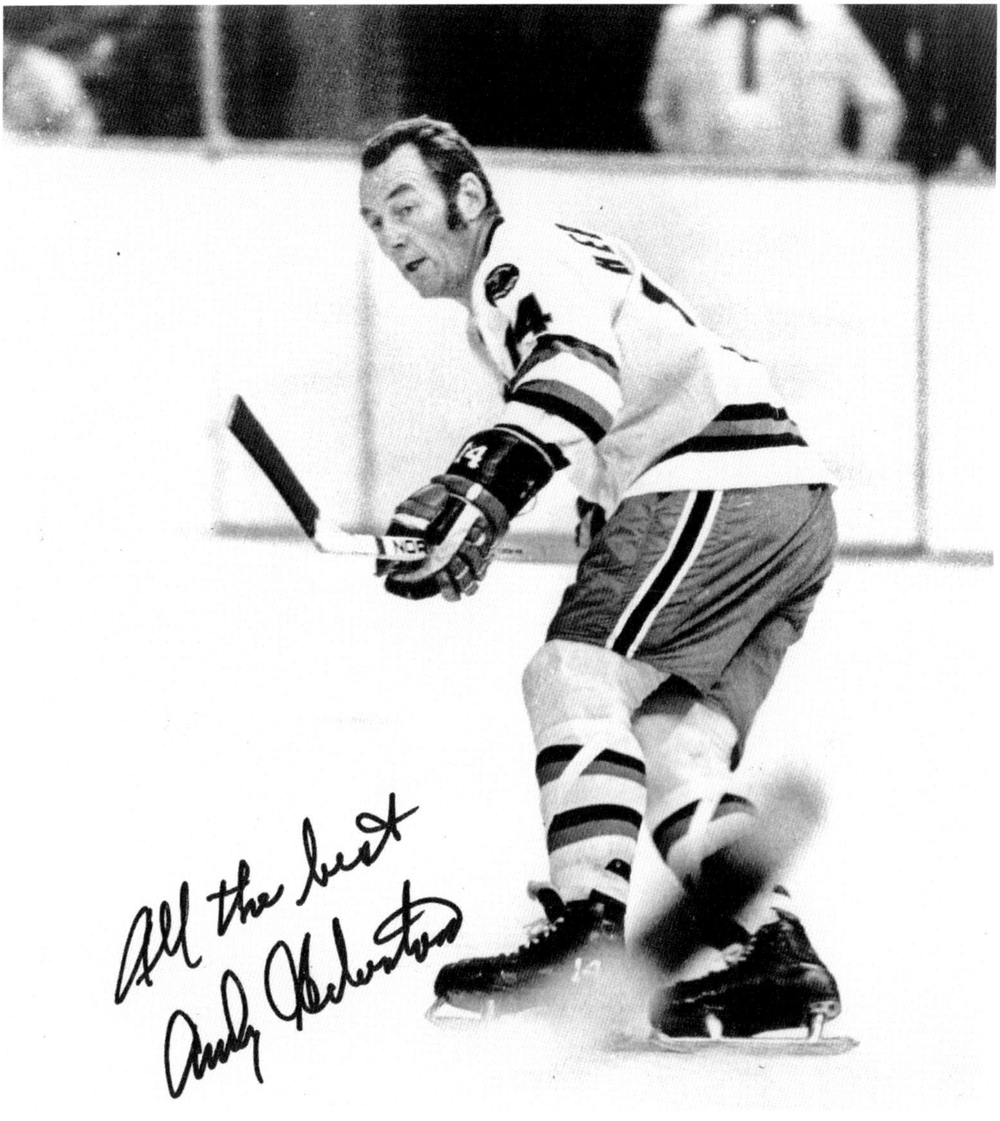

Andy Hebenton (Right Wing). In Buckaroos' history, Hebenton is third all time in points (557) and assists (328), fourth all time in goals (229), and sixth all time in games played (580). He also had 125 PIM during his eight seasons with Portland (1964–1965 and from 1967 to 1974). The right-winger was a member of two Buckaroo Patrick Cup–winning teams in 1964–1965 and 1970–1971. Hebenton was named the WHL's most gentlemanly player six times—more than anyone in league history. In WHL history, Hebenton is tied for third all time in goals (425), fourth all time in points (957), fourth all time in games played (1,056), and eighth all time in assists (532). He was a WHL All-Star five times and won two other league playoff championships with the Victoria Cougars in 1950–1951 and the Victoria Maple Leafs in 1965–1966. A veteran of nine NHL campaigns from 1955 to 1964, Hebenton accumulated 391 points, 202 assists, and 83 PIM in 630 games. He won the NHL's Lady Byng Memorial Trophy (most gentlemanly player) in 1956–1957.

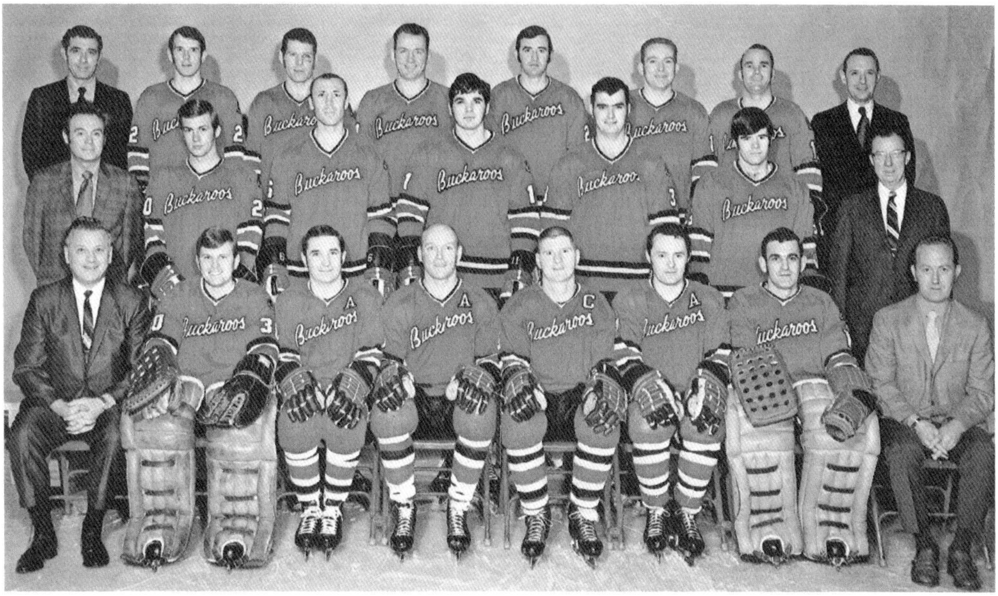

Portland Buckaroos, 1969–1970. Pictured from left to right are the following: (first row) Gordon Fashoway (coach), Dave Kelly, Cliff Schmautz, Norm Johnson, Art Jones, Bill Saunders, Jim McLeod, and Berlyn Hodges (trainer); (second row) Dr. Larry Mudrick (team dentist), Paul Terbenche, Larry Leach, Jerry Korab, Rick Foley, Dennis Kearns, and Dr. Frank Smith (team physician); (third row) Harry Glickman, Roger Bellerive, Mel Pearson, Andy Hebenton, Dick Van Impe, Ken Campbell, Mike Donaldson, and George Rickles (business manager).

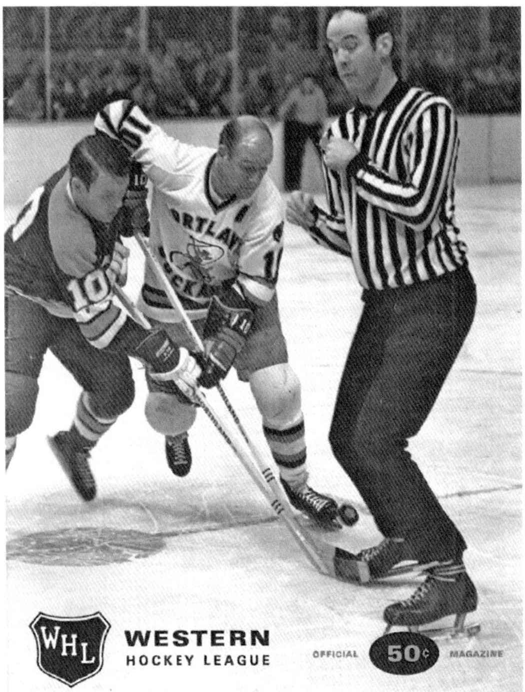

Buckaroos program featuring Norm Johnson Facing-Off against a San Diego Gulls Player, 1969–1970. The Vancouver Canucks were the last WHL Canadian-based team in 1969–1970. The City of Vancouver had a team in the PCHL/WHL for 26 consecutive seasons, dating back to the league's inception in 1944–1945. After the 1969–1970 season, the WHL Canucks were forced to fold with the arrival of NHL expansion.

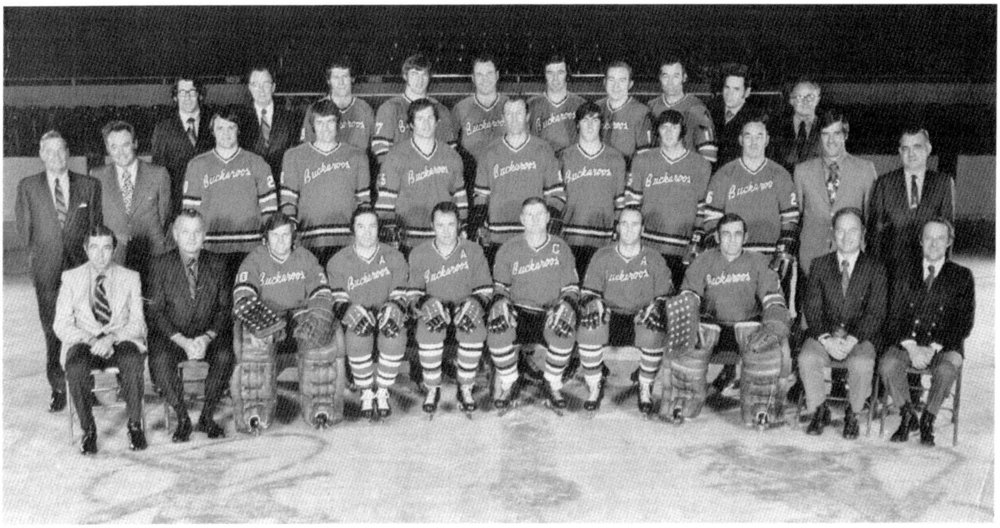

PORTLAND BUCKAROOS, 1971–1972. Pictured from left to right are the following: (first row) Harry Glickman (president), Gordon Fashoway (coach), Dave Kelly, Cliff Schmautz, Bill Saunders, Art Jones, Mike Donaldson, Jim McLeod, Berlyn Hodges (vice president), and George Rickles (business manager); (second row) Bill Anderson (radio announcer), Dr. Larry Mudrick (team dentist), John Barber, Bob Jones, Barry Long, Larry Leach, John Van Horlick, Jake Rathwell, Connie Madigan, Dan Trutanich (promotion director), and John White (publicity director); (third row) Mike Hope (assistant publicity director), Dr. Frank Smith (team physician), Mel Pearson, Barry Cummins, Andy Hebenton, Dick Van Impe, Ken Campbell, Guyle Fielder, Cam Hammett (trainer), and Dr. Irv Puziss (physician).

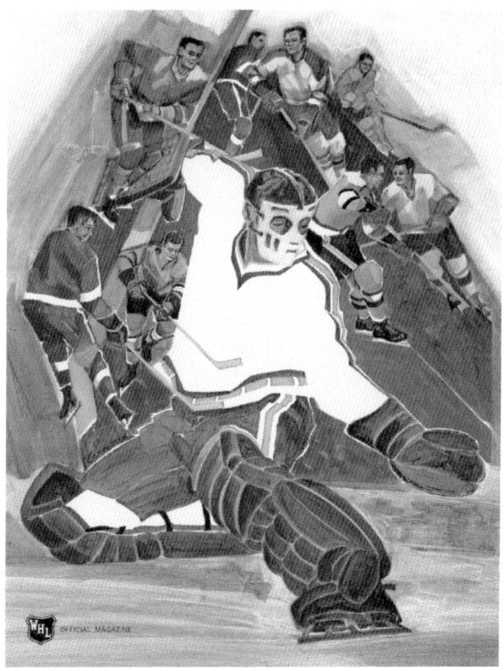

BUCKAROOS PROGRAM, 1970–1971. Portland captured its third Patrick Cup title in 1970–1971. The Vancouver Canucks hold the WHL all-time record for the most playoff championships won—four—since the league turned professional in 1948–1949. The Buckaroos, the Edmonton Flyers, and the Seattle Totems are tied for the second-most WHL playoff championships won with three.

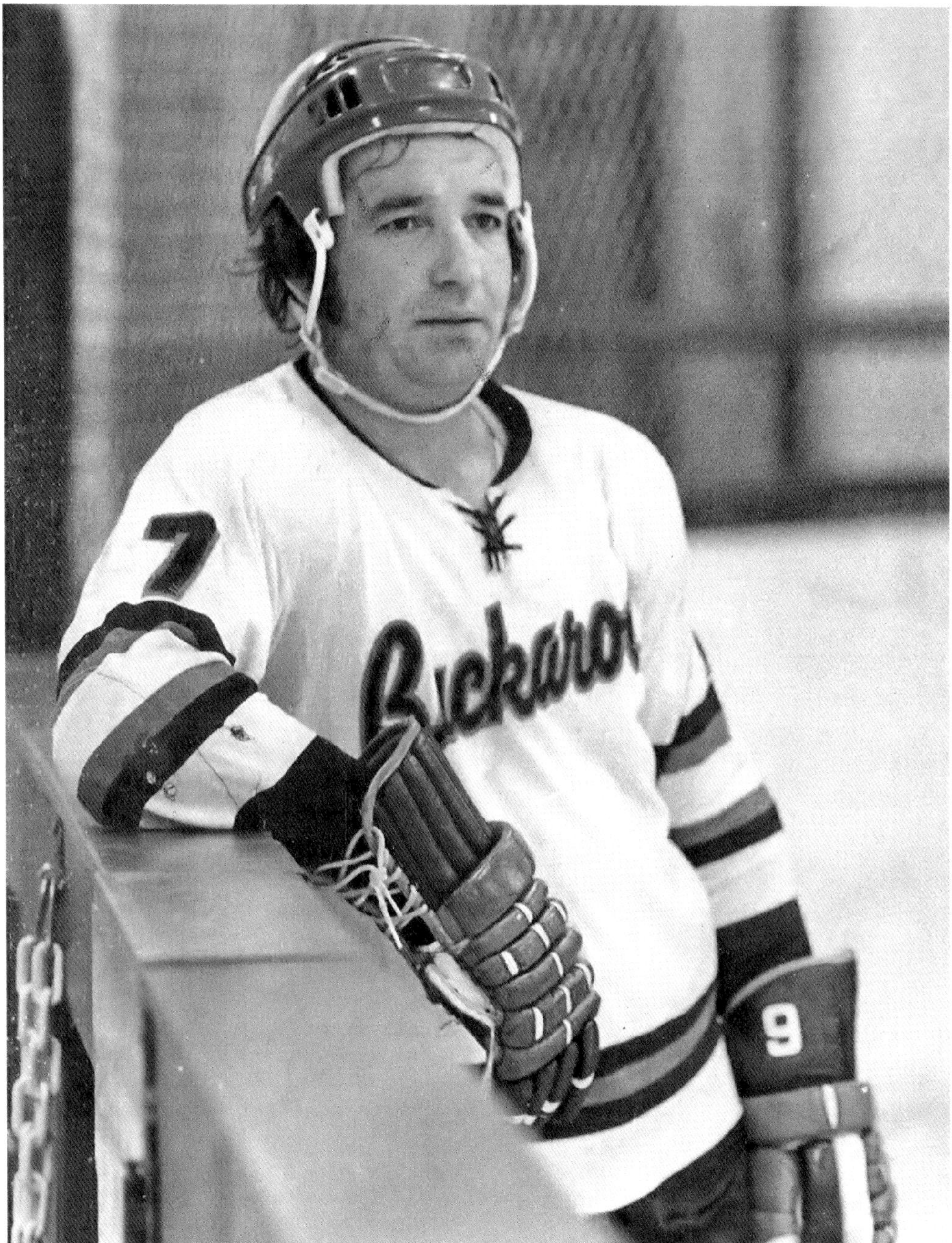

CLIFF SCHMAUTZ (RIGHT WING). Schmautz is third all time in goals (261), fourth all time in points (550), fifth all time in assists (289), and eighth all time in games played (552) in Buckaroos' history. He accumulated 384 PIM during nine seasons with Portland from 1963 to 1970 and 1971 to 1973. Schmautz won a Patrick Cup with Portland in 1964–1965. He led the WHL in points in 1965–1966 and was selected to the WHL All-Star Team twice. Arnie Schmautz is Cliff's brother.

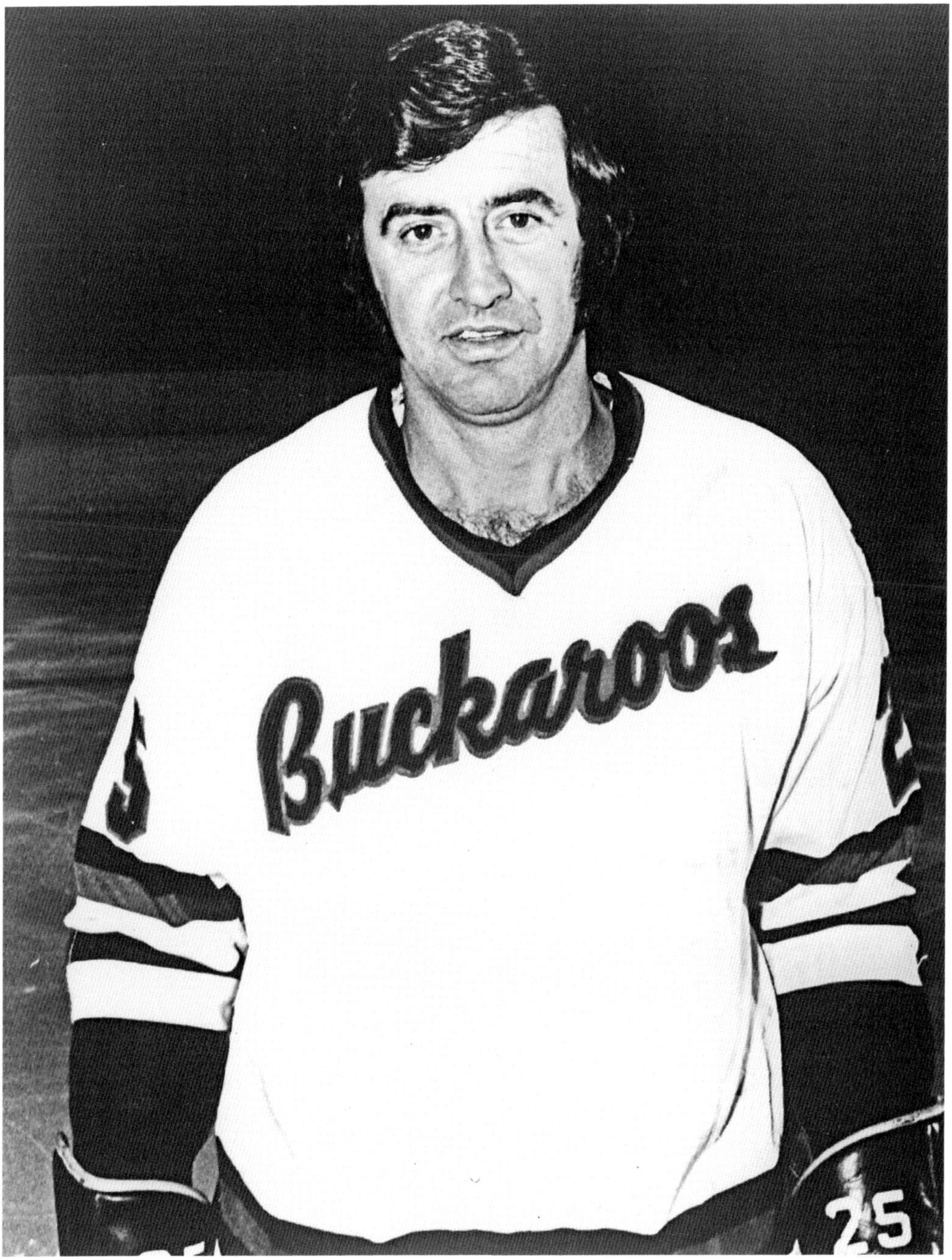

Dick Van Impe (Left Wing). Van Impe ranks fifth all time in points (397), sixth all time in assists (257), seventh all time in goals (140), and ninth all time in games played (543) in Buckaroos' history. He also amassed 310 PIM during 10 seasons with Portland, from 1963 to 1973. Van Impe was a member of two Buckaroo Patrick Cup–winning teams in 1964–1965 and 1970–1971.

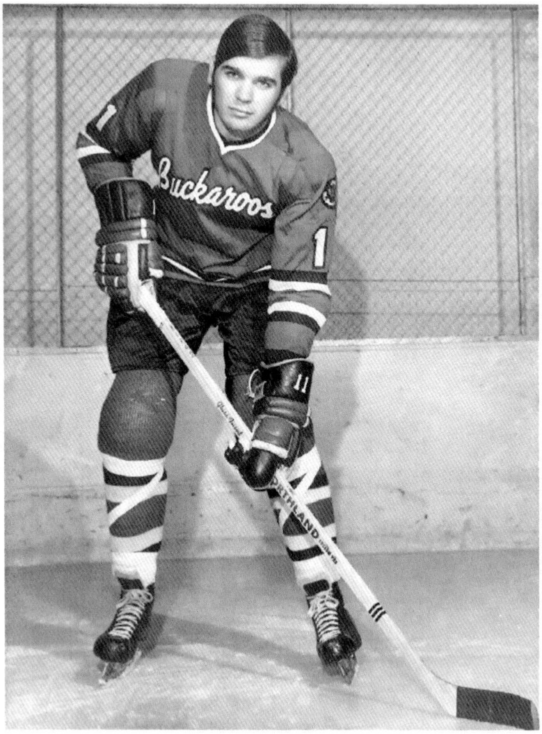

Jerry Korab (Defense). A veteran of 15 NHL seasons, from 1970 to 1985, Korab accumulated 1,629 PIM, 455 points, and 341 assists in 975 games. The defenseman was a member of the Buckaroos' 1970–1971 Patrick Cup team. He garnered 29 points, 17 assists, and 247 PIM in 85 games with Portland from 1969 to 1971. Korab also spent time in the IHL in 1968–1969 and the AHL from 1983 to 1985.

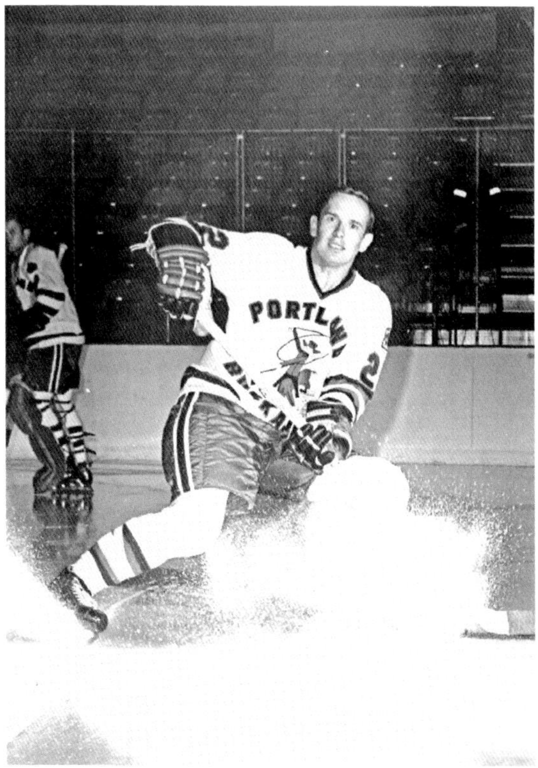

Roger Bellerive (Left Wing). The left-winger was a member of Portland's 1970–1971 Patrick Cup team. Bellerive garnered 103 points, 57 goals, and 43 PIM in 211 games during three seasons with the Buckaroos, from 1968 to 1971. He also played in the WHL with Salt Lake City from 1971 to 1974, and he spent time in the CPHL from 1964 to 1968.

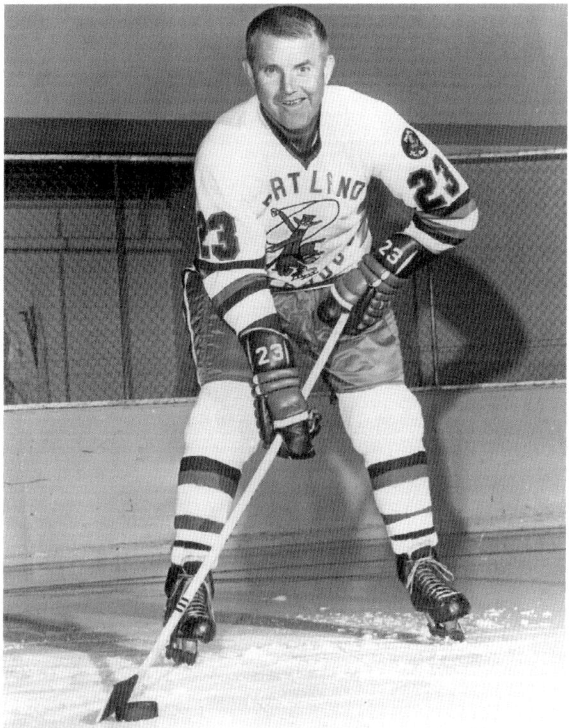

Jim Hay (Defense). From 1964 to 1969, Hay spent five seasons with Portland, accumulating 96 points, 85 assists, and 425 PIM in 333 games. He also played with the Buckaroos during the 1969–1970 postseason. The defenseman was a member of Portland's 1964–1965 Patrick Cup–winning team. In WHL history, Hay ranks second all time in PIM (1,462) and sixth all time in games played (961).

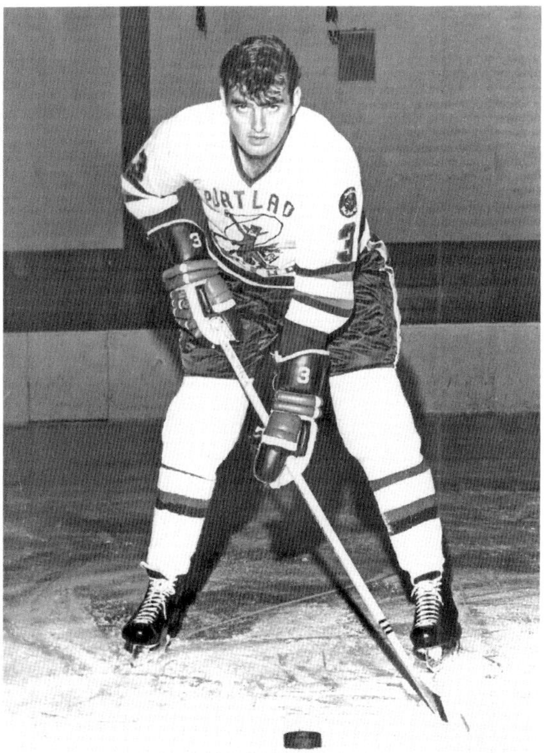

Rick Foley (Defense). Foley amassed 543 PIM, 116 points, and 92 assists in 142 games during three seasons with Portland, from 1968 to 1971. He was a member of the Buckaroos' 1970–1971 Patrick Cup team. The defenseman skated in three NHL seasons between 1970 and 1974, garnering 180 PIM and 37 points in 67 games. Foley holds the all-time WHL single-season PIM mark (306), which he set in 1970–1971.

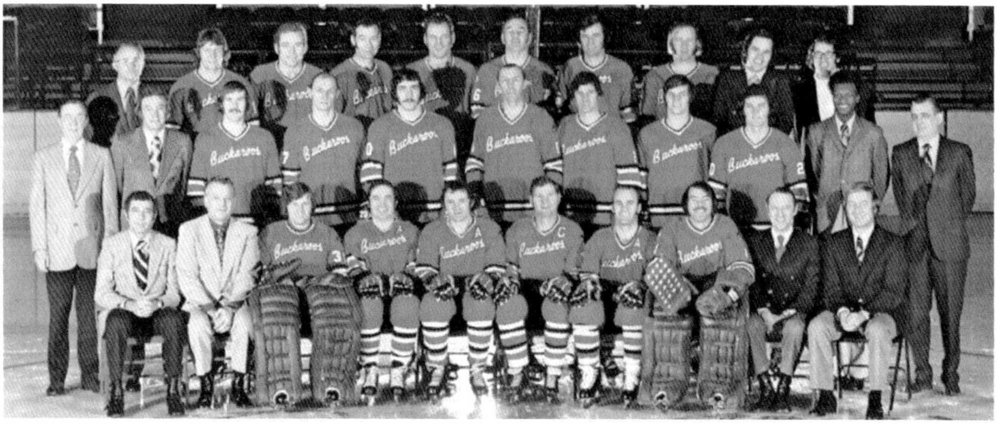

PORTLAND BUCKAROOS, 1972–1973. Pictured from left to right are the following: (first row) Harry Glickman (president), Gordon Fashoway (general manager), Dave Kelly, Cliff Schmautz, Bill Saunders, Art Jones, Mike Donaldson, Phil Headley, George Rickles (business manager), and Berlyn Hodges (vice president/coach); (second row) Dr. Frank Smith (team physician), Dr. Larry Mudrick (team dentist), Mike Keeler, Bill Orban, Glen Toner, Larry Leach, Gary Kilpatrick, Derek Black, Jim Stanfield, Wallace Scales (director of promotions), and John White (publicity director); (third row) Dr. Irv Puziss (team physician), Tom Foxcroft, Ken Campbell, Guyle Fielder, Andy Hebenton, Connie Madigan, Dick Van Impe, Gordon Nelson, Cam Hammett (trainer), and Mike Hope (assistant publicity director).

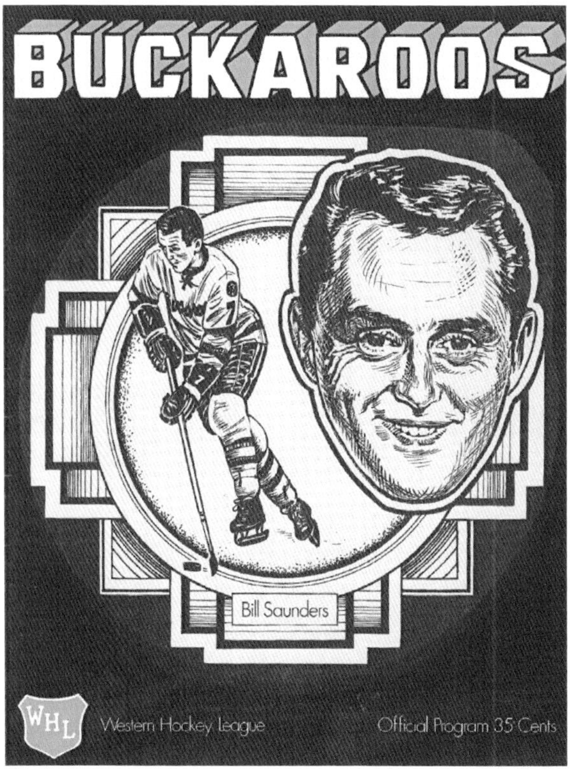

BUCKAROOS PROGRAM FEATURING BILL SAUNDERS, 1971–1972. The Coleman E. Hall Cup was awarded to the WHL's regular-season champion. (When the league had two divisions, the honors were shared by both teams.) The trophy was originally called the Governors' Cup, from 1948–1949 to 1968–1969, but was renamed after Coleman E. Hall for the 1969–1970 campaign. Hall owned several franchises in the WHL and was influential in the league's success.

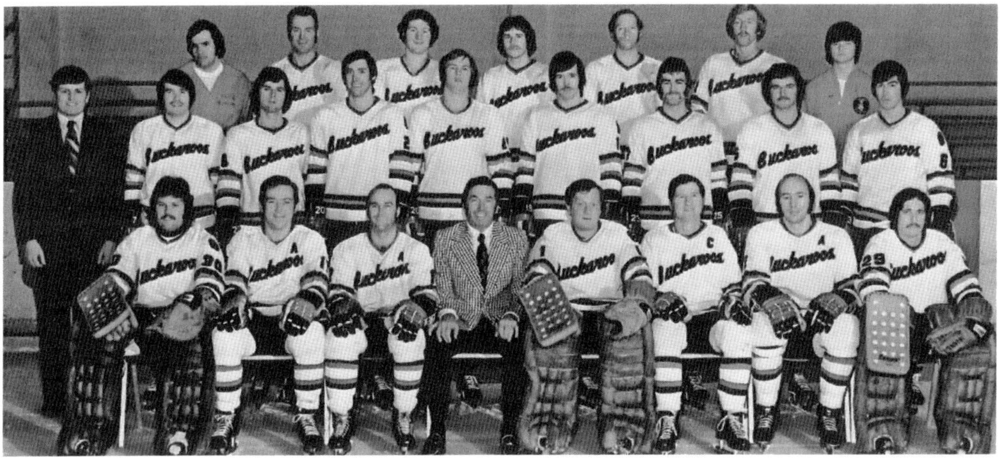

PORTLAND BUCKAROOS, 1973–1974. Pictured from left to right are the following: (first row) Dave Kelly, Ken Campbell, Mike Donaldson, Ron Stewart (coach), Rick Charron, Art Jones, Larry McNabb, and Bob Vroman; (second row) John Wolf (manager), Karl Haggarty, Pokey Trachsel, Jimmy Peters, Doug Buhr, Dale Lewis, Dennis Abgrall, Jim McElmury, and John Van Horlick; (third row) Cam Hammett (trainer), Andy Hebenton, Dennis Giannini, Bob Poffenroth, Howie Hughes, Ron Wilson, and Jack Kennedy (assistant trainer).

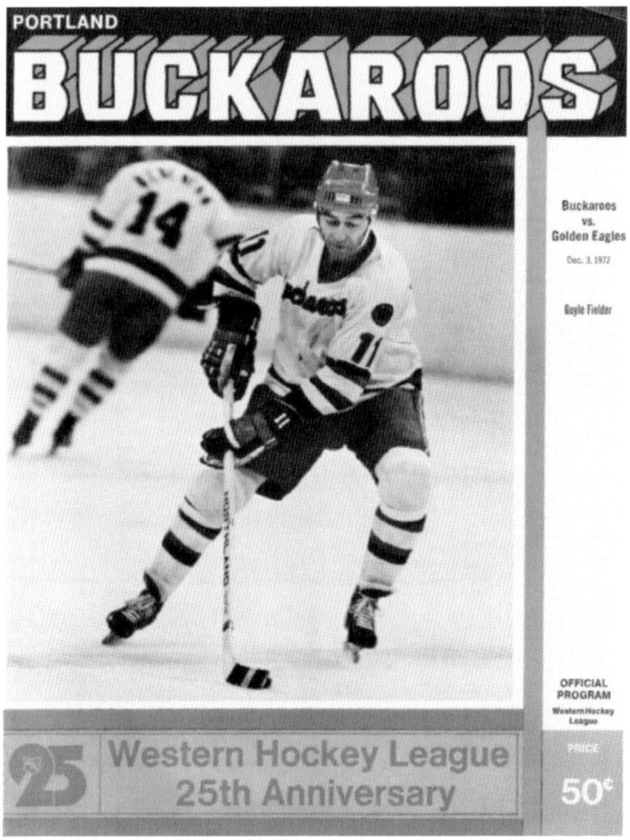

BUCKAROOS PROGRAM FEATURING GUYLE FIELDER, 1972–1973. Fielder is minor league hockey's all-time leader in points (1,929), assists (1,491), and games played (1,487). Fielder became the all-time regular-season point king in professional hockey history during the 1971–1972 season, when he surpassed Gordie Howe's record of 1,857 points. Howe regained the record from Fielder during the 1973–1974 campaign. Fielder also held the all-time professional hockey regular-season assist record for over three decades.

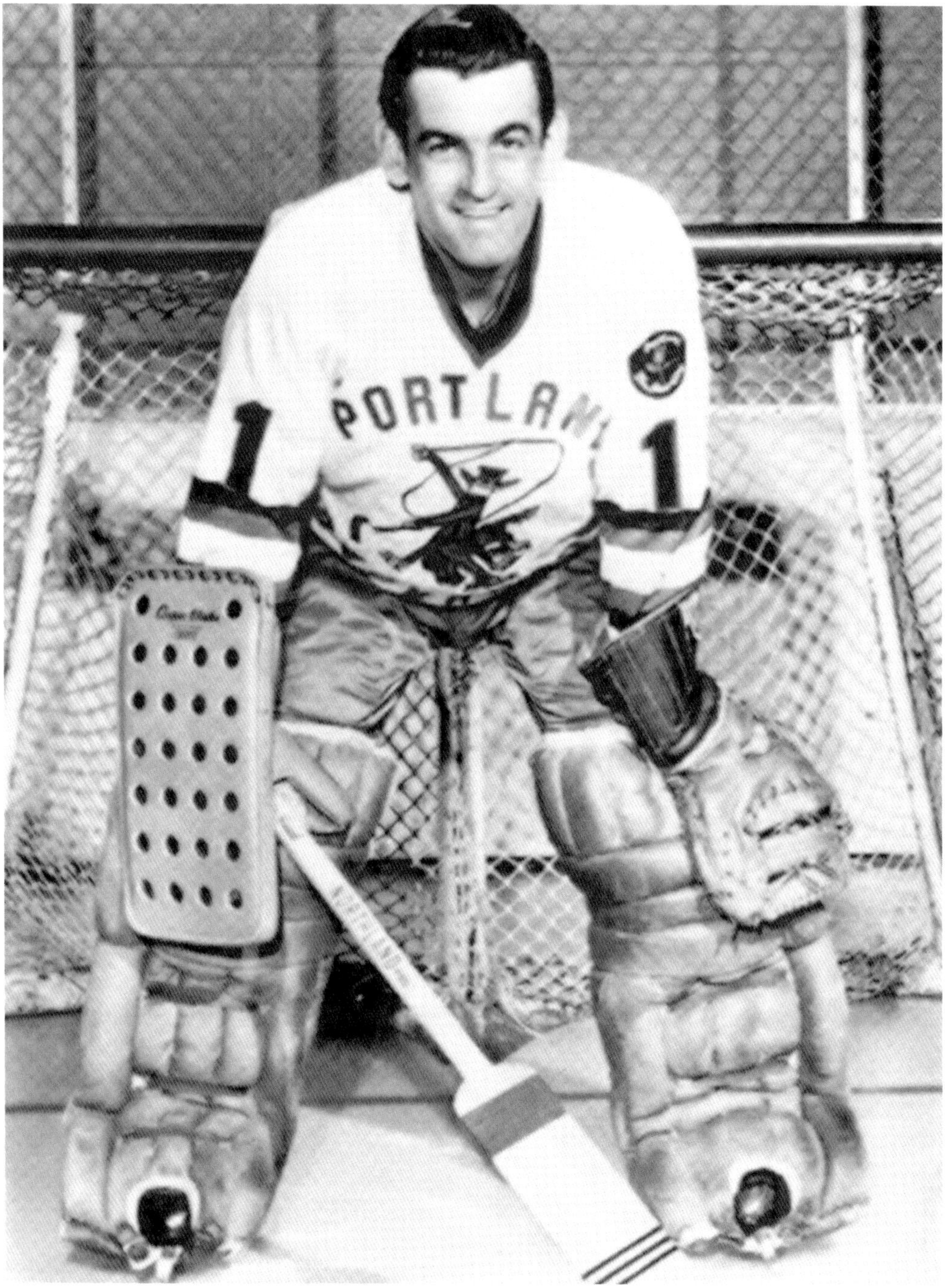

JIM MCLEOD (GOALIE). McLeod is the Buckaroos' all-time leader in career GAA (2.65). He also compiled a 103-41-15 record and earned 12 shutouts in 168 games with Portland from 1967 to 1972. The goalie was a member of three Patrick Cup–winning teams—San Francisco in 1962–1963, Seattle in 1966–1967, and Portland in 1970–1971. He won the WHL Outstanding Goalkeeper Award four times (twice shared) and was selected to the WHL All-Star Team four times.

PATRICK CUP FINALS PROGRAM, 1970–1971. Portland defeated Phoenix four games to one in the 1970–1971 WHL finals to win its third Patrick Cup. Art Jones and Larry Leach are the only two players to be members of all three Buckaroos' Patrick Cup championship teams (1960–1961, 1964–1965, and 1970–1971).

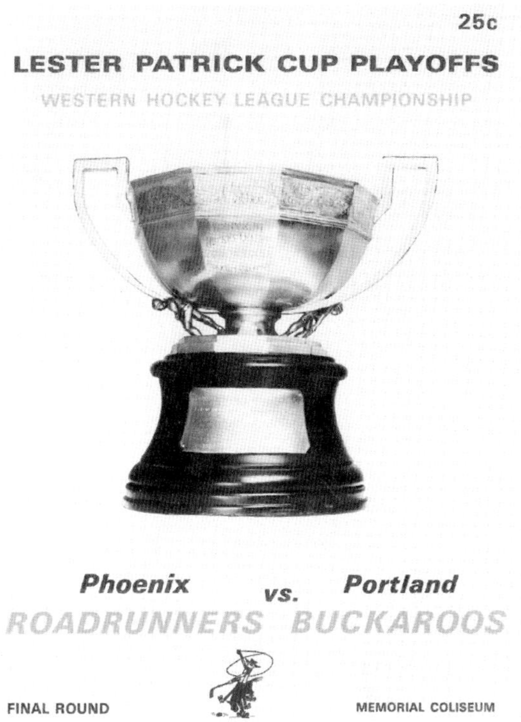

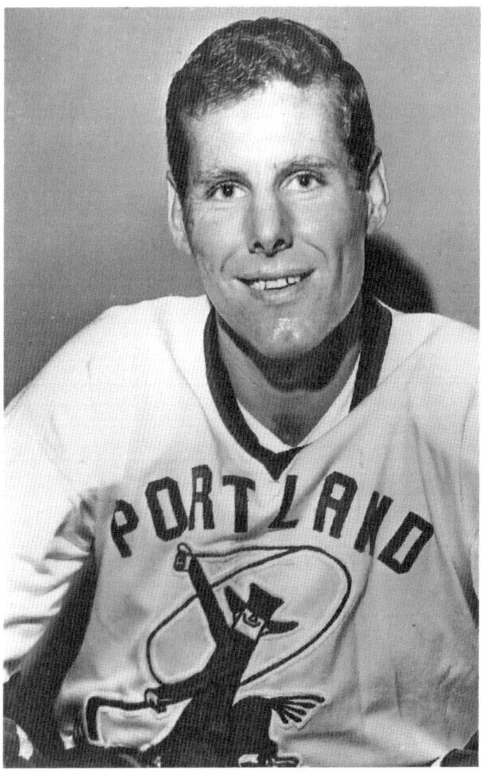

MEL PEARSON (CENTER). In five campaigns with the Buckaroos, from 1967 to 1972, Pearson tallied 233 points, 108 goals, and 181 PIM in 358 games. He was a member of Portland's 1970–1971 Patrick Cup–winning team. In five seasons, the center garnered 8 points, 6 assists, and 25 PIM in 38 NHL games between 1959 and 1968. He also won an Adams Cup with St. Paul (CPHL) in 1964–1965.

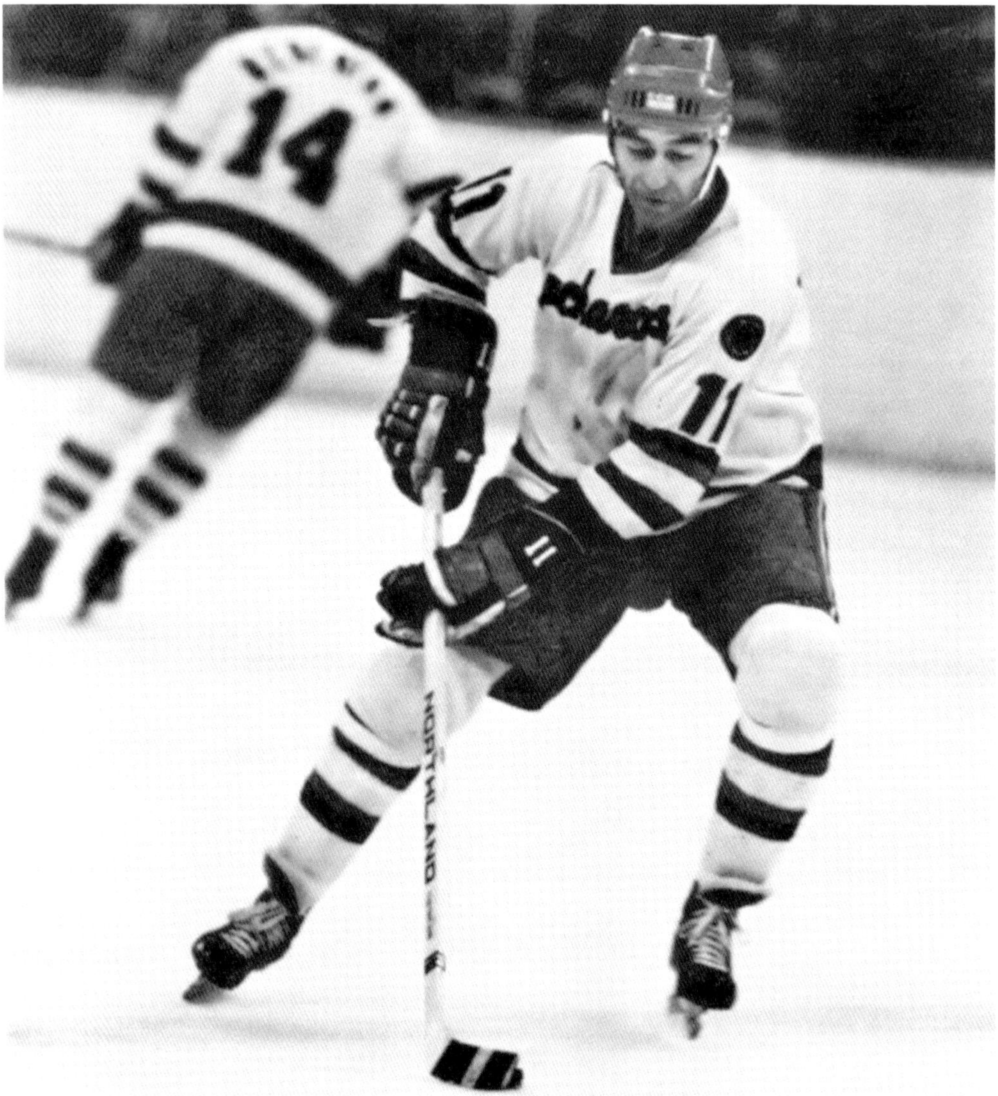

GUYLE FIELDER (CENTER). Fielder is the WHL's all-time leader in points (1,846), assists (1,430), games played (1,425), and seasons played (22). In WHL history, he also ranks fifth all time in goals (416). The center was the WHL's leading point scorer (nine times), WHL's MVP (six times), and was named to the WHL All-Star Team (12 times), more times than any other player in league history. Fielder also won the WHL's most gentlemanly player award three times, was named WHL Outstanding Rookie in 1951–1952, and was chosen as the AHL Outstanding Rookie in 1952–1953. He played with the Buckaroos from 1971 to 1973 and produced 107 points, 87 assists, and 14 PIM in 110 games. The center also played in the PCHL/WHL with New Westminster in 1951–1952 and 1954–1955; Edmonton in 1952–1953; Seattle in 1953–1954 and from 1955 to 1969; and Salt Lake City from 1969 to 1972. He won three Patrick Cups with Seattle in 1958–1959, 1966–1967, and 1967–1968. Fielder is the only player to appear in all six WHL All-Star Games.

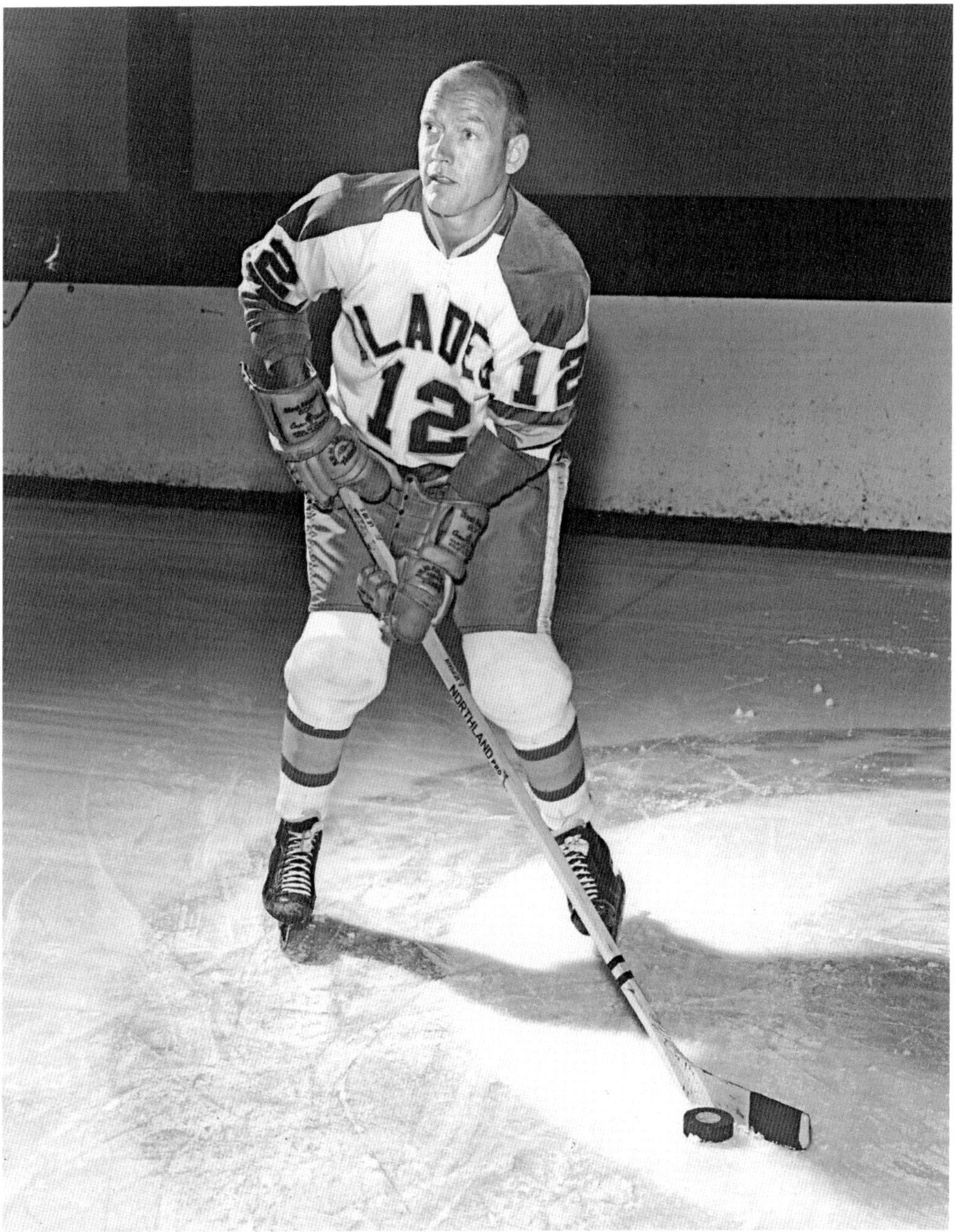

NORM JOHNSON (CENTER). Johnson is ninth all time in points (341), goals (137), and assists (204) in Buckaroos' history. The center also had 184 PIM in 286 games during four campaigns with Portland from 1967 to 1971. He was a member of the Buckaroos' 1970–1971 Patrick Cup–winning team and was a WHL All-Star four times. Johnson ranks third all time in points (1,082) and assists (691) and sixth all time in goals (391) in WHL history. He also won a WHL playoff championship with Brandon in 1956–1957. A veteran of three NHL seasons, from 1957 to 1960, Johnson garnered 25 points, 20 assists, and 41 PIM in 61 games.

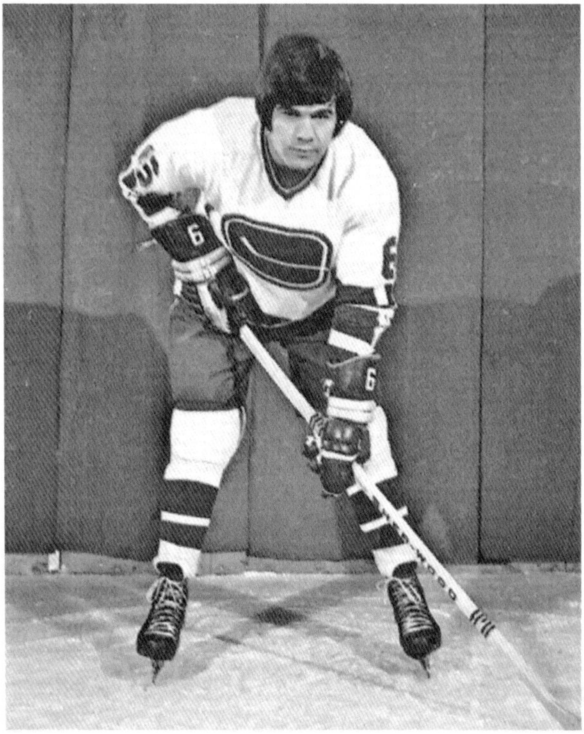

DENNIS KEARNS (DEFENSE). In three seasons with Portland, from 1967 to 1970, Kearns tallied 117 points, 99 assists, and 210 PIM in 214 games. He is a two-time WHL All-Star. The defenseman spent 10 campaigns in the NHL, from 1971 to 1981, accumulating 321 points, 290 assists, and 386 PIM in 677 games. He also played in the CHL in 1970–1971.

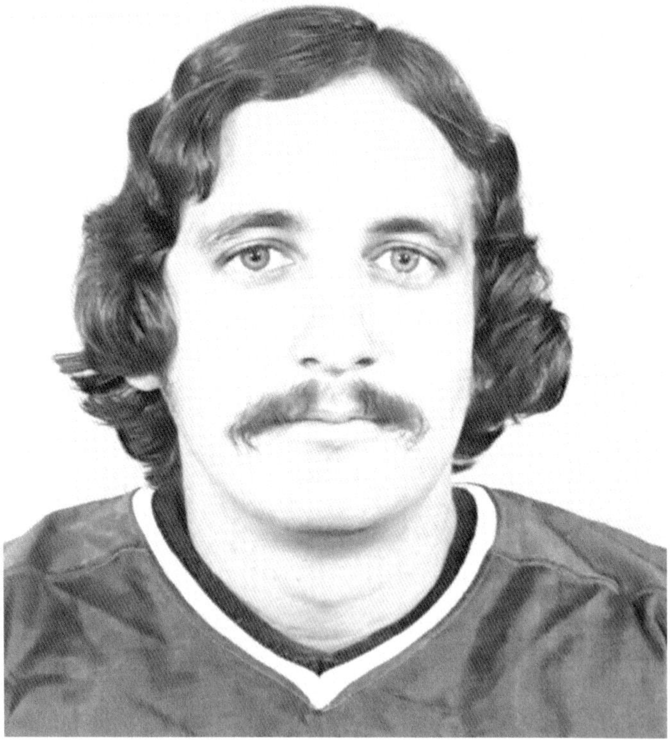

BOB VROMAN (GOALIE). Vroman was in net for 11 games with Portland during the 1973–1974 campaign, compiling a 4.35 GAA and a 2-5-1 record. The goaltender also spent time in the EHL from 1970 to 1972, the AHL from 1971 to 1973, and the CHL in 1973–1974.

PORTLAND VERSUS THE HOCKEY RUSSIAN NATIONALS PROGRAM. The Buckaroos hosted the Russian Nationals on January 6, 1973, in front of 10,493 fans at the Portland Memorial Coliseum. The Russians won the match 11-4, behind the goaltending of Vladislav Tretiak. Portland led 4-3 after one period with goals from Art Jones, Mike Keeler, Ken Campbell, and Andy Hebenton. Phil Headley and Dave Kelly split the goaltending duties for Portland.

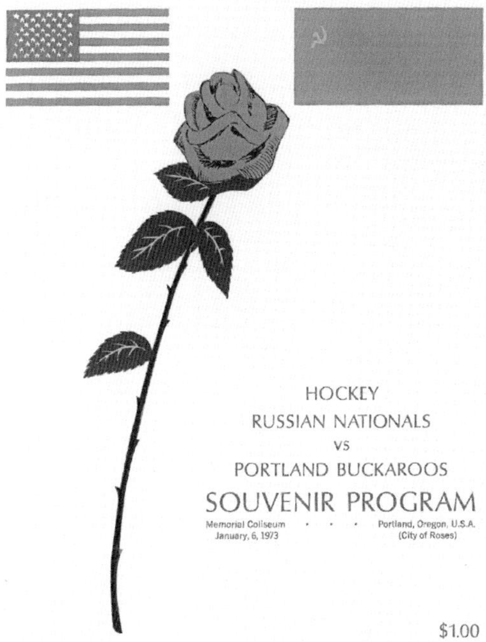

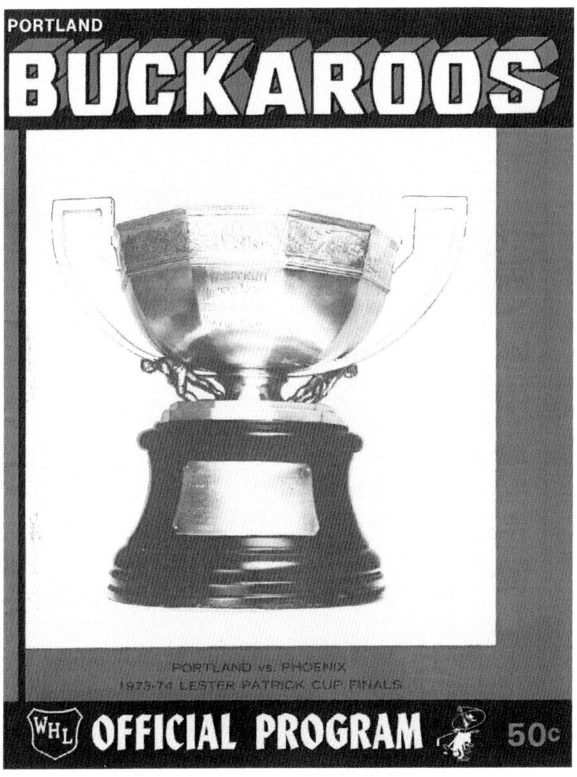

PATRICK CUP FINALS PROGRAM, 1973–1974. Although Phoenix defeated Portland in the last Patrick Cup finals series in 1974, the Buckaroos have the distinction of hosting the last WHL game ever played (game five of the finals on April 28, 1974) and Buckaroos' player Howie Hughes has the honor of scoring the final goal in WHL history at 19:12 of the third period in game five of the finals.

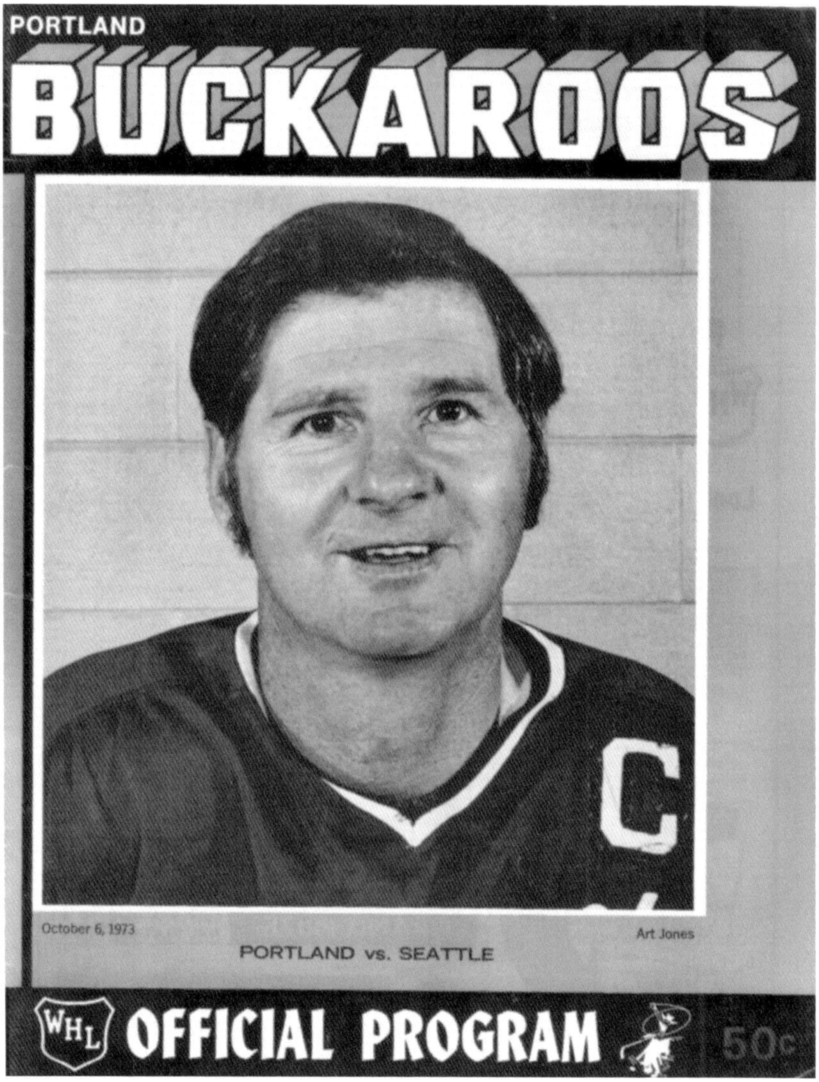

BUCKAROOS PROGRAM FEATURING ART JONES, 1973–1974. The final season of the WHL was 1973–1974. The WHL brass voted to suspend operations for one year over the summer of 1974 because of World Hockey Association (WHA) franchises landing in Phoenix and San Diego for the 1974–1975 season coupled with a decision by the Los Angeles Kings not to operate the Portland Buckaroos. The Kings (NHL) cited the uncertain future of the WHL as the primary reason for not continuing to operate the Buckaroos team. The WHL, which owned the Portland franchise, opted not to operate the team as well. The San Diego Gulls (WHL) were unable to negotiate a lease at the San Diego Arena as a result of the WHA coming to town. The NHL granting conditional franchises to Denver and Seattle for the 1976–1977 season also influenced the WHL to take the sabbatical. The Central Hockey League, threatened with possible extinction of its own with only four teams ready to operate for the 1974–1975 season, was given new life with the addition of three WHL teams shifting to the league for the 1974–1975 campaign (Denver Spurs, Salt Lake City Golden Eagles, and Seattle Totems).

9

A Memorabilia Tribute to the Buckaroos

A WHL Dynasty

This chapter is a memorabilia tribute to the Portland Buckaroos, who are one of the greatest and most colorful teams in minor league hockey history. The Buckaroos players were not just great at the game of hockey; they also had a unique loyalty to their fans and gave back to the Portland community. One of the greatest illustrations of the Buckaroo players' benevolence and dedication towards area fans occurred after the 1973–1974 WHL campaign when both the WHL and the Portland Buckaroos hockey club suspended operations.

Former WHL Buckaroos players organized and initially financed a senior team in the established Western International Hockey League (WIHL) for the 1974–1975 season. The new Portland Buckaroos home games were played at Portland's Jantzen Beach Ice Arena. The team was led by player/coach Andy Hebenton and was composed of several all-time WHL Buckaroos fan favorites, including Art Jones (team captain), Roger Bellerive, Bill Davidson, Mike Donaldson, Don Head, Dave Kelly, Connie Madigan, Dick Meissner, Bill Saunders, and Arnie and Cliff Schmautz. Teams in the WIHL that season were the Cranbrook Royals, Kimberley Dynamiters, Nelson Maple Leafs, Spokane Flyers, and Trail Smoke Eaters. The champion of the WIHL competed for the Allan Cup—symbolic of the senior champions of Canada. The Buckaroos only played a partial schedule in the WIHL, and the results of the club's games were only counted towards their opponent's record in official WIHL standing. Portland went 10-13-2 in 25 games that season (other WIHL teams played 53 games).

The Buckaroos returned for one more season in 1975–1976. The club competed in the amateur North West Hockey League (NWHL), and Hebenton stayed on as the team's player/coach. There was a smaller nucleus of former WHL Buckaroos that second season but Jones, Bellerive, Davidson, Donaldson, Kelly, and Madigan stayed on to thrill the fans for one more campaign. The highlight of the season was a game against the U.S. Olympic team on October 5, 1975, at the Portland Memorial Coliseum. The Buckaroos lost the game 10-4, but it was a memorable night.

The Portland Buckaroos players are true champions—both on and off the ice!

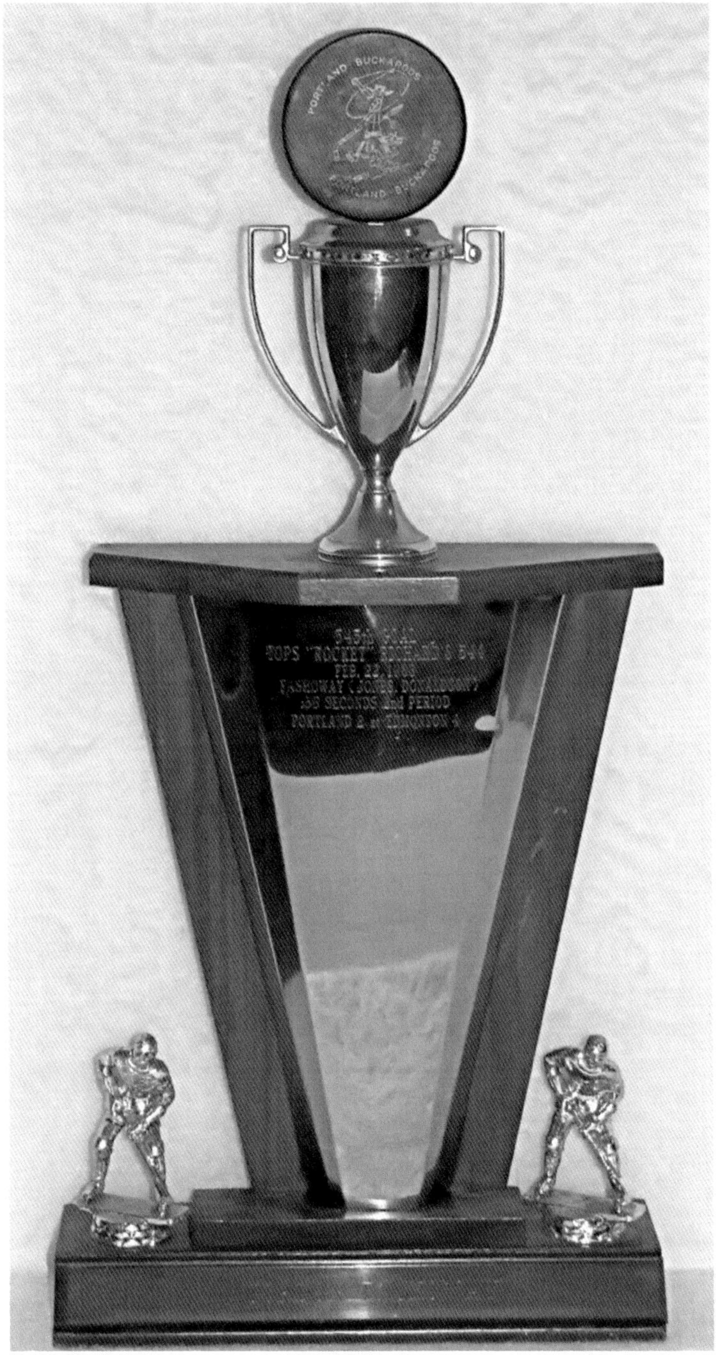

GORDON FASHOWAY'S 545TH GOAL TROPHY. This trophy was presented to Gordon Fashoway on February 22, 1963, for surpassing Maurice Richard's professional record of 544 regular-season goals to become the all-time leading regular-season goal scorer in professional hockey. Fashoway scored his record 545th goal at 36 seconds of the second period, assisted by Art Jones and Mike Donaldson, in a game at Edmonton.

NORM JOHNSON'S 1,000TH WHL POINT TROPHY WITH GAME-USED PUCK. Norm Johnson became the third and final player in WHL history to reach the 1,000th point mark. He achieved the milestone during the 1970–1971 season while playing with the Buckaroos. Guyle Fielder and Art Jones are the other two players to reach the 1,000th point plateau in WHL history.

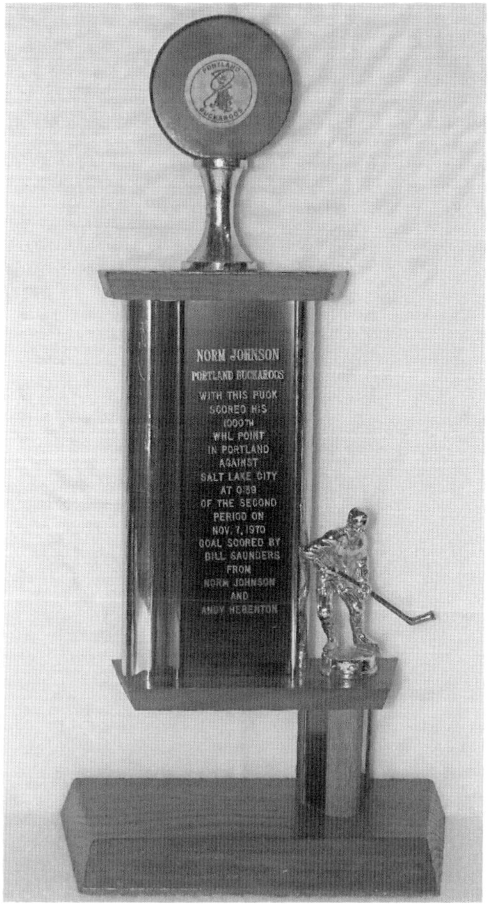

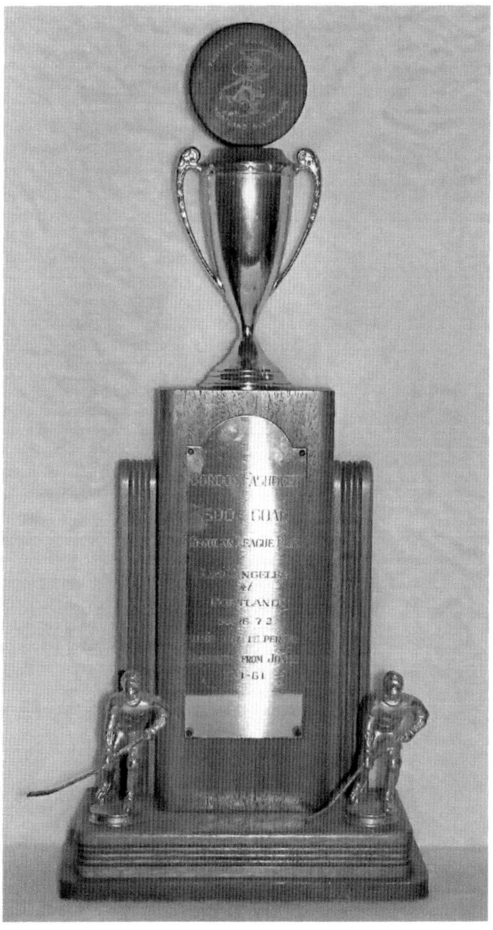

GORDON FASHOWAY'S 500TH GOAL TROPHY. This trophy was presented to Gordon Fashoway by the WHL and Buckaroos management for scoring his 500th goal in professional regular-season play on November 1, 1961, against Los Angeles at Portland. He scored the goal at 1:17 of the first period, assisted by Art Jones. At the time, Fashoway was one of only three players (along with Gordie Howe and Maurice Richard) to score 500 regular-season goals professionally.

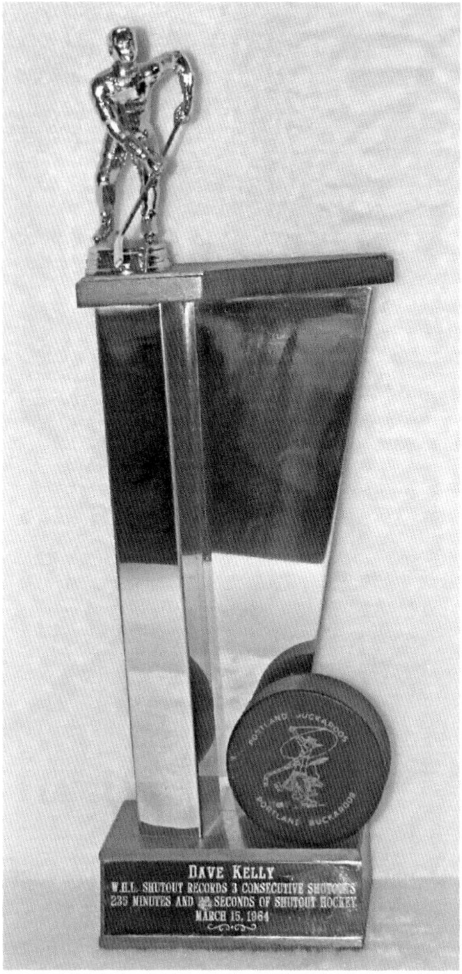

DAVE KELLY'S WHL ALL-TIME SHUTOUT RECORD TROPHY. This trophy was presented to Dave Kelly for recording the WHL all-time record for longest shutout sequence by a goaltender—235 minutes and 22 seconds (three consecutive complete shutout games plus)—which he set during the 1963–1964 season. The streak started on March 8, 1964, at home against Seattle and ended at home on March 15, 1964, against Vancouver at 11:38 of the third period.

TROPHY PRESENTED TO GORDON FASHOWAY FOR WINNING THE FRED J. HUME CUP FOR 1960–1961 SEASON. Fashoway won the WHL's inaugural Fred J. Hume Cup as the league's most gentlemanly player, which was first awarded for the 1960–1961 season. The Hume Cup was won more times by a Buckaroo player (seven times—Fashoway once and Andy Hebenton six times) than by players from any other club.

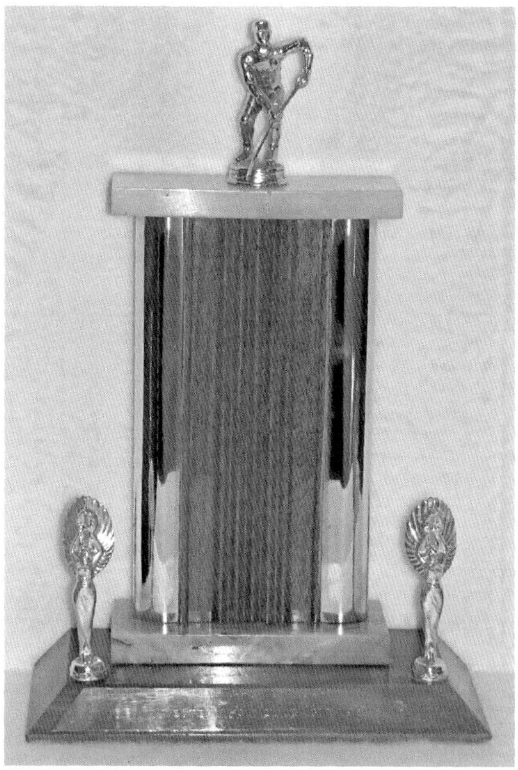

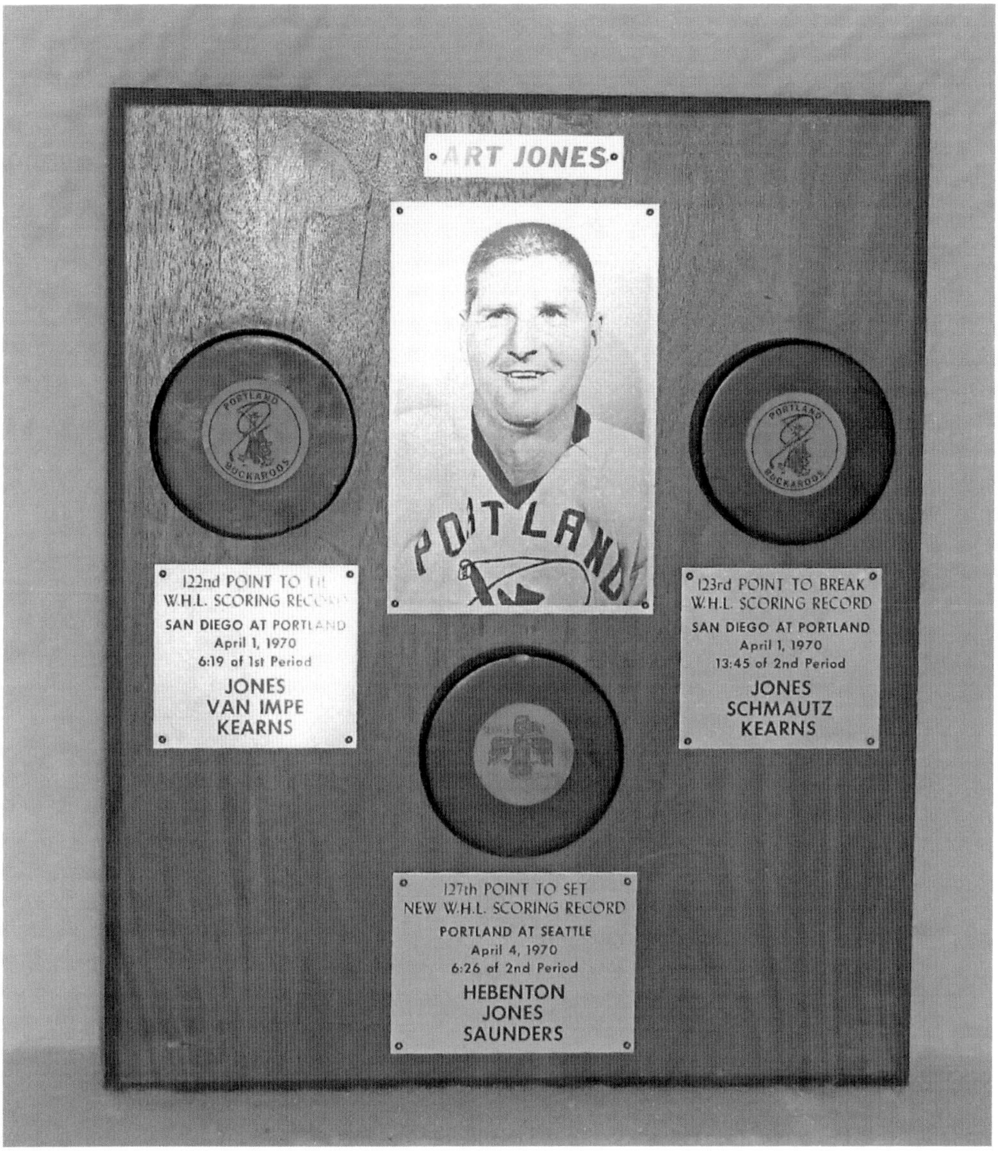

ART JONES'S WHL RECORD 127TH POINT PLAQUE. On April 4, 1970, Art Jones broke Guyle Fielder's WHL single-season point record of 122 points (set in 1956–1957) with his 123rd point. Jones achieved the highest single-season point total in WHL history that season with 127 points. The plaque displays the actual pucks that tied (left) and broke (right) the old record, and the one that set the new record of 127 points (center).

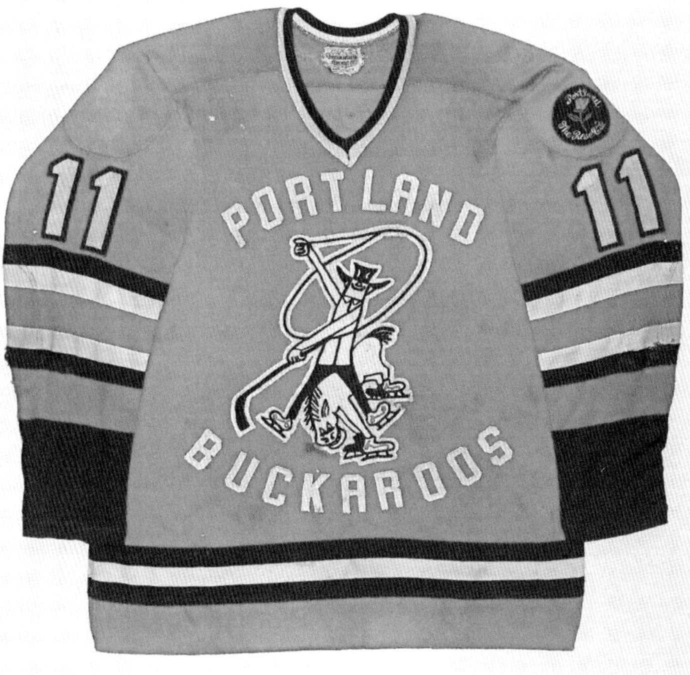

GUYLE FIELDER'S GAME-USED BUCKAROOS JERSEY FROM THE 1972–1973 SEASON. Many hockey historians regard Fielder as the greatest minor league hockey player of all time. The minor league hockey legend spent most of his career with Seattle (WHL), but the Buckaroos were fortunate enough to obtain Fielder in a trade with Salt Lake City (WHL) in January 1972, along with Jake Rathwell for Lyle Bradley and Fred Hilts.

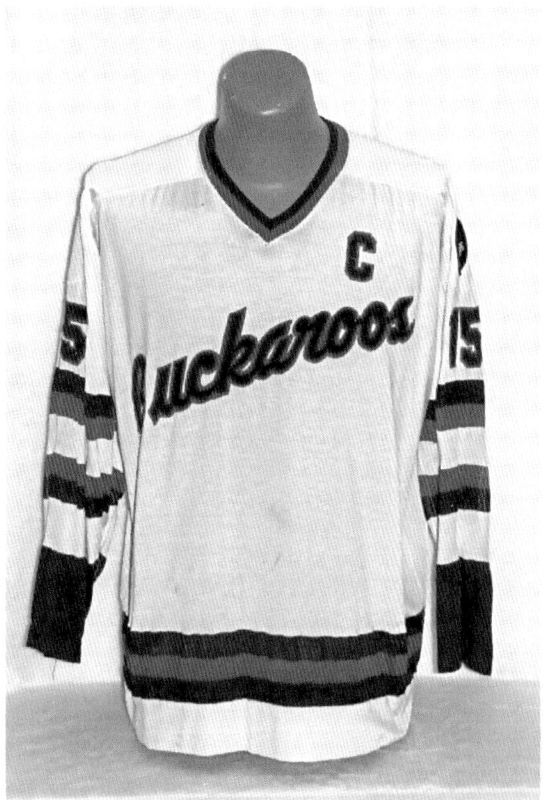

ART JONES'S GAME-USED BUCKAROOS JERSEY FROM THE 1973–1974 SEASON. Art Jones is the WHL's all-time leader in postseason points (149), goals (59), assists (90), and games played (140). Jones led the WHL in playoff scoring in 1960–1961 with 18 points, 1967–1968 with 17 points, and 1968–1969 with 14 points (tied with Cliff Schmautz).

JIM MCLEOD'S GAME-USED GOALIE MASK. McLeod helped led the Buckaroos to a Patrick Cup championship in 1970–1971. The goaltender led the WHL in GAA (2.70), wins (32-10-3 record in 47 games), and shutouts (five) that season. He also shared the WHL Outstanding Goalkeeper Award and earned a WHL Second All-Star Team selection in 1970–1971.

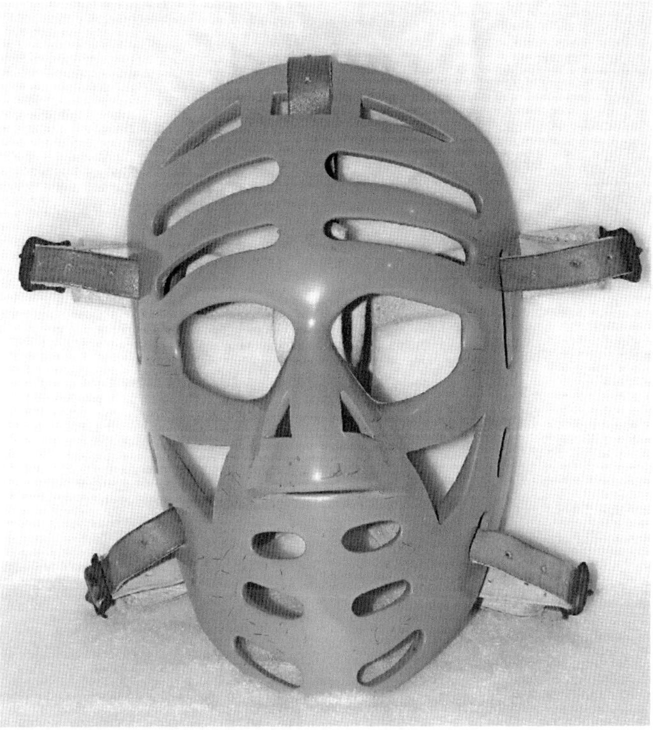

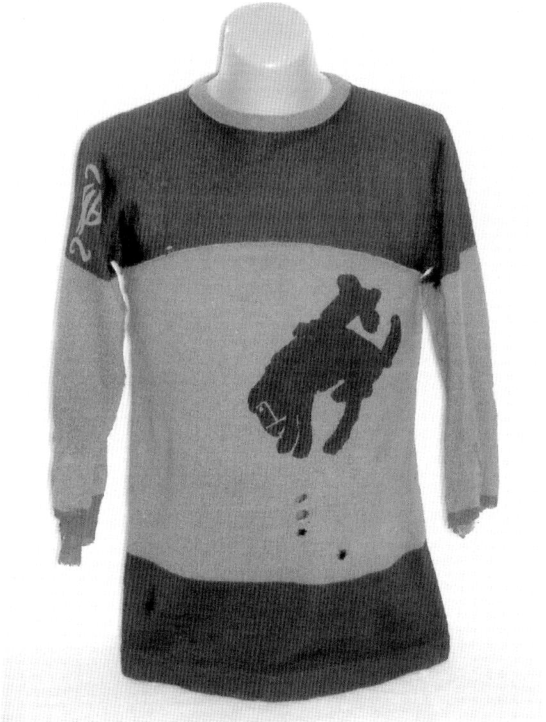

ANDY AITKENHEAD'S GAME-USED BUCKAROOS JERSEY FROM THE 1936–1937 SEASON. In 1936–1937, Aitkenhead led Portland to a PCHL regular-season and playoff championship with a league-leading 1.80 GAA and seven shutouts, while posting a 22-13-5 record in 40 games. In the playoffs that season, the Buckaroos received a direct bye into the finals and the goaltender helped Portland sweep Spokane three games to none with a 1.00 GAA and a 3-0 record.

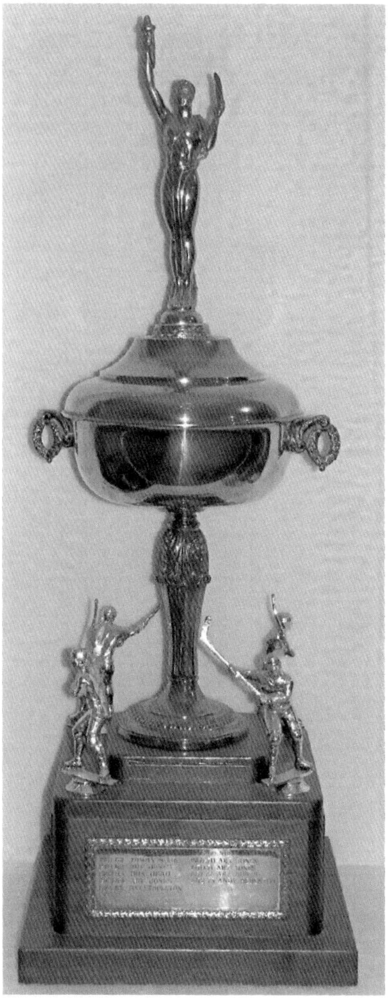

Ted Gamble Trophy. From 1960–1961 to 1972–1973, this trophy was presented to the Buckaroos' most valuable player by the Portland Buckaroo Hockey Club. Recipients include Don Head (1960–1961 and 1962–1963), Andy Hebenton (1972–1973), Norm Johnson (1968–1969), Art Jones (1961–1962*, 1963–1964, 1967–1968, 1969–1970, 1970–1971, and 1971–1972), Connie Madigan (1966–1967), Tom McVie (1961–1962*), Cliff Schmautz (1965–1966), and Pat Stapleton (1964–1965). Ted Gamble was one of the principle investors in the Buckaroos. (*Tied for selection).

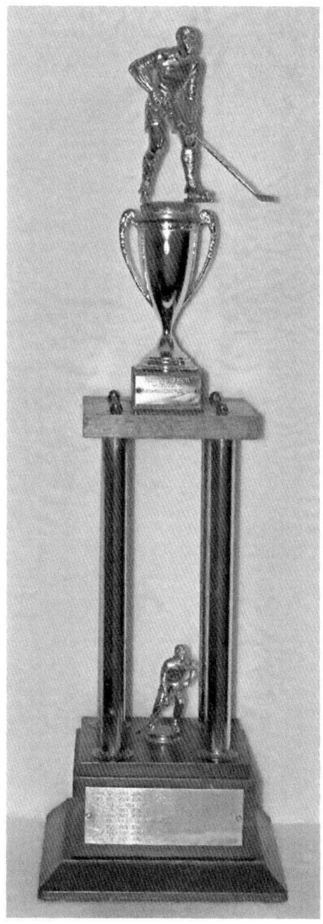

Morris Rogoway Leading Goal Scorer Trophy. This trophy was presented annually to the Buckaroos leading goal scorer from 1960–1961 to 1972–1973. The award was sponsored by Morris Rogoway, a prominent jeweler in the Portland area who was a large supporter of the Buckaroos. Art Jones won the award in every season but two. Gerry Goyer captured the trophy in 1962–1963, and Cliff Schmautz was presented the award in 1965–1966.

PORTLAND BUCKAROOS MOST POPULAR PLAYER TROPHY. This trophy was awarded from 1961–1962 to 1972–1973 by the Portland Buckaroos Booster Club. Recipients include Roger Bellerive (1968–1969), Ken Campbell (1969–1970), Andy Hebenton (1964–1965 and 1972–1973), Dave Kelly (1963–1964), Connie Madigan (1965–1966), Tom McVie (1961–1962), Bill Saunders (1966–1967), Arnie Schmautz (1962–1963), and Mel Pearson (1967–1968, 1970–1971, and 1971–1972).

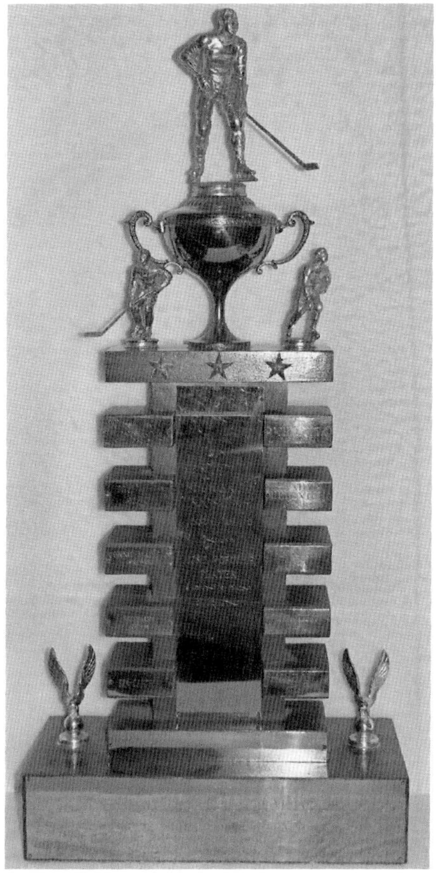

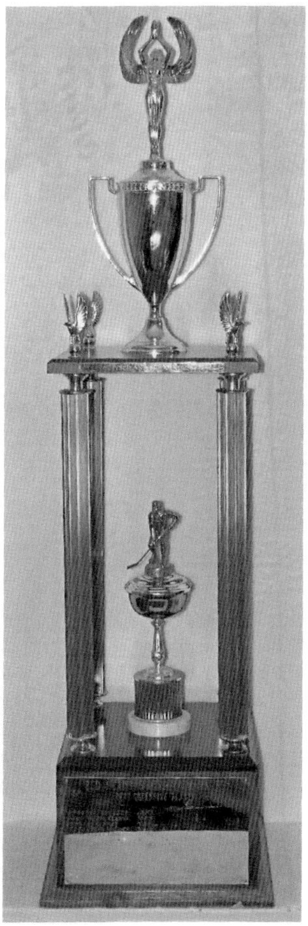

BUD MEADOWS PERPETUAL AWARD. This award was presented to the Buckaroos' best defensive player from 1967–1968 to 1971–1972. Recipients include Mike Donaldson (1967–1968), Rick Foley (1969–1970), Dennis Kearns (1968–1969), Larry Long (1971–1972), and Connie Madigan (1970–1971). Bud Meadows, a well-known car dealer in Portland, was a big supporter and one of the prime sponsors of the Buckaroos.

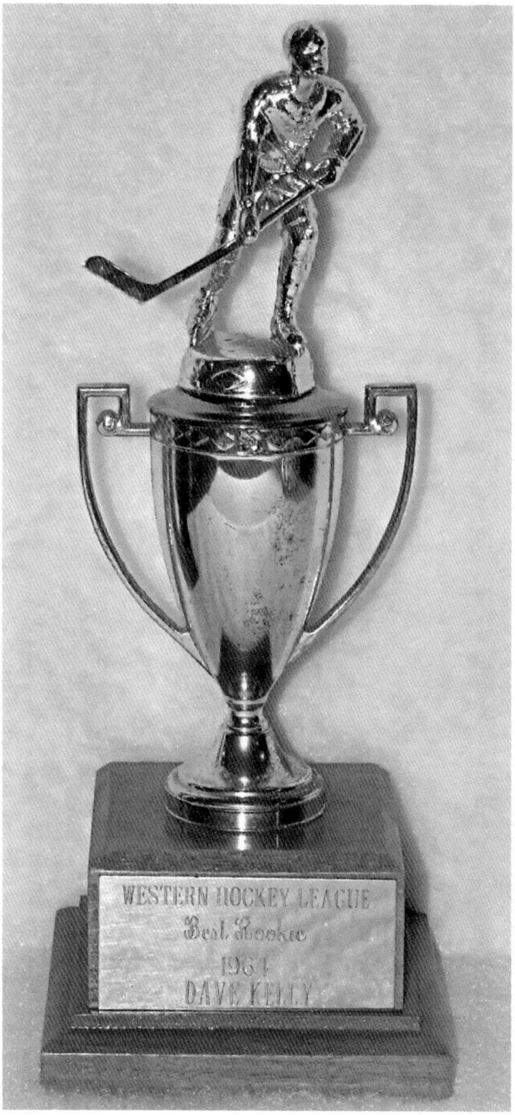

DAVE KELLY'S 1963–1964 WHL ROOKIE AWARD. Kelly posted the second lowest GAA (3.10) in the WHL during the 1963–1964 season and established the league record for longest shutout sequence by a goaltender (235 minutes and 22 seconds) to earn the WHL Rookie Award. Kelly was also one of the youngest goalies in professional hockey that year at 20 years of age.

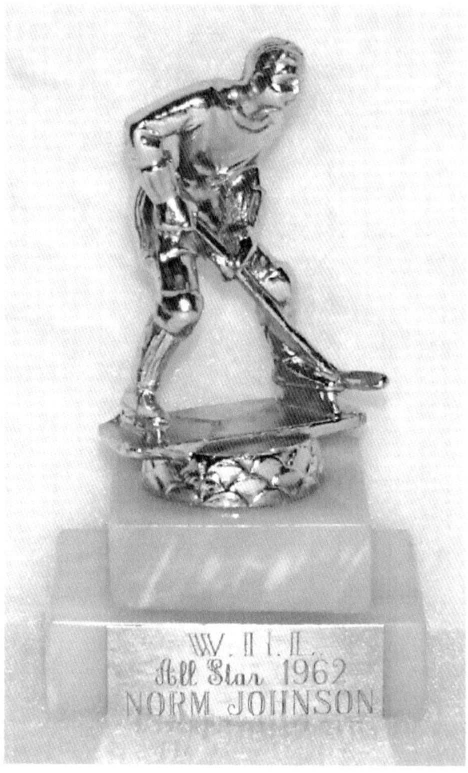

NORM JOHNSON'S 1961–1962 WHL ALL-STAR TROPHY. Norm Johnson was given this trophy by the WHL for being named to the WHL All-Star Team in 1961–1962 as a first-team center. He was a member of the Calgary Stampeders that season. Johnson was also named to the WHL All-Star Team in 1956–1957, 1960–1961, and 1968–1969.

ARNIE SCHMAUTZ. Schmautz was one of the smallest players (5 feet 7 inches, 135 pounds) to play in the WHL and in professional hockey during his career. He played with the heart of a giant and was a vital part of the Buckaroos' success for eight seasons. He became a fan favorite because of his willingness to do whatever it took to win games.

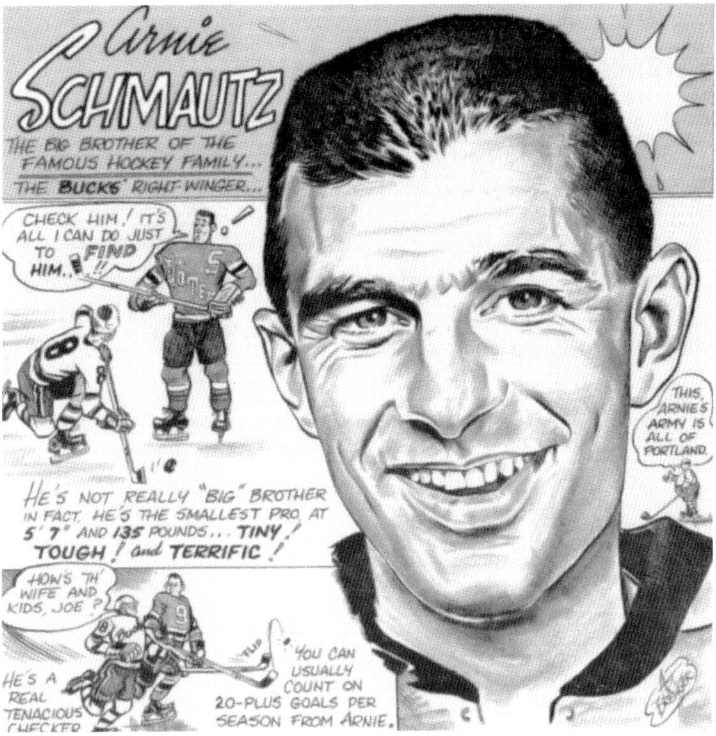

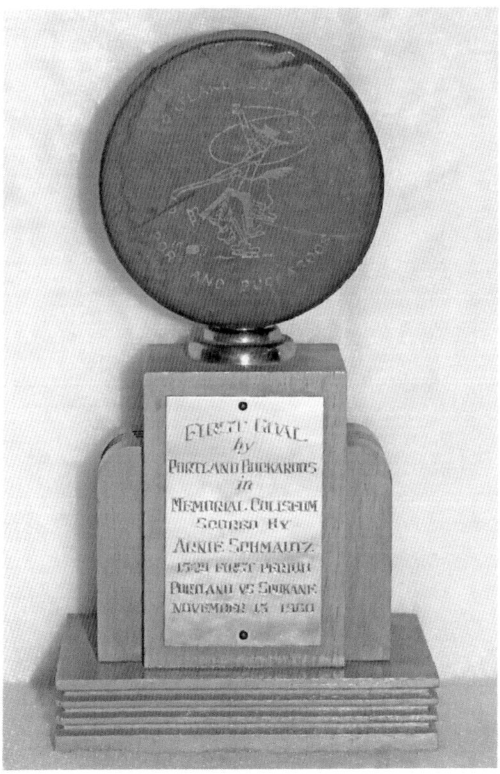

ARNIE SCHMAUTZ'S FIRST GOAL AT THE PORTLAND MEMORIAL COLISEUM TROPHY. Schmautz's historic first goal at the Portland Memorial Coliseum was tallied at 15:29 of the first period when the Buckaroos hosted the Spokane Comets on November 15, 1960, for their inaugural season home opener. In recognition of this accomplishment, the Buckaroos' management had the puck made into this trophy, which they presented to Schmautz several nights later.

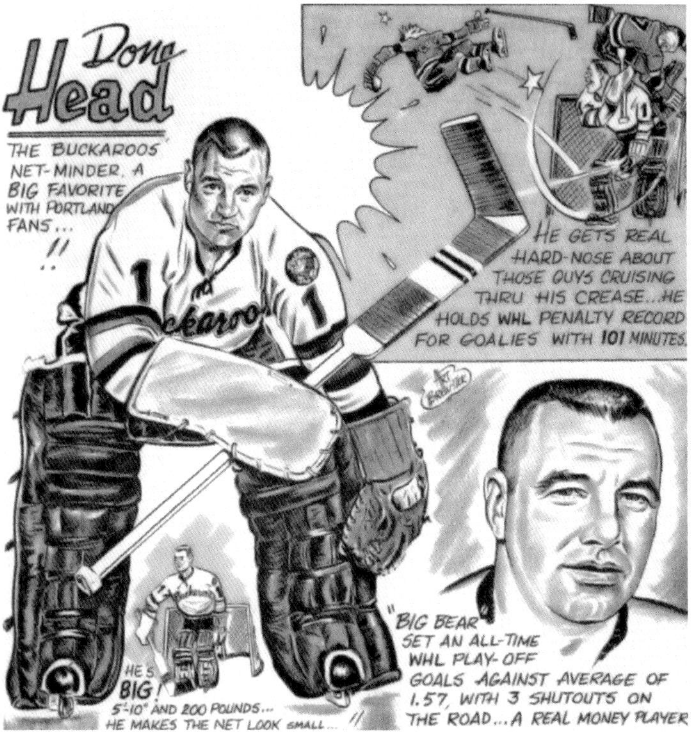

DON HEAD. He helped lead Team Canada to a silver medal at the 1960 Winter Olympic Games at Squaw Valley, California. His performance in the Olympics earned him a contact offer from the Buckaroos for the 1960–1961 season.

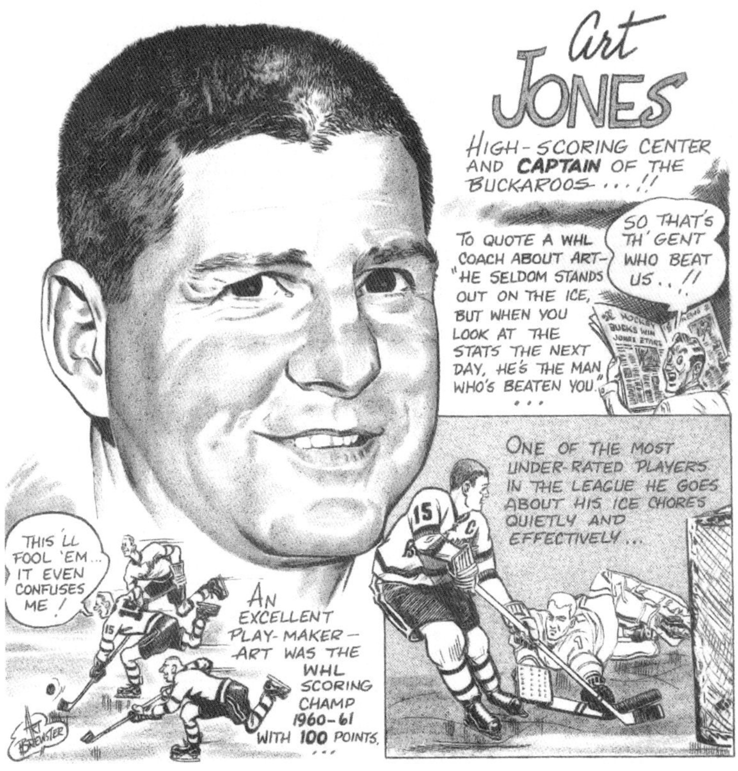

ART JONES. Known as "Mr. Buckaroo" in Portland, Jones was "the one who got away" in Winnipeg because he was cut by the WHL's Winnipeg Warriors before going on to one of the greatest careers in minor league hockey history with the Buckaroos. *The Hockey News* named Jones Minor League Player of the Year for the 1970–1971 season.

BILL SAUNDERS. He shares the WHL all-time record for most goals in a period with four, which he accomplished on October 15, 1967, against Vancouver at Portland (third period). Two of the other three players who also registered four goals in a period in WHL history up to that point were members of the Portland Eagles/Penguins—Pat Desbiens (November 24, 1948, against San Francisco) and Joe Ciuman (November 9, 1949, against Seattle).

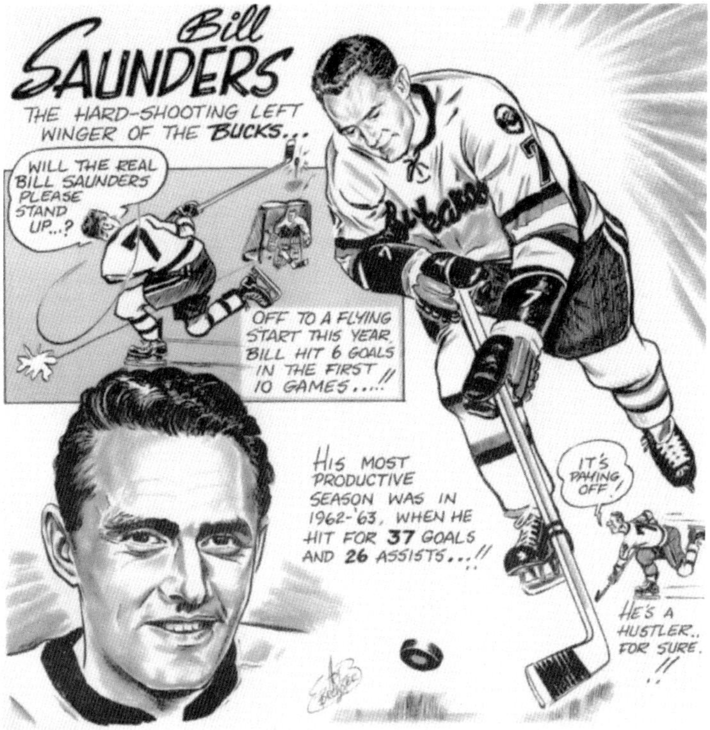

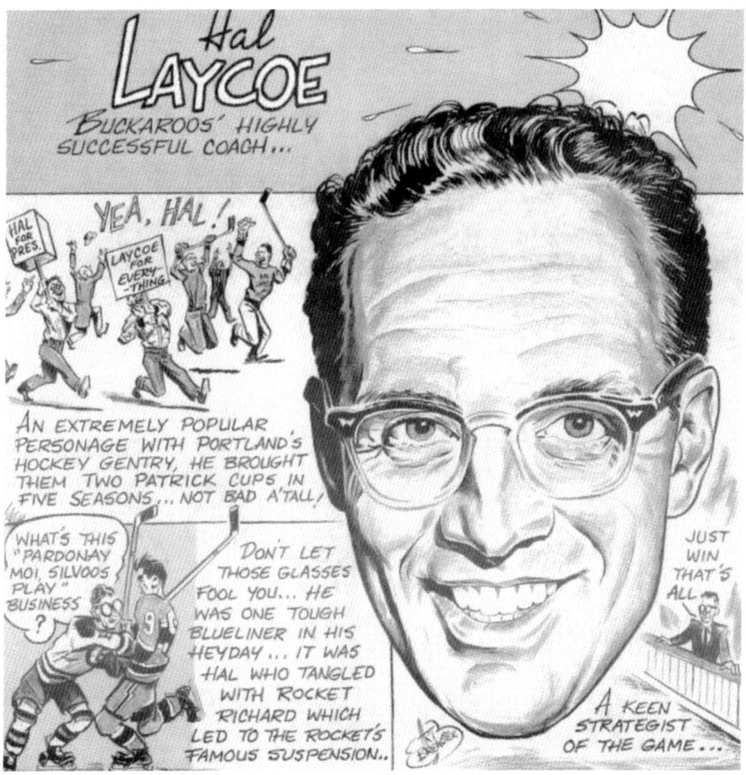

HAL LAYCOE. Not only one of the greatest coaches in minor league hockey history, Laycoe was also an 11-year veteran of the NHL. Laycoe, a defenseman, garnered 102 points, 77 assists, and 292 PIM in 531 NHL games with New York, Montreal, and Boston from 1945 to 1956. *The Hockey News* named him Minor League Coach of the Year for 1968–1969.

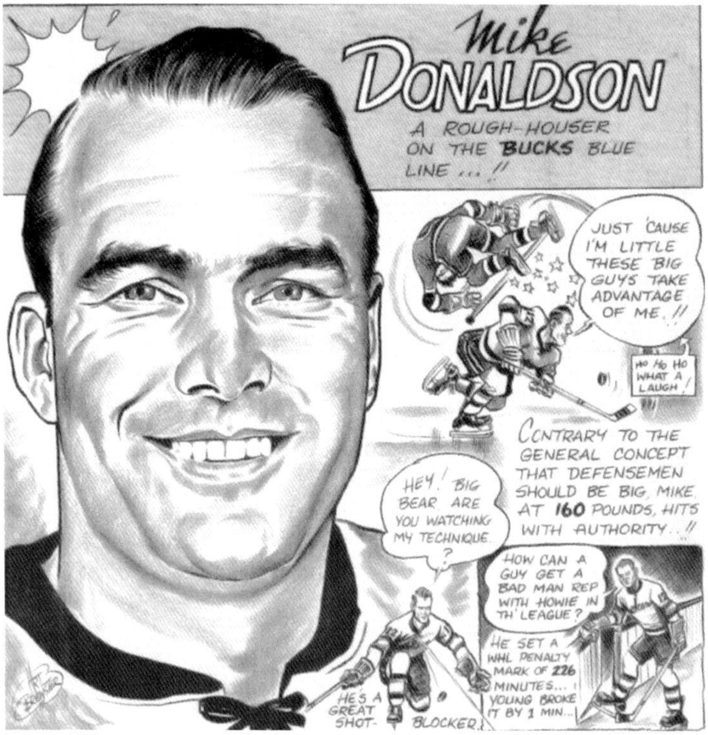

MIKE DONALDSON. Considered a good positional player and a rugged defenseman, Donaldson once held the WHL record for the most penalty minutes in a season with 226 PIM and ranks as the eighth-most penalized player in WHL history with 1,146 PIM.

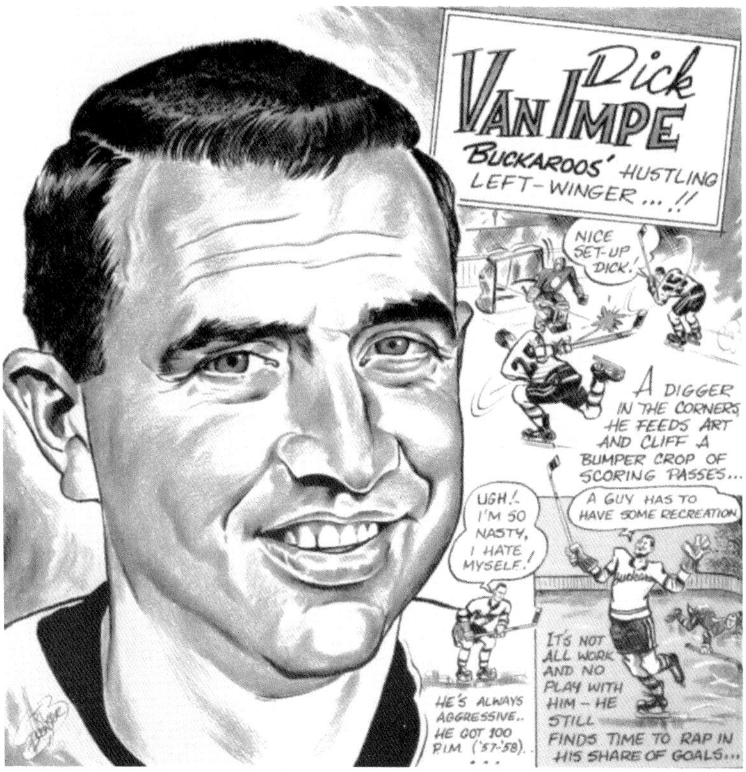

DICK VAN IMPE. An important part of two Buckaroos' Patrick Cup championship teams in 1964–1965 and 1970–1971, Van Impe registered 47 points and 16 goals for Portland in 1964–1965 and 45 points and 15 goals in 1970–1971.

Tom McVie. McVie coached in the NHL and WHA after his Buckaroo playing days were over. He compiled a 126-263-73 (.352) record in eight NHL seasons with Washington, Winnipeg, and New Jersey between 1975 and 1992. McVie was a late-season coaching replacement for Winnipeg (WHA) in 1978–1979 and earned an 11-8-0 (.579) regular-season record before leading his team to the Avco Cup championship.

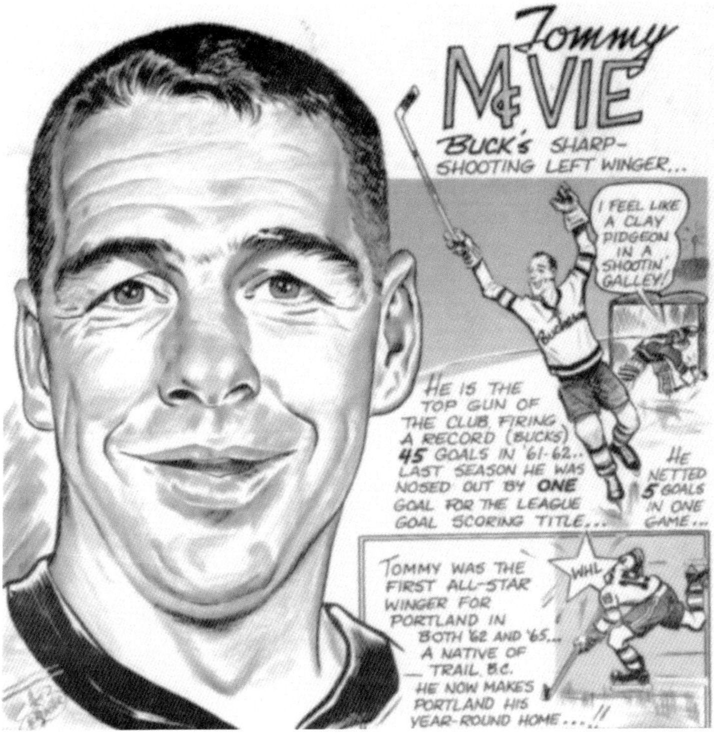

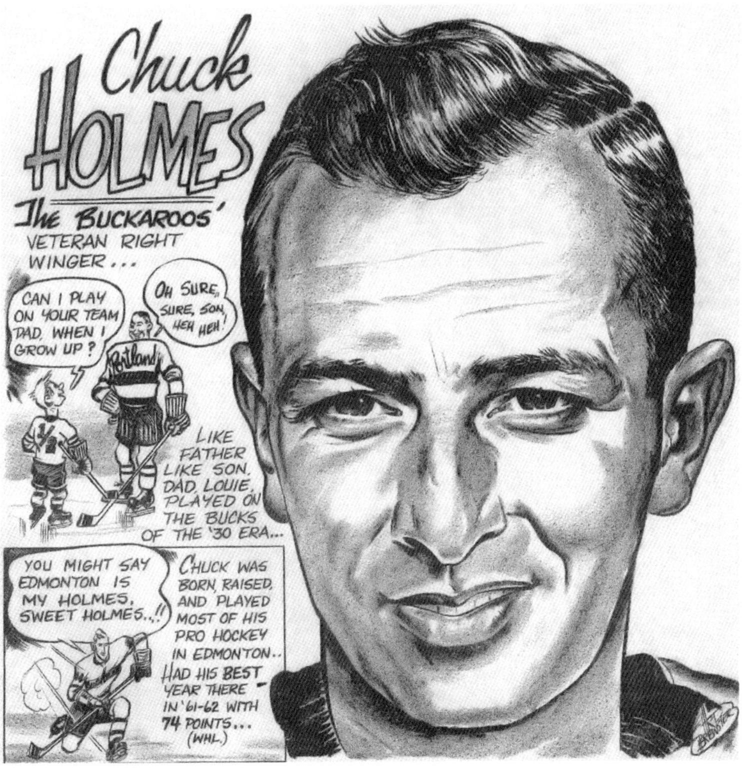

Chuck Holmes. He is the son of WCHL/NWHL/PCHL Buckaroos' player Lou Holmes, who skated with Portland in the late 1930s. Both Chuck and Lou are one of the few father-and-son combinations to skate in the NHL. Chuck played two seasons with Detroit (NHL) between 1958 and 1962, and Lou played from 1931 to 1933 with Chicago.

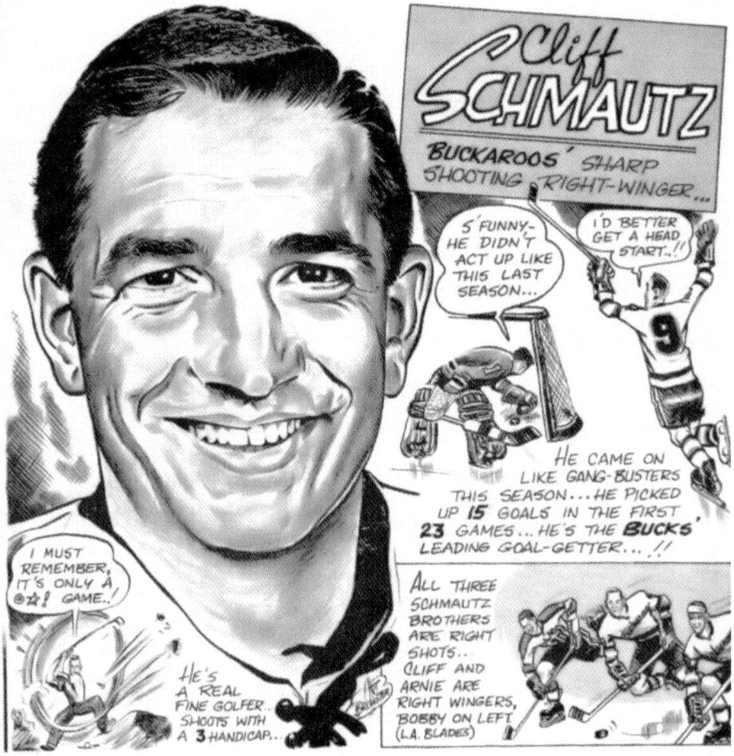

CLIFF SCHMAUTZ. A member of the Buffalo Sabres (NHL) during the team's inaugural season in 1970–1971, Cliff was claimed by Buffalo in the interleague draft and also played with Philadelphia (NHL) that year, his only season in the NHL. He shares the WHL record for assists in a game with six, which he set on April 3, 1966.

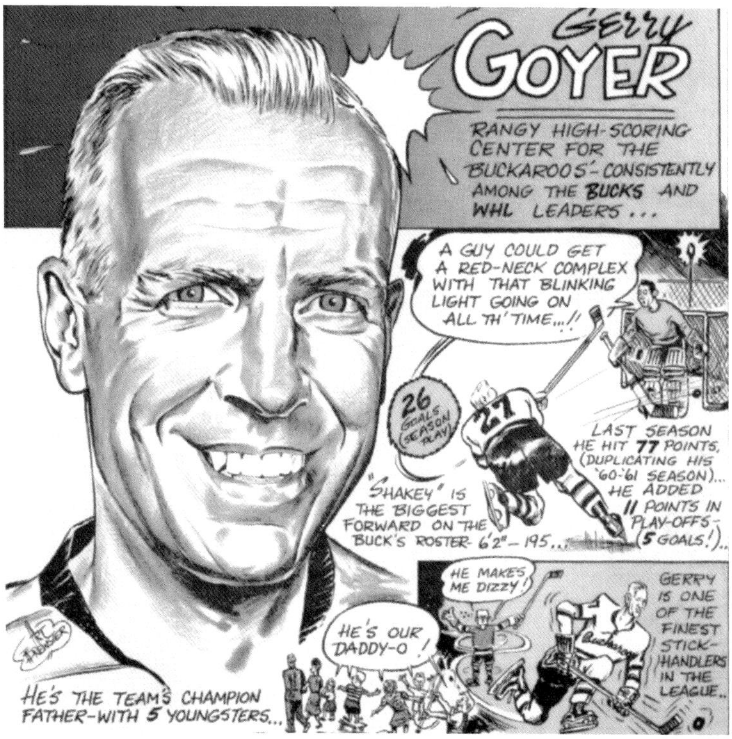

GERRY GOYER. Goyer was a steady goal scorer in the WHL as he topped the 20-goal mark in 11 seasons with Victoria (Cougars), Los Angeles, Portland, Vancouver, and San Diego between the 1960–1961 and 1972–1973 campaigns. Goyer led the WHL in playoff scoring twice in 1964–1965 with Portland and in 1969–1970 with Vancouver (he tied with another player for the lead in 1969–1970).

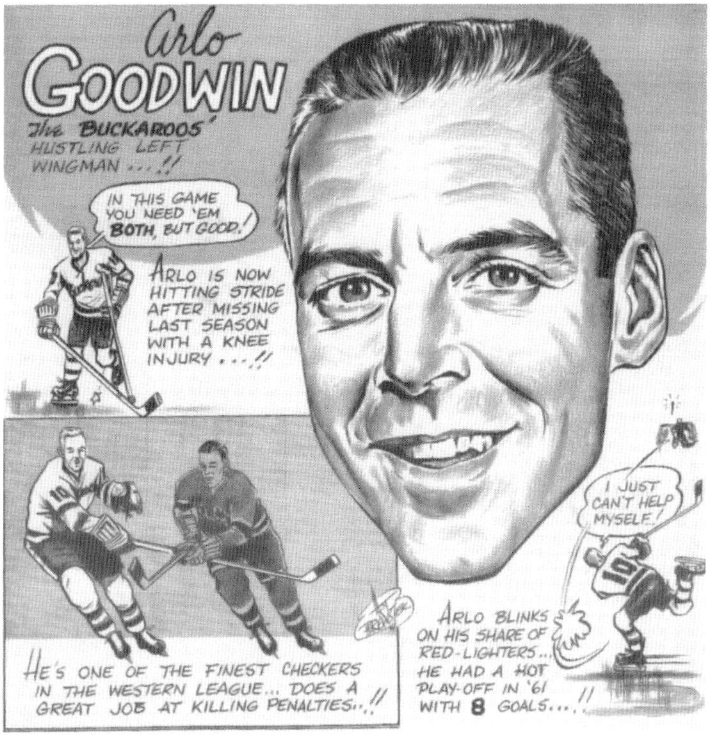

ARLO GOODWIN. One of the toughest checkers and top penalty killers during his years in the WHL, Goodwin was nicknamed "Bones" by his teammates because he broke a lot of them in his professional hockey career.

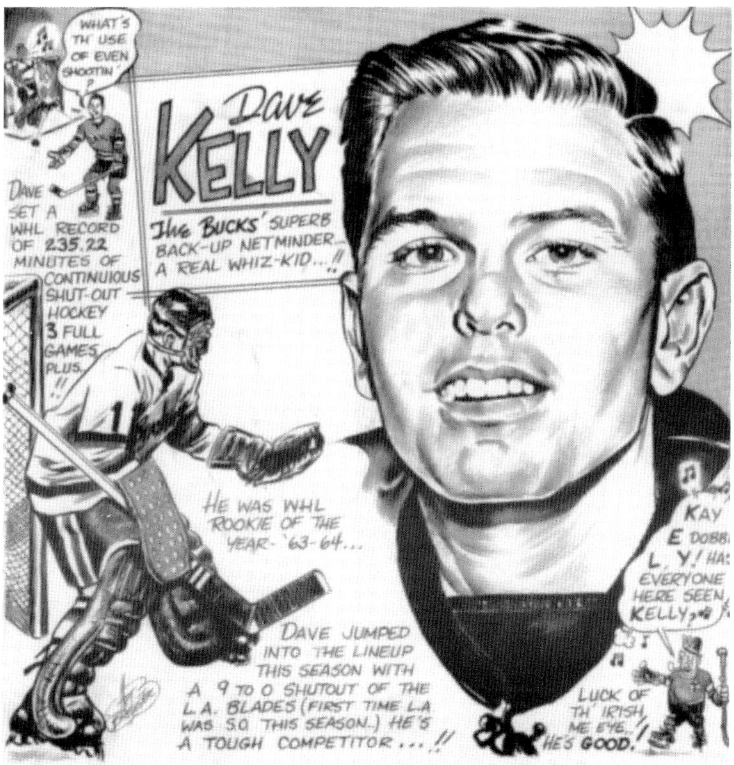

DAVE KELLY. In his 11-year career in the WHL with Portland, Los Angeles, and San Diego, from 1963 to 1974, Kelly posted a 3.42 GAA and 20 shutouts in 397 WHL games.

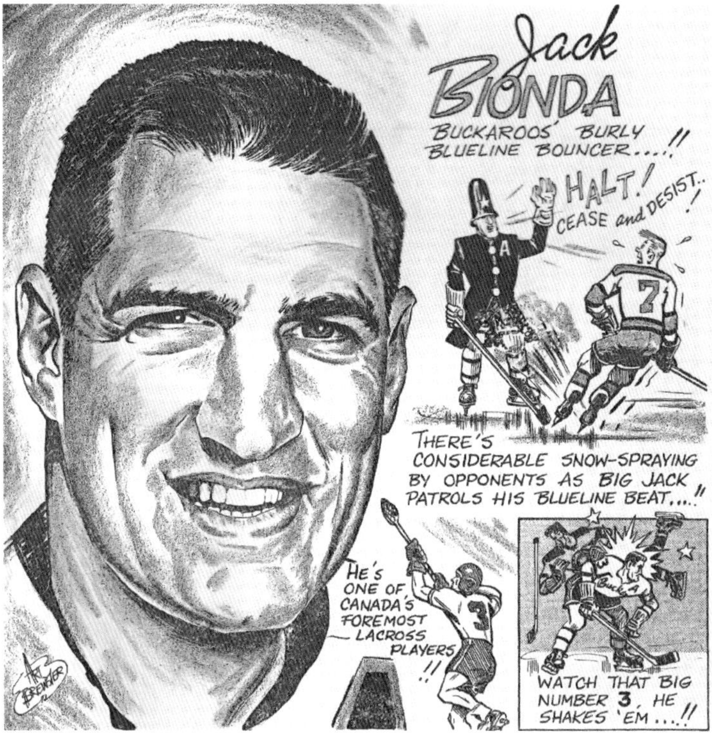

JACK BIONDA. The first true superstar of lacrosse in Canada, Bionda is considered by many to be the finest player the sport has ever produced. Bionda was a true lacrosse legend, earning several Mann Cup victories and league MVPs.

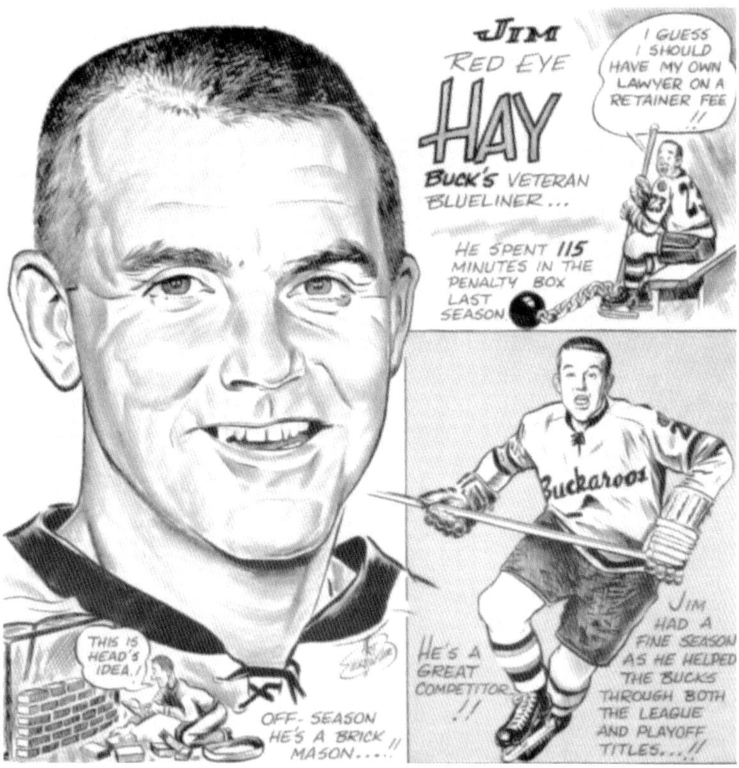

JIM HAY. With the distinction of being a member of more WHL teams than any other player in league history, Hay skated with a total of eight WHL clubs—the Edmonton Flyers, Brandon Regals, Victoria Cougars, Los Angeles Blades, San Francisco Seals, Seattle Totems, Portland Buckaroos, and the Salt Lake City Golden Eagles. Of his eight WHL teams, the defenseman never took the ice for Los Angeles.

FRED HILTS. Hilts tallied 67 points, 34 goals, and 30 PIM in 76 games during two seasons with the Buckaroos—1965–1966 and 1971–1972. Hilts also skated in the WHL with Calgary in 1958–1959, San Diego from 1966 to 1971, and Salt Lake City from 1971 to 1973. The left-winger won a Foley Trophy with Hull-Ottawa (EPHL) in 1961–1962.

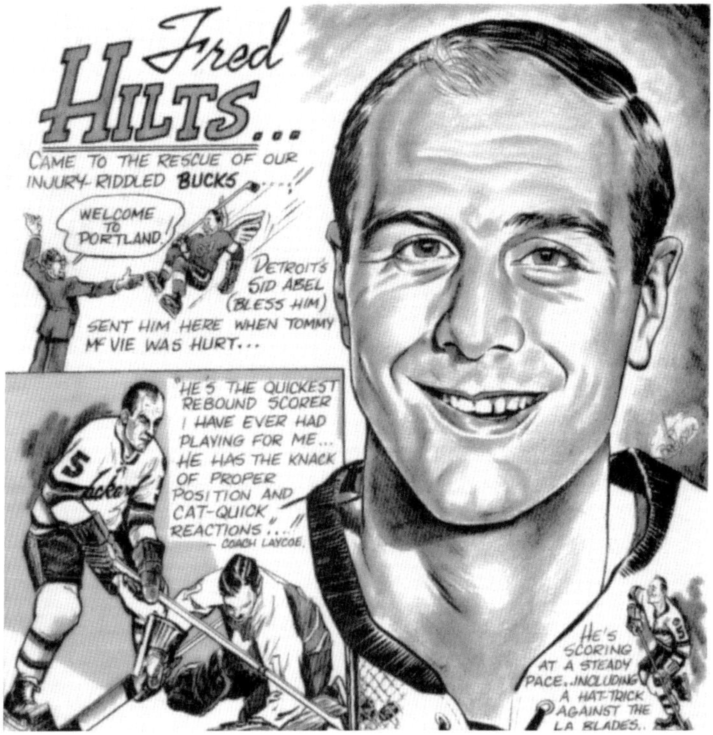

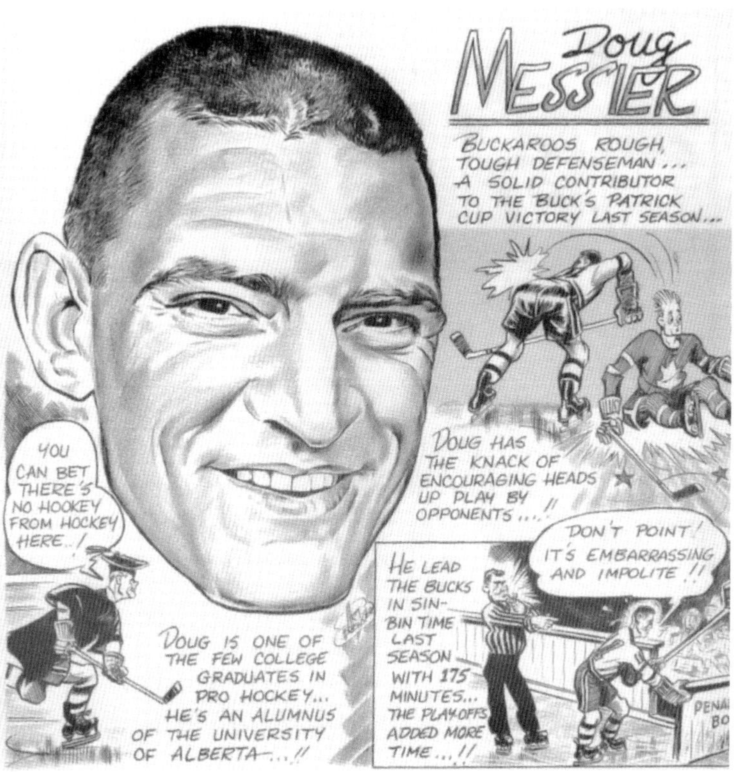

DOUG MESSIER. Doug is the father of all-time hockey great Mark Messier. While Mark was developing into one of the NHL's top stars with the Edmonton Oilers, Doug was coaching the Oilers' (NHL) top farm club, the Moncton Alpines (AHL), from 1982 to 1984.

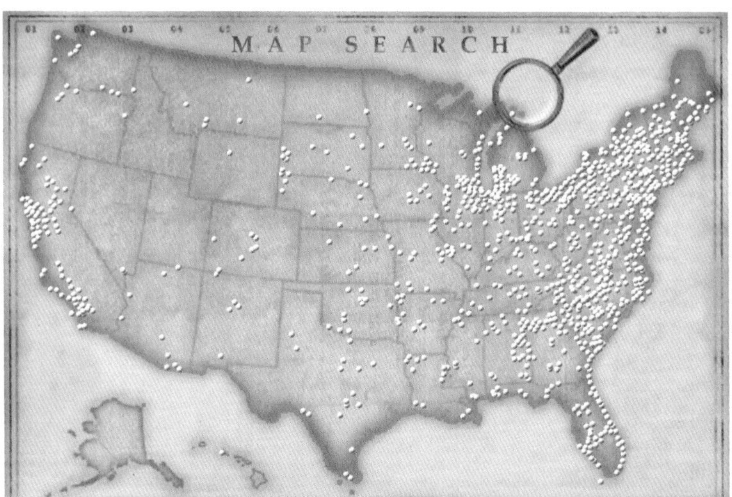
MAP SEARCH